Throughout his life and career at the Proms, Henry Wood considered it his duty to nurture public taste and improve access to classical music. The Proms upholds this mission today with a diverse range of free talks, workshops and participatory events on offer during the festival, as well as events for families and relaxed and British Sign Language-interpreted performances.

PROM 24 • 6 AUGUST

See also page 107

The Proms moved to the Royal Albert Hall in 1941, when the festival's original home, the Queen's Hall, was gutted by fire after being bombed in an air raid. Concerts in the 1941 season began at the earlier time of 6.30pm to make the most of the evening before the blackout and after six weeks of Proms, on 16 August, Henry Wood gave his first Last Night speech, inaugurating another Proms tradition that continues to this day.

LAST NIGHT OF THE PROMS
14 SEPTEMBER

When the BBC took over the running of the Proms in 1927, Henry Wood remarked, 'With the whole-hearted support of the wonderful medium of broadcasting I feel that I am at last on the threshold of realising my lifelong ambition of truly democratising the message of music and making its beneficent effect universal.'

Every Prom is broadcast live on BBC Radio 3.
24 Proms are broadcast on BBC Television

A plaque adorns the wall at the site of the Queen's Hall, the first home of the Proms

Deaf poet and British Sign Language interpreter Donna Williams at the Relaxed Prom in 2018

CITY OF WESTMINSTER
THE QUEEN'S HALL
1893-1941
SITE OF BRITAIN'S
LEADING CONCERT HALL

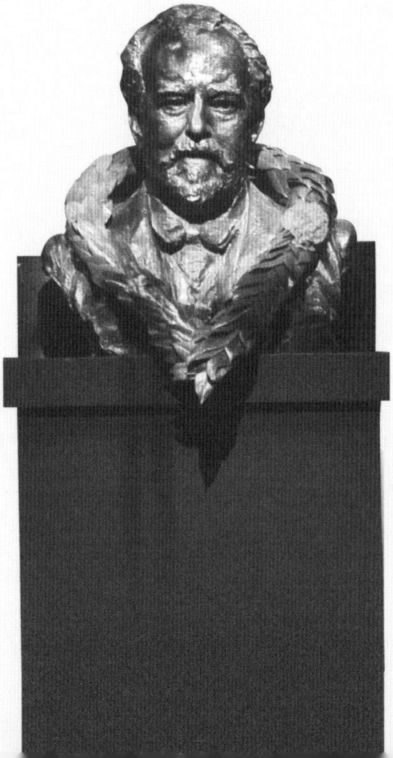

Petroc Trelawny presenting the Proms on BBC Radio 3

For image credits, see page 181

Contents

The Sound of Space **14**

Music, Inspiration … Education **20**

A Birthday 'Enigma' **24**

New Directions **42**

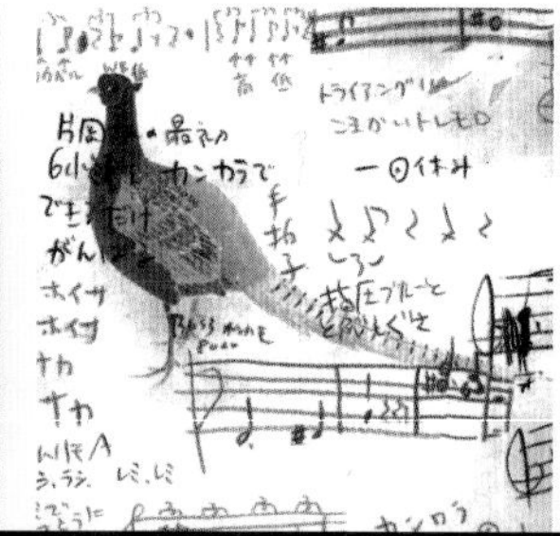

A Vehicle for Virtuosity? **64**

Welcome

4 / BBC Proms Director David Pickard introduces the 2019 festival; poet Debris Stevenson reflects on 'The Breaks'

Beyond the Bust

8 / Hannah French honours Proms founder-conductor Henry Wood's legacy, 150 years after his birth

The Sound of Space

14 / In the 50th-anniversary year of the first manned Moon landing, Neil Brand turns his lens on music and the cosmos

Music, Inspiration … Education

20 / Former BBC Young Musician finalist Jess Gillam on the benefits of a musical education from an early age

A Birthday 'Enigma'

24 / John Pickard on a new set of 'Enigma' Variations, commissioned for the 60th birthday of conductor Martyn Brabbins

A Life with Berlioz

36 / John Allison talks to Sir John Eliot Gardiner about his affinity for Berlioz and the composer's colourful intensity

New Directions

42 / As the role of the composer has become increasingly multifaceted, Errollyn Wallen reflects on her musical journey

Lost Words in the Name of the Earth

48 / Radio 3's Petroc Trelawny looks at the connections between music and the natural world

These Are the Breaks

52 / Angus Batey talks to conductor Jules Buckley ahead of a Prom that takes street dance to the Royal Albert Hall

A Vehicle for Virtuosity?

64 / Violinist Daniel Pioro reviews the changing form of the violin concerto, from a performer's viewpoint

Music for the Dream Factory

70 / Mervyn Cooke revisits the music from the Warner Bros. studio that helped to define the 'Hollywood Sound'

In Parlour and Palace

74 / In the bicentenary year of Queen Victoria's birth, Matthew Sweet asks how musical the monarch was

A History of Classical Music **78**

Chinese Revolutions **92**

I Put a Spell on You **100**

A Musical Trip to the Moon **104**

Concert Listings **121**

A History of Classical Music

78 / An illustrated history of classical music by Kate Romano to accompany the Proms at … Cadogan Hall concerts

Chinese Revolutions

92 / Jindong Cai and Sheila Melvin place the popularity of Western Music in China in the context of the country's past

Lost Legacies

96 / Anna Beer on pioneering anniversary women composers Barbara Strozzi and Clara Schumann

I Put a Spell on You

100 / As the Proms dedicates a concert to Nina Simone, Courtney Patterson-Faye reflects on the singer's influence

A Musical Trip to the Moon

104 / Get ready to become a musical astronaut at this year's CBeebies Proms!

Proms on Radio, on TV, Online

106 / Bringing the festival to you – follow the Proms on radio, on TV and online

Free Events

107 / Highlights of this year's pre-Prom events, talks and workshops

Concert Listings

121 / Full listings and details of all the 2019 Proms concerts

Booking

163 /

- Ticket Prices 164
- Last Night of the Proms 165
- Prom on the day 166
- Access at the Proms 166
- Venues 168

Indexes

180 /

- Index of Artists 180
- Index of Works 182

The BBC Proms 2019 Festival Guide is also available as an audio book, in Braille and as a text-only large-print version.
See page 167 for further information.

Welcome to the 2019 BBC Proms

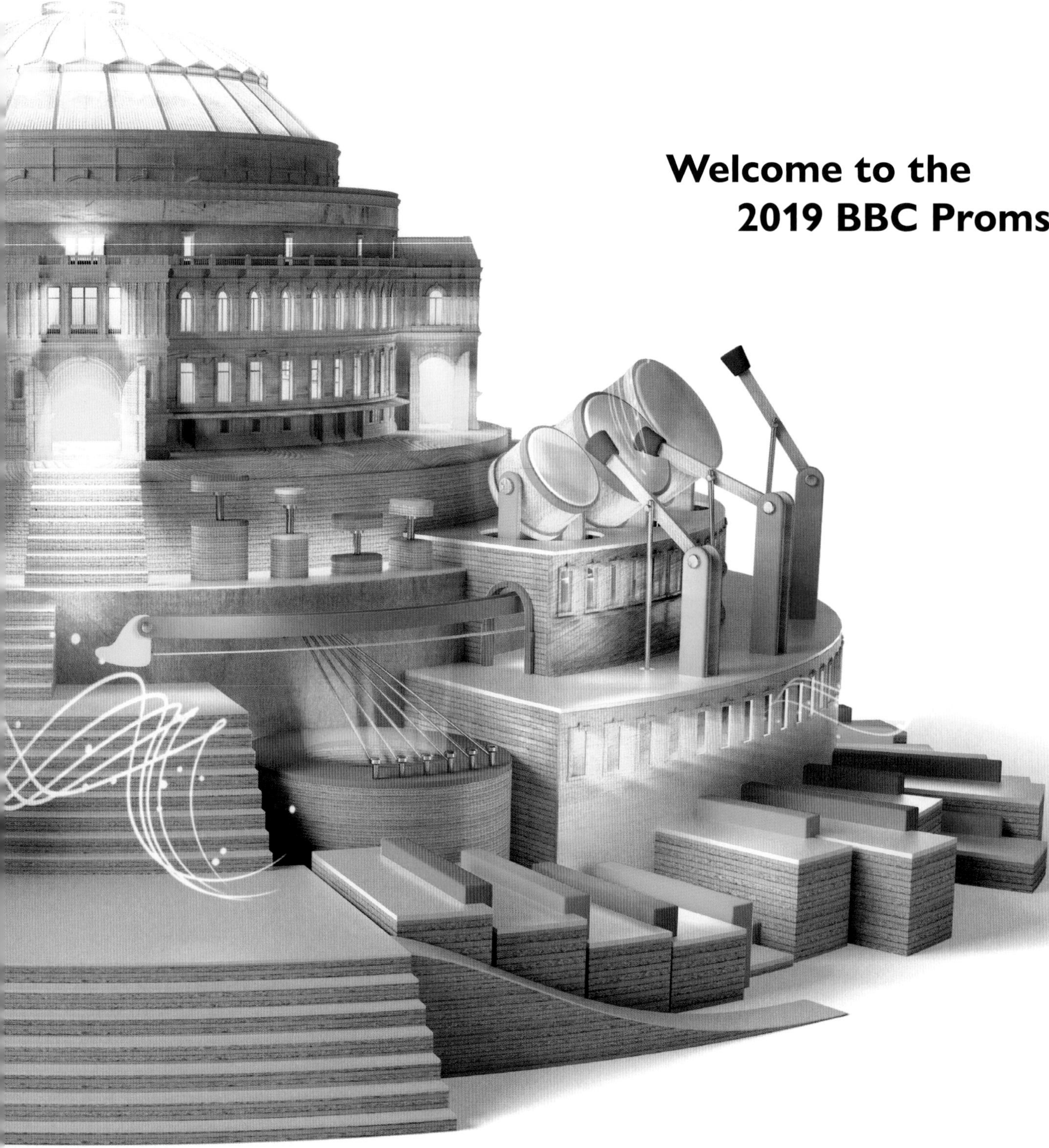

Welcome to the 2019 BBC Proms – the 125th season of this celebrated music festival. I hope you will enjoy the range of music that we have on offer from some of the finest orchestras, artists and ensembles from across the globe.

This year sees another special anniversary – 150 years since the birth Henry Wood, founder-conductor of the Proms. It's a tribute to the strength of his vision that the underlying principles of the festival remain unchanged from his original mission – to bring the finest works of classical music to the widest possible audience in an informal setting. For all the musical riches on offer, what remains the beating heart of the Proms is its audiences and, not least, the energy and enthusiasm of the 'Prommers', who stand in the Arena or up in the Gallery. Promming tickets at £6.00 are still the best bargain in classical music. Talk to any of the artists who have performed at the Proms and they will tell you that one of the greatest thrills of taking part is to be only inches away from one of the largest and most attentive audiences in the world. It would surely have pleased Wood that the audience he hoped to reach continues to grow – not just in the Royal Albert Hall, but through the revolution of streaming and downloads that he could never have imagined.

And what would Sir Henry make of the programme itself and how it has developed over the years? I think he would be delighted that many of the new works (or 'novelties') that he introduced to the UK have now become core classics. Indeed, it has not been difficult to include a broad selection of the staggering number of premieres he brought to this country, including as they do major works by Debussy, Janáček, Mahler, Sibelius, Rachmaninov, Ravel and Tchaikovsky.

And what of the range of concerts this summer that veer away from core classical repertoire? Wood himself featured lighter popular music of the time in the second half of many concerts, and this year we include a new work from boundary-crossing composer Jonny Greenwood, a performance by the eclectic West-African singer Angélique Kidjo and a tribute to Duke Ellington's Sacred Concerts.

One of the most significant changes since Wood's death is the number of new works commissioned by the Proms, and the range of that work is broader now than ever before. Even 50 years ago, in 1969 – when William Glock, a great champion of new music – was director of the Proms, only five BBC commissions featured in the season. This year there are more than 20, and they range from works by established international composers such as Louis Andriessen and Hans Zimmer to exciting young talent being heard at the Proms for the first time, including Zosha Di Castri, Daniel Kidane and Outi Tarkiainen.

When Wood died in 1944, he could not have imagined that just 25 years later a man would be walking on the Moon, and we celebrate that anniversary not just through space-related works from across the musical spectrum, but also through a broader look at the link between music and the world around us. The Lost Words Prom takes Robert Macfarlane and Jackie Morris's book about some of the vanishing language of nature and uses it as a starting point for a family concert of words, music and art that celebrates the huge diversity of our musical culture and influences. In another concert for younger audiences, the CBeebies Prom offers a journey to the Moon and back. And, in the flagship project of our learning and participation programme, John Luther Adams's *In the Name of the Earth* presents an opportunity for four community choirs to participate in a huge choral work that is inspired by landscape and will fill the entire space of the Royal Albert Hall's rotunda.

Concerts outside the RAH have become a firmly established part of the Proms in recent years. This year our Proms at … Cadogan Hall chamber series takes on the impossible task of reflecting the history of classical music in just eight concerts, celebrating some women composers of the past along the way. For the first time, we also take the Proms to the newly reopened Battersea Arts Centre and to Holy Sepulchre (aka St Sepulchre), Holborn, where Henry Wood is buried.

So I hope that Sir Henry would approve of the Proms in 2019 and that you too will find much to enjoy, whether attending in person or listening and watching through the many different broadcast possibilities offered by the BBC. ●

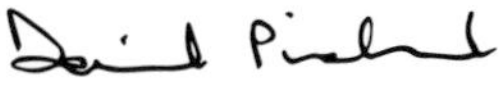

David Pickard Director, BBC Proms

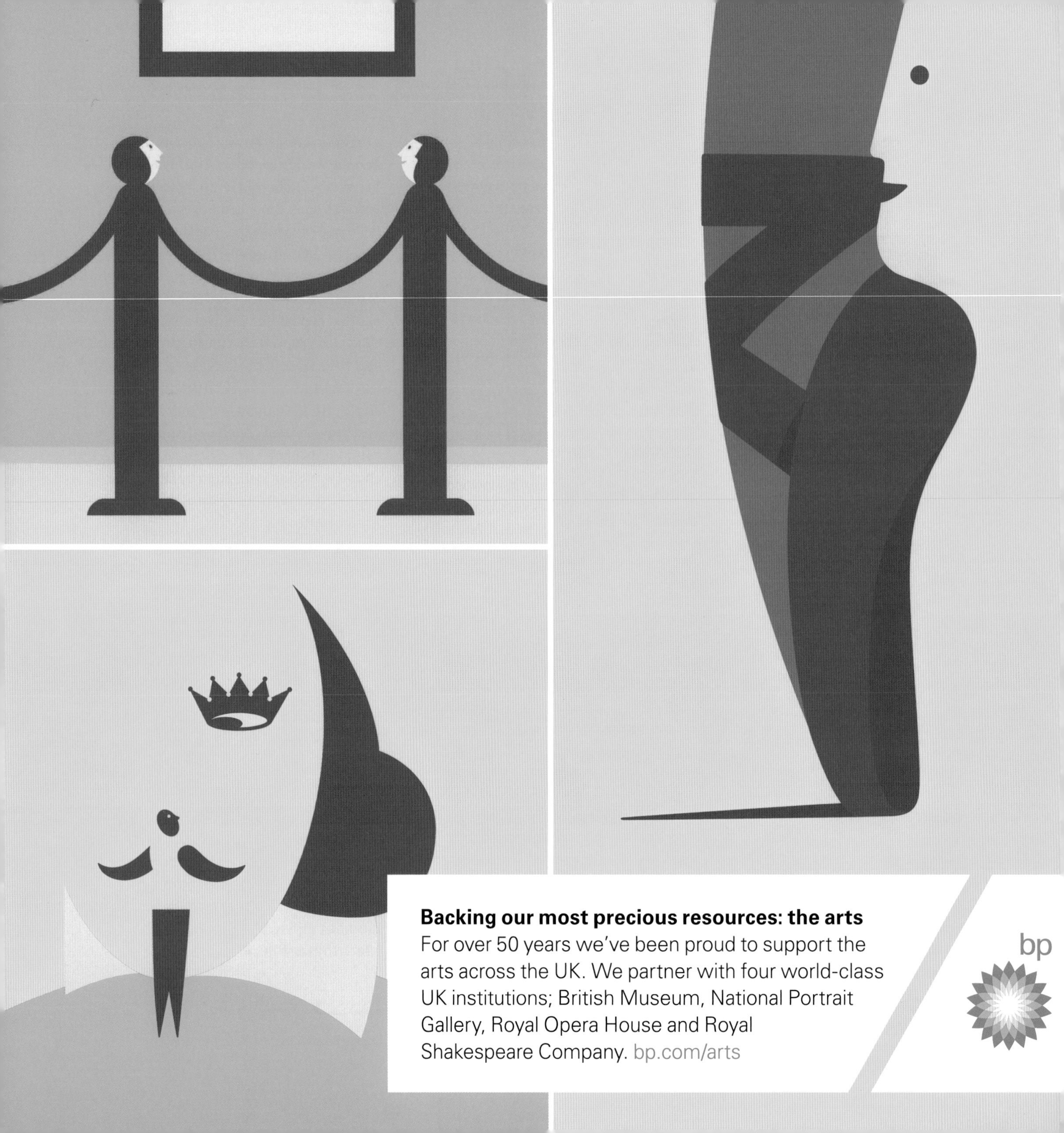
Backing our most precious resources: the arts
For over 50 years we've been proud to support the arts across the UK. We partner with four world-class UK institutions; British Museum, National Portrait Gallery, Royal Opera House and Royal Shakespeare Company. bp.com/arts
bp

The BBC Proms represents the best of classical music-making now from around the world today, and the fact that this wonderful gathering of the world's musicians is made possible by the BBC is something to celebrate and cherish – something that makes us the envy of the world. The BBC orchestras and choirs remain the bedrock of the world's greatest classical music festival, alongside international and British orchestras. This year's Proms season begins with a world premiere that marks the culmination of *Our Classical Century*, the year-long survey across the BBC of the past 100 years of classical music in the UK.

As ever, BBC Radio 3 will be broadcasting every Prom in HD Sound and you can also listen again for 30 days on the BBC Sounds app, with some unique added content too. BBC Television will also capture a large number of concerts, all available to view whenever it suits you on BBC iPlayer.

I can't wait for you to join us this summer in whichever way you choose, and together we'll experience the greatest classical music festival in the world. ●

Alan Davey Controller, BBC Radio 3

This year, 'The Breaks' (Prom 64) brings the world of breaking (aka breakdancing) to the Proms for the first time. Inspired by a forward-looking quote from Proms founder-conductor Henry Wood, poet and performer **DEBRIS STEVENSON** brings two diverse worlds together

The Breakables

'Stick to it, gentlemen! This is nothing to what you'll have to play in 25 years' time.'

Henry Wood while rehearsing Schoenberg's *Five Orchestral Pieces* in 1912

I spy a man a-about eighty-three,
he is spinning on a stage with a guitar
cogged in his teeth,
he charmed it: a mobile up to his lips –
his dentures, they are mechanising strings:
is it a trick?

Then it's the time for the drummer to smash
through static.
The ground it starts to tremble:
he's shifting solid traffic.
Do you know you were once dancing like,
this baby?
You would dance before you said a word!

The break – a toddler again.
When you hear the drummer, you are
being born again.
The break – it's the mo-ment.
You pluck your own strings and hear
the music of your brain.

I spy a lady as she starts to flow
soon a geyser from the stage with
a baton rainbow.
She scatters her directive right through
her hands,
so, the violin bows glide as if the breeze
across the sand.

Then it's the time for the bassoons
to ripen magic.
The ground it starts to grow:
rain after a famine.
And here I am, back row, dancing like this, baby,
I start to dance: no-one's said a word.

The break – a toddler again.
When I hear the cello, I'll hit record,
play again.
The break – it's the mo-ment.
You sample someone's strings
and hear the music
of their brain.

It's that re-mix that we're all trying to conjure;
record, pause, play (half-speed), make bass
longer till it's rapid, rapid: crowds be jumping,
rapid, rapid: the trumpets be pumping.

Capture the magic: vinyl scratching.
Tubas erratic: I'm feeling something
rapid, rapid: sampling, sampling
rapid, rapid: sampling, sampling.

Something in your feet's alive, shifting
my tombstone.
Extract the music from my thighs: dance
etched into bone.

You only need two steps to break
new ground, my love,
and then: we
can let go.

Beyond the Bust

In the 150th-anniversary year of Henry Wood's birth, HANNAH FRENCH celebrates the vision and legacy of the Proms founder-conductor, who single-handedly steered the festival for almost 50 years

The mere thought of Henry Wood conjures up strong images: the regal bust presiding over the Royal Albert Hall stage; the robust bearing and well-trimmed beard; the conductor in full flight, carving the air with his trademark oversized baton. His presence is especially felt in this, the 125th Proms season, and 150 years since his birth. But what do these snapshots reveal about the man who shaped one of the world's best-loved classical music festivals?

In his 1938 memoir, *My Life of Music*, Wood charts his early progress from playing chamber music with his parents at their home on London's Oxford Street to studying the organ at the Royal Academy of Music and, after that, vocal teaching, composing and giving organ recitals. While some memories are not strictly accurate, it's clear that the young man who turned to conducting at the age of 18 was above all a thoroughly practical musician. Early opportunities presented themselves with the D'Oyly Carte and Carl Rosa opera companies, and conducting the British premiere of Tchaikovsky's opera *Eugene Onegin* at the Olympic Theatre, London, in 1892. With a touch of Bow Bells in his speech, Wood was a natural communicator who could get the best out of his performers.

Wood's home-grown raw talent was exactly what Robert Newman was seeking to lead his latest scheme at the newly built Queen's Hall: a festival of promenade concerts. The artist manager and impresario wanted to disrupt the demographic of British concert-going and predicted that an off-season festival with cheap tickets and an unpretentious atmosphere would attract a new audience for classical music. The 26-year-old Wood seized the challenge, taking to the podium on Saturday 10 August 1895 to open the inaugural eight-week season. This first season was not a roaring success, financially or artistically, but the Proms (as the festival was known by 1912) was built on a sound concept. It would weather the storms of finance, management-change and war but, as the years went by, it became apparent that it survived above all because of its association with Wood.

The young conductor certainly looked the part. Queen Victoria herself enquired of him in 1898: 'Are you quite English? Your appearance is rather un-English!' In an age of prejudice against British musicians, he had modelled himself both physically and musically on the Hungarian conductor Arthur Nikisch. Yet, despite first impressions, here was a British conductor ushering in a musical sea change in the London concert scene.

A quick comparison of Proms programmes across Wood's lifetime serves to highlight the shift in tone he achieved. True to the spirit of a promenade concert – which offered an informal air, refreshments and the ability to wander about – Wood and Newman's early programmes comprised large numbers of short popular works, vocal or instrumental solos, waltzes,

Henry Wood in his garden, playing
with his Scottish terrier Michael

Portrait of Henry Wood by Spy (Sir Leslie Ward), published by *Vanity Fair* in 1907

marches and parlour songs. But over the years new works were introduced, first halves becoming more serious and second halves remaining informal; and, over the course of half a century, the programmes evolved into symphonic conceptions worthy of any modern concert hall.

From the very first season, with its Wagner Mondays, themed nights provided structure to the festival. These were an immediate success – but Newman insisted that the second half should continue to include a mix of English popular songs and European favourites, to satisfy every taste. Soon Beethoven Fridays and Popular Saturdays were introduced, while Wednesdays were increasingly reserved for Bach and Handel or Brahms – a practice that continued throughout Wood's lifetime.

Newman's goal was to make each concert as attractive as possible so that people wouldn't want to miss a single night of the season. It was no mean feat, programming music that catered for all tastes and filled around 16 hours each week. Introducing new works was paramount and Wood's appetite for new music, whether newly composed or newly discovered, was insatiable. He also possessed boundless energy for preparing orchestral and vocal parts, producing arrangements and revisiting old scores. It was all about earning the audience's trust: Wood and Newman learnt quickly that new repertoire was best introduced steadily, even stealthily. They fostered a sense that Promenaders might 'overhear' something new and exciting, even if they were queuing for refreshments at the time.

The vast number of Proms premieres given under Wood's baton – more than 700 works by over 350 composers – attests to his wide tastes, and to his ambition and success as an orchestral experimenter and tireless promoter of new music. Whether sourced from the neglected 'ancients' of Bach or Handel, the French Impressionists, the Second Viennese School or contemporary British composers, Wood dubbed them 'novelties'. He was conducting Scriabin, Mahler and Schoenberg before the First World War, and had the perfect platform to promote the latest works by composers he knew personally, from Richard Strauss and Sibelius, to Rachmaninov and Elgar. He also encouraged composers to conduct their own premieres and, while some novelties may have been forgotten by the following morning, others endured to become part of the public psyche.

A note found in Wood's wallet on the day that he died read: 'There is no gain in art without labour of mind and body.' It could have been his lifelong mantra, and it certainly reflected his labour of love at the Proms.

His collaboration with the Queen's Hall Orchestra, *his* orchestra, defined his approach. As a fledgling ensemble, they required Wood's methodical rehearsal technique and crystal-clear beat. Initially there was only time to rehearse a fraction of the works performed every week, prompting meticulous detail in marking up the players' orchestral parts, every pencil stroke of which was entered by Wood himself. He was the first to admit that 'rehearsing with your watch in your hand – every minute precious – is no joke either for conductor or orchestra'. He was, in fact, partial to a joke, but his serious reforms, such as his abolition of the practice that allowed players to send substitutes to rehearsals, made those who accepted his decisions even more respectful of his desire for quality. Wood and the Queen's Hall Orchestra developed a distinctive on-stage chemistry that reflected his temperament. For example, in rehearsal he carefully gave each member the tuning note as they walked on stage – then, like clockwork, with white carnation in place and oversized baton in hand, he took to the podium, then, after a glance to left and right, the music would begin. Newcomers to the orchestra would be given the same encouragement: 'Don't worry! You may be reading at sight in public, but you can't possibly go wrong with *that* stick in front of you!' Little wonder such trademarks earned Wood the nickname 'Timber', not only a play on his name and baton, but a mark of his reliability.

Wood made a point of encouraging emerging talent and the Proms offered the ideal opportunity for those who had passed his audition. Even while he worked with the greatest artists of his day, such as the violinists Joachim, Kreisler and Ysaÿe, he would continually seek out new musicians to add to his roster. Teamwork was the hallmark of the enterprise. It's easy to forget that, for the best part of half a century, a single conductor and orchestra performed six nights each week for the entire season – and regular soloists might feature up to a dozen times. With such consistency of musicians, the Promenaders really got to know the orchestra, and soloists too, seeking out familiar faces and trusting them to introduce new repertoire.

In sponsorship of the Proms, early partnerships with the music-loving ear, nose and throat specialist Dr George Cathcart, and banker Edgar Speyer had been advantageous – principally because they had not demanded artistic control. However, things changed in 1916 when the publishers Chappell & Co., headed by William Boosey, took on financial responsibility. Their progressively difficult terms, including an insistence on programming ballads to advertise their catalogue and a resistance to broadcasting, irked Wood. He did not share Beecham's opinion that broadcasting was 'devilish work' that didn't adequately recompense the efforts of composers and performers and would render concert halls deserted within a decade, so with Newman he began investigating a collaboration with the BBC. Amid escalating tensions Newman died suddenly in 1926 and by March the following year Chappell's declared themselves finished with the Proms. Reeling, but no stranger to negotiations, Wood finally secured the BBC's backing by the start of the 1927 season.

The BBC had begun wireless broadcasting from concert halls in 1924, and Wood's instincts were right. His characteristic precision was ideally suited to an age of recording and broadcasting, and through them he was able to reach a hitherto unimaginably large audience. Initially, the Corporation sought continuity over reform, allowing Wood to keep his players, under the guise of 'Sir Henry J. Wood and his Symphony Orchestra', and offered extra rehearsal time. There is little doubt that the BBC brought with it a new era of professionalism, perhaps best

Wood the Painter

'What after all is music but a picture?'

In 1911, the same year that Henry Wood was knighted for his services to music, he staged an exhibition of some 50 of his own oil paintings at the Piccadilly Arcade Gallery. The image of Wood the painter, brush rather than baton in hand, is not one that we regularly associate with him but many photographs show him in this guise, and in 1938 he declared 'painting is my real love'.

Wood's painting, and his skill at carpentry, were no mere amateurish dabblings. 'He could have been equally distinguished in this art,' claimed Jessie Wood (his common-law wife), and his landscapes were positively reviewed by Royal Academy cognoscenti. He had received formal training and claimed to have attended the prestigious Slade School of Art – though no official registration can be proved.

Capturing sights from his travels across the UK and Europe, Wood worked swiftly, usually finishing a piece in just two sittings. As with his near-contemporary Winston Churchill, painting was an escape from the day job; latterly, when rest was enforced, he would suggest, 'Let's go where I can paint.'

Old masters infused his musical interpretations: for example, he cited Rembrandt's *Descent from the Cross* as inspiration in preparing for Bach's *St Matthew Passion*. In performance, meanwhile, he asserted: 'I paint the picture with the point of my baton.'

demonstrated by the foundation of the BBC Symphony Orchestra in 1930, which comprised many of the finest orchestral musicians of the day. However, the relationship was not always an easy one. Disputes ranged from disagreements over programming and artist engagement to heated negotiations regarding Wood's contract. With the onset of the Second World War, the BBC withdrew its support for three years, during which time Wood was forced once again to find sponsorship elsewhere. When the Queen's Hall was razed to the ground in the Blitz of 1941, one of the few surviving objects among the rubble was Donald Gilbert's famous bust of Wood. It was a fitting metaphor: through thick and thin, he was the one who would stand firm.

Wood was knighted in 1911, awarded the Gold Medal of the Royal Philharmonic Society in 1921 and made a Companion of Honour in 1944. He remained a lifelong loyal British subject, turning down lucrative positions in America, and continuing his work countrywide through the dark days of wartime, even when his own London home was bombed. The legacy of the Proms dwarfs his other considerable projects: conducting a plethora of musical festivals, innumerable concerts in London and the provinces, and his charity work – including raising funds to build a replacement Queen's Hall and to provide beds for musicians in London hospitals.

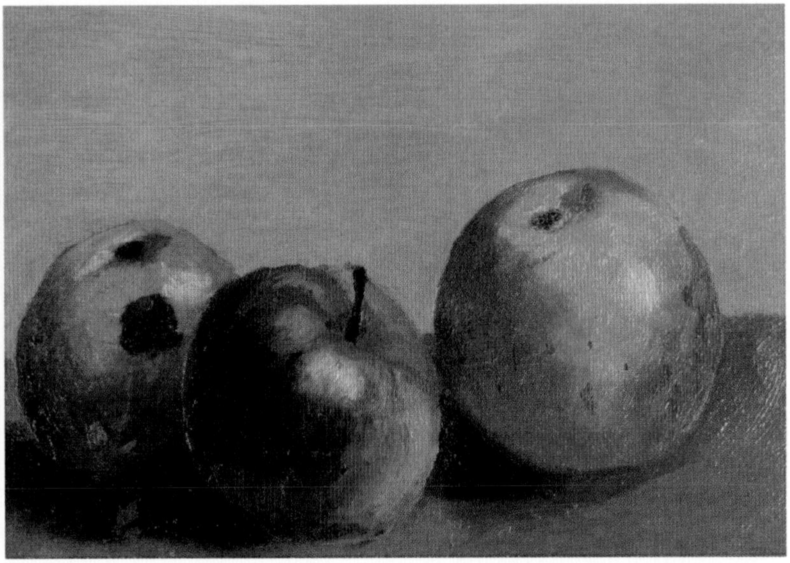

LEFT Portrait by Flora Lion (1876–1958) of Wood's third 'wife', Lady Jessie Wood; their marriage was in name only as Wood's second wife, Muriel, refused to grant him a divorce

RIGHT *Apples* (1880): an early example of Wood's skill as a painter, produced at the age of 11 or 12

Wood had a complicated family life, which inevitably revolved around the Proms. His first wife, the soprano Olga Michailoff, performed at the festival annually until her death in 1909. His second wife, Muriel, had little passion for music, and so increasingly he chose to stay at the Langham Hotel for the entire season. She refused to give him a divorce, so Jessie Linton became his third 'wife', changing her name by deed poll to 'Lady Jessie Wood'. As a former professional

Wood the Feminist?

The Proms provided an ideal platform for Wood's advocacy of women performers. He continually sought out leading female artists, from Astra Desmond to Myra Hess and Jelly d'Arányi. At the same time he spotted and nurtured new female talent, and directed the many women in the student orchestra at the Royal Academy of Music.

Wood admitted women into the Queen's Hall Orchestra in 1913, before the war necessitated it, and from 1916 they played in the full Proms season. He was the first to appoint a female leader of a British orchestra – Marie Wilson, of the BBC Symphony Orchestra, in 1934; encouraged the formidable composer Ethel Smyth to conduct her own works; and entrusted Rosa Newmarch with his first biography and with the descriptive notes for the printed programmes.

He may have posited at one point that 'if women are in too great a proportion, I find their presence is apt to slacken the standard of the other men', but in 1921 he declared: 'I shall never conduct an orchestra without [women] in future, they do their work so well … They are sincere, they do not drink, and they smoke less than men. In the Queen's Hall they have given a certain tone to our rehearsals, and a different spirit to our performances.'

Wood was surrounded by strong women. He formed a musical power couple with his first wife, the soprano Olga Michailoff; produced two headstrong daughters with his second wife, Muriel; and his third partner, Jessie, fought to secure his legacy. As a singer, she understood the artistry and practicalities of the music industry and helped restore his *joie de vivre* in the final decade of his career.

What of Wood's lasting reputation? It was said he lacked the brilliance of Beecham, the illustriousness of Boult and the showmanship of successors such as Sargent, but he was arguably unparalleled in turning around the artistic reputation of a country. William Glock, Controller of the Proms from 1960 to 1973, famously quipped that he 'fell short of genius but rose above mannerism', but his interpretations at the Proms were not those for which he had the opportunity to invest prolonged thought or rehearsal time. In a sense his reputation was flawed by his paranoia that work might dry up, which resulted in his accepting almost every opportunity and creating an exhaustive workload. Ultimately it was *what* he did, rather than *how* he did it that became his legacy, and the epitaph at his resting place at Holy Sepulchre (aka St Sepulchre), Holborn, sums up the achievement: 'He opened the door to a new world of sense and feeling to millions of his fellows. He gave his life for music, and brought music to the people.'

A workaholic to the end, there's no image of Wood as the doddery senior figure. He died in harness aged 75. We're left with the final gesture of each season when, after numerous recalls to accept applause, he would appear on stage in his coat and hat to indicate that he really must be off home. ●

Hannah French is a broadcaster, academic and Baroque flautist. She regularly presents BBC Radio 3's *Early Music Show* and is the author of *Sir Henry Wood: Champion of J.S. Bach*, to be published in June.

'Novelties'

Works whose UK or world premieres were conducted by Wood

PROMS 1, 7, 8, 17, 18, 20, 22, 23, 24, 25, 28, 33, 35, 41, 46, 52, 56, 58, 61, 67, 69 & 75

Composer-themed nights

Wagner Night

PROM 68 • 9 SEPTEMBER

Bach Night

PROM 71 • 11 SEPTEMBER

Beethoven Night

PROM 74 • 13 SEPTEMBER

Proms at … Holy Sepulchre London
The BBC Singers under Sofi Jeannin perform at the church where Henry Wood is buried, and whose St Cecilia stained-glass window overlooks his grave in its Musicians' Chapel

PROMS AT … HSL • 17 AUGUST

Russian Premieres
The London Philharmonic Orchestra under Vladimir Jurowski performs Russian works premiered by Henry Wood

PROM 41 • 17 AUGUST

Cross-Channel Premieres
The BBC Concert Orchestra under Bramwell Tovey performs English and French works premiered by Henry Wood

PROM 56 • 31 AUGUST

Students Turning Professional
Henry Wood studied at London's Royal Academy of Music, whose orchestra he trained for 20 years; students from the RAM and New York's Juilliard School unite in a Prom conducted by Edward Gardner

PROM 6 • 22 JULY

See Index of Works for composers championed by Wood, eg. Debussy, Grieg, Rachmaninov, Tchaikovsky

◀ Exploring new frontiers: a still from Christopher Nolan's 2014 sci-fi thriller *Interstellar*, scored by Hans Zimmer

The Sound of Space

Fifty years after the *Apollo 11* mission landed on the Moon, NEIL BRAND ponders on how composers across the centuries have imagined and created the sound of space

Space has long represented 'the final frontier' to more of us than just the crew of the starship *Enterprise* – the idea of a universe of unexplored potential has challenged visionary artists in all fields throughout history, from writers, to scientists, to film-makers, to composers. The creative challenge, imagining worlds and environments that have never previously existed, lies alongside the practical challenge, imagining humanity at large in those worlds: the strangeness, the isolation, the staggering scale of distances and the superhuman task of surviving them. And music has played its part in immersing us in those experiences.

When *Apollo 11*'s lunar lander touched down on the Moon's surface on 20 July 1969, it somehow broke the spell of the unknown – mankind now stood on a distant, inhospitable planet. Only a year earlier, Arthur C. Clarke and Stanley Kubrick had foreseen the Moon as merely a starting point in mankind's journey to the stars with *2001: A Space Odyssey*, in which utterly realistic-seeming spaceships prowled into the void to the existing music of Richard and Johann Strauss, Ligeti and Khachaturian. Kubrick had famously rejected the excellent, avant-garde original score of Alex North in favour of these composers, but I think there is good reason for that. The smooth confidence and timelessness of *Also sprach Zarathustra* and the waltz *By the Beautiful, Blue Danube* helped anchor the mindblowing images in a more secure, 'human' world that audiences could relate to – even if Ligeti's *Atmosphères* seemed an entirely 'new' sound, the quintessence of a headlong rush through cosmic infinity.

In a more mundane reality, the 1969 landing triggered, alongside new pieces from Duke Ellington and Pink Floyd, one musical masterpiece. A pop single called 'Space Oddity', inspired by Kubrick's film, was released a few days before *Apollo 11*'s launch. Thus began David Bowie's own odyssey, which would influence music right down to the present day … and beyond.

Cinema first became obsessed with outer space as early as 1902, when Parisian film-maker and magician Georges Méliès sent his wizards into a cinematic miracle of cardboard sets and double-exposed stunts on *A Musical Trip to the Moon*. The CBeebies Proms this year mirror exactly that personal lunar journey, one which every child somehow understands and can imagine, just needing the music (in this case an inclusive melange of composers from Puccini to John Adams) to help bring the trip to life.

And when film composers were set the task of contributing to our immersion in strange new worlds, they used an equally wide array of musical styles with which to accomplish it. In 1935, Arthur Bliss composed arguably the first great British film score, for William Cameron Menzies and H. G. Wells's futuristic fantasy *Things to Come*, the soundtrack a heady mix of Elgarian melodies and complex harmonies driven by urgent percussion. Thirty years later Alex North produced his original, sweeping avant-garde orchestral score for Kubrick's *2001*, full of bold textures

Buzz Aldrin (with fellow astronaut Neil Armstrong reflected in his visor) experiencing what he recalled as the 'utter desolation' of the Moon's surface upon landing on 20 July 1969

and harmonic clashes in an attempt to find a new 'voice' for Kubrick's visions. But 10 years before even Alex North's humiliating rejection, New York-based avant-garde electronic music pioneers Bebe and Louis Barron had scored MGM's *Forbidden Planet*. Their 'electronic tonalities' (some created by literally overloading circuits until they burned out) were an entirely successful attempt to give a completely new soundscape to distant worlds; everything within the film's soundtrack, from spaceships, to guns, to the roars of the invisible monster, had an electronic voice, one any sci-fi fan of today would recognise. And, *pace* John Williams's stunning return to Golden Age scoring with 1977's *Star Wars*, space has since primarily sung with the unpredictable textures of rapidly improving music technology – think Vangelis's *Blade Runner* soundtrack, Brian Eno's *Dune*, Clint Mansell's *Moon*, Hans Zimmer's *Interstellar*, and perhaps most adventurously Mica Levi's shimmering *Under the Skin* (2013), which somehow seemed to bring the otherworldliness of deep space onto the streets of Glasgow.

But what of the realities of space itself, its physical properties and gravitationally contained sound-worlds, which must, surely, somewhere, pierce the silence of airlessness?

The idea of the Music of the Spheres, celestial tones made by the Solar System's bodies interacting in motion with each other, was first proposed by the Greeks and taken up by Cicero in his philosophical treatise, *The Dream of Scipio*. The idea of 'unheard heavenly music' still held sway when the astronomer and astrologer Johannes Kepler (1571–1630), a contemporary of Galileo, used mathematical calculations and observation through early telescope lenses to establish laws of motion for the entire Solar System. He argued in his *Harmonices mundi* ('The Harmony of the World', 1619) that the motions of the six known planets could be described in terms of musical intervals and harmonies.

In a sense, he was quite correct, the later mathematical calculations of distance, gravitational pull and even the nature of the Universe itself were akin to the calculations of sound-waves, resonances and tonal shifts that are the physical manifestation of musical tones to the human ear. Largely thanks to Kepler, the connection between music, mathematics and astronomy had a profound impact on scientific history, resulting in music's inclusion in the quadrivium, the medieval curriculum that comprised arithmetic, geometry, music and astronomy; along with grammar, logic and rhetoric, these together make up the seven liberal arts that are still the basis of higher education today. Yet another positive argument, were one needed, for the improvement of music provision to schools.

Kepler's scientific descendant, astronomer and composer William Herschel, would, in 1781, add a seventh planet to the cosmos, Uranus, discovered through careful calculation with superb new and enormously large optical telescopes. And in June 1792 Joseph Haydn visited Herschel's observatory in Slough – where he may (or may not) have discussed Herschel's findings with Herschel's sister Caroline, after which he may (or may not) have taken away the notion of describing the heavens bursting into God-given light in his great oratorio of 1796–8, *The Creation*.

> When *Apollo 11*'s lunar lander touched down on the Moon's surface on 20 July 1969, it somehow broke the spell of the unknown – mankind now stood on a distant, inhospitable planet.

What is not subject to speculation is how profoundly Haydn captured the sense of the void that exists before Verse 3 of the Book of Genesis. After the gradual diminution of that massive opening chord on the note C, Haydn's audience would have found his Representation of Chaos entirely unpredictable and ambiguous, as chaotic and unknowable to 18th-century ears as the Bible's own description of that same void – 'And the earth was without form, and void; and darkness was upon the face of the deep.' And Haydn's picture-painting continues – orchestra and choir remain hushed, sparse, empty through these opening verses, until the explosion of sound that brings light to this darkness, the great C major chord, surely the loudest human-made sound to have been heard up to that time.

And there we have the building bricks of our idea of 'space' in musical terms – darkness, sparsity, often with long resonances, echoing into an immeasurable distance – the idea of unpredictable, ambiguous tonalities, atonal, unstructured, dimensions suggested more by orchestral texture than volume of sound. In the past half-century we have developed a world of unexplored textures available through electronics – sound-design, tonalities both musical and non-musical. Emptiness suggested through sound.

The philosophy of such music is that man, adrift in space, is alone and confused – all sense of community, warmth, security is irretrievably lost. There is no order in space, ergo there can be no God. Like the sea, we make space represent whatever we want it to. And it is not a place into which mankind is, in any way, welcomed.

It's a vast and chilling concept captured beautifully in Icelandic composer Anna Thorvaldsdottir's *Metacosmos*, a 14-minute piece that seems to navigate the abyssal depths of space with bold strokes of orchestral colour – as critic David Wright wrote after its New York premiere last year, 'Listening to [Thorvaldsdottir's] piece, one couldn't help thinking of the saying attributed to the scientist J. B. S. Haldane, that the Universe is not only stranger than we suppose, it is stranger than we can suppose.' And to Edward Sava-Segal it seemed that 'at points one has the impression of vistas without borders. Elsewhere, huge, unknown beings, heavily breathing, seem to be very close.'

Much other modern music has also been inspired by the very process of grappling with these enormous themes – Philip Glass's 1992 opera *The Voyage* posits the dilemma of the crew of a spaceship crashing onto an unknown planet (actually ice-age Earth), set alongside the voyage of Christopher

The Planets and Holst

Professor Brian Cox reflects on how what we now know about the planets of our Solar System affects how we hear Holst's *The Planets*, over 100 years on

When Holst completed *The Planets* in 1917, little was known about the worlds he represented musically, and he didn't care. His inspiration was astrological and his focus terrestrial; War, Peace, Jollity, Old Age, Messenger, Magician and Mystic.

Today we have visited all the planets, and at first sight this new knowledge might appear to jar with Holst's work, but this would be a superficial conclusion. Set against what we now know, the work catalyses new ideas that enrich and inform debates in progress today, as art with depth must do.

Mars was once Earth-like. Life may have begun on the red planet and may exist today. The discovery of a second genesis in our Solar System would have profound cultural consequences: it would mean that we are not alone in the Universe.

Venus was also once Earth-like, but a runaway greenhouse effect has turned a potential paradise into a vision of hell. Listen to Holst's Venus with this in mind, and the piece becomes a requiem for a failed planet, a reminder that planets – just as human beings – were once born and will one day die. It is this fragility that makes them precious.

2019 SEASON
REGENT'S PARK OPEN AIR THEATRE
16 May – 08 Jun
OUR TOWN
by THORNTON WILDER
14 – 22 Jun
HANSEL AND GRETEL
by ENGELBERT HUMPERDINCK
in a co-production with English National Opera
28 Jun – 27 Jul
A MIDSUMMER NIGHT'S DREAM
by WILLIAM SHAKESPEARE
02 Aug – 21 Sep
EVITA
lyrics by TIM RICE
music by ANDREW LLOYD WEBBER
As You Like It (2018). Photo: David Jenson/Feast Creative
THE ROYAL PARKS
Season Partners
scala RADIO
The Telegraph
THE MARYLEBONE
DOYLE COLLECTION • LONDON
0333 400 3562*
openairtheatre.com
* Lines open 9am – 9pm. A £1.80 per ticket telephone booking fee applies.

Columbus to the Americas, surely an odyssey worthy of the name. Górecki's enormous Second Symphony is a meditation on the works of Copernicus, who established the solar cosmography of our planetary system, and was composed for the astronomer's 500th anniversary. And Karlheinz Stockhausen, perhaps more than any other 20th-century composer, anchored his musical inspiration to the stars, and myriad concepts of the idea of space. His narrative pieces *Sirius* and *Licht* grapple with these cosmic complexities and gain enormous strength from his deep research and understanding both into the physics of electronic sound-creation and his fascination with astronomy.

But space as a vital element of an audience's listening experience was also Stockhausen's currency. The concept of spacialisation in music – distributing sound across space – was not new. Indeed, it had been a recognised element in the work of Palestrina and many others in the 16th century, in which the position of musicians in relation to the audience was a crucial element in performances of his works. Stockhausen's wish for 'new kinds of concert halls, more suited to Spatial Music' was at least partially realised with the construction of a spherical auditorium, whose performances he oversaw and composed for, at the Expo '70 exhibition in Osaka.

Arguably the best-known work inspired by the Cosmos must be Holst's suite *The Planets*, which itself adheres to a Keplerian view of space in 'humanising' the planets according to their cosmological and astrological associations. And this year Huw Watkins continues the theme of planetary-inspired music with a new piece, *The Moon*, for orchestra and choir including settings of poems by Shelley, Larkin and Whitman, especially commissioned for this anniversary of the 1969 Moon landing.

Meanwhile, in space itself, nobody can hear you scream … or sing … or emit any noise at all … Or can they?

For years, NASA has been recording radio emissions from space – plasma waves, magnetic emissions, solar winds and ionospheres – and collecting them in their sound-archive. In 2002 astrophysicist Donald A. Gurnett was responsible for capturing these sounds recorded by the *Voyager* spacecraft on its journey to the stars and creating the means to make them audible. NASA suggested using Gurnett's recordings as the basis for a musical piece, which composer Terry Riley and the Kronos Quartet created under the title *Sun Rings*.

And, continuing the theme of music and 'found sound', Public Service Broadcasting recreate their groundbreaking 2015 concept album *The Race for Space*, a superb mix of music and broadcast recordings combining to tell the, sometimes dark, tale of the US/Russian space race of the 1950s and 1960s with wit and deep insight.

It seems that, even today, space itself is getting closer, not farther away. Probes and landers are sending back new information daily from Mars and the dark side of the Moon, deep-space probes pierce ever further beyond our Solar System. And, at the beginning of this year, a new observatory in Canada detected a very unusual repeating signal, coming from a galaxy about 1.5 billion light years away. Our ability to 'hear' these signals grows year by year. And surely the actual experience of deep-space travel, for which man has been preparing so diligently for as long as civilisation has existed, can only be a matter of a generation or so away.

But, thanks to the work of these visionary musicians, perhaps we have already 'heard' it … ●

Neil Brand is a pianist, composer, writer and broadcaster best known for his work on BBC Radio 4's *The Film Programme*, and his *Sound of…* series for BBC Four, which have covered film music, sound technology and stage and screen musicals. He has written orchestral scores for silent films including Hitchcock's *Blackmail* and Fairbanks's *Robin Hood*, composed as a result of his nearly 40-year-career as an improvising silent-film pianist.

CBeebies Proms: A Musical Trip to the Moon
PROMS 3 & 5 • 21 & 22 JULY

Holst The Planets; **Adams** Short Ride in a Fast Machine
PROM 4 • 21 JULY

Anna Thorvalsdottir Metacosmos
UK premiere
PROM 6 • 22 JULY

The Race for Space (Public Service Broadcasting)
PROM 10 • 25 JULY

Messiaen Des canyons aux étoiles …
PROM 13 • 28 JULY

The Sound of Space: Sci-Fi Film Music
PROM 27 • 7 AUGUST

Huw Watkins The Moon
BBC commission: world premiere
PROM 28 • 8 AUGUST

◀ Jess Gillam – saxophonist and music education advocate – making her Proms debut aged 19, at the Ten Pieces Prom in 2017

Music, Inspiration ... Education

As the BBC Proms continues its series of events aimed at getting the whole family involved in music-making – regardless of age or ability – former BBC Young Musician finalist JESS GILLAM highlights the impact early access to musical engagement has made on her career and musical life

Exploration and excitement are constant features in our youth, but it's not often that something entirely captures the imagination to the extent that you don't want to do or try anything else. I was lucky enough to have this experience at the age of just 7; one of my most vivid memories is picking up a saxophone for the first time at the Barracudas Carnival Arts Centre in Barrow-in-Furness. I was utterly enthralled and in love with the instrument.

On reflection, the vigour, excitement and liveliness of a carnival was the perfect place to start. We met twice a week to rehearse – once with the band and once with the dancers, stilt walkers and backpackers. I instantly felt like I was part of a community – a team of people who had a shared vision, together creating a huge sound and splash of colour. The band toured all over the country playing at some of the UK's biggest carnivals. It was a hub for creativity and joy, and a celebration of what the arts could achieve. The Barracudas provided so many people – from a huge range of backgrounds, ages and abilities – with a sense of belonging and purpose.

I have never forgotten that feeling of unity and it's something that I carry with me in everything I do now – even if it's a solo recital. I believe a sense of belonging is something every child deserves to feel and it's something that the arts, especially music, provide in reams. Whether it's as part of an orchestra, carnival band, choir or any other ensemble, making music together unites people. It demands a deep level of empathy and communication that cannot be taught in a classroom or in a traditional working environment – an unspoken yet deep form of interaction.

At the age of 11, I was extremely lucky to have access to a Primary Tuition Scheme run by the local secondary school. This was a scheme whereby older students in the sixth form would pass on their skills by teaching primary schoolchildren for just £2.00 a week. In this method of teaching, the teacher can consolidate their own knowledge while simultaneously imparting it to a younger student. However, music did not (and rarely does) feature as a core part of the curriculum in schools. It seems unfathomable to me that, even though music is central to human experience and part of the fabric of our society, it does not feature heavily in the basic education of most British children.

It is for this reason that I am so keen to play to children of all ages in schools and other educational establishments around the country – with the aim to inspire and ignite a spark for music in young people. Even though we live in a society where information and resources are so accessible, music education is continually being cut back, making learning an instrument and accessing music ever more difficult.

Whether or not a young person chooses to pursue music as a career, it can teach and develop so many key life skills: determination, co-operation, empathy, resilience, discipline and confidence, to name just a few.

The role of the performer has evolved in recent decades and professional musicians are now becoming seen as 'musical citizens' helping to promote the role of music in society, and classical music no longer exists only in concert halls. Recently, it has become common for concerts to be linked to an educational programme or community project: I think this is essential at a critical time for engaging with the community.

Never too young to pass on experience: Jess Gillam giving a masterclass at a school in Preston, 2017

Live music is absolutely electric – there is something so special about a performance existing only in that moment in time and being shared by performer and audience; a concert is like a capsule of energy. I believe that exposing young children to live music is one of the most effective ways of encouraging them to engage with music and their surroundings. An especially memorable experience for me was playing to a room full of children aged 7 to 11. The concert was held at the local hall and there was a buzz of excitement as the children sat in rows and watched the concert. I was amazed by their level of concentration, focus and engagement, and completely shocked when I performed the final piece: the whole hall erupted and spontaneously rose. They were on their feet, dancing, spinning, clapping, laughing and grooving! To see this instinctive, intuitive reaction to music was truly incredible and I felt an overwhelming sense of inspiration. At that moment I decided that working with young people had to become an essential part of my performing career.

At the age of 12, I began studying at the Junior Royal Northern College of Music in Manchester. This was a key part of my music education, a place brimming with creativity and passion, where I was surrounded by peers with a hunger to learn. To be with these like-minded young people was utterly inspiring. Had I not had parents who encouraged me and appreciated the value of music, I would never have had the opportunity to study at a Saturday school such as the Junior RNCM. Again, this experience really fuels my determination to reach as many young people as possible who may not have this opportunity.

I came to learn about the BBC Young Musician competition through being a student at the Junior RNCM and I applied aged 14. I reached the Woodwind final and in 2016 re-entered and reached the Grand Final. I learnt more from the process of BBC Young Musician (about myself as a musician and a person) than from any experience in my life so far. It made me ask crucial questions about what kind of a musician (and communicator) I wanted to be, what music really means and how best to communicate emotion. I am so grateful to the BBC for providing young people with an opportunity to share and showcase their passions while inspiring and promoting excellence. This is a prime example of how music teaches far more than just the learning of an instrument.

The number and range of education and outreach projects have rocketed recently and a huge project I was also very lucky to be involved with was the BBC's Ten Pieces scheme. The multi-dimensional approach of the initiative – whereby children listen to music, learn about its history and creatively respond to it – is really fantastic! Performing at the Ten Pieces Proms in 2017 was a special experience for me: to see the Royal Albert Hall filled with babies, toddlers and young people enjoying a wide variety of classical music was unforgettable. I think the notion of participation in music is fundamental, and it is a key aspect of Ten Pieces: for young children to have the opportunity and freedom to react creatively and be a part of the music-making process (as in Kerry Andrew's specially composed *No Place Like*).

If music remains an add-on to our education system and if there isn't a significant shift to appreciating the value of music within our society, I believe we are in danger of crushing innovation, creativity and expression. The immeasurable entity we call 'music' is wonderfully inexplicable. It can transform lives, force us to ask fundamental questions and provide a sense of hope, joy and worth. We must do everything we can as a society to ensure that every single child is given the opportunity to be captivated by its magic. ●

Classical BRIT-winner Jess Gillam won the woodwind final of BBC Young Musician in 2016. She performed at the Proms in 2017 and 2018 and in April joined Radio 3 as presenter of *This Classical Life*.

BBC Proms Learning

BBC Proms Learning supports the Proms' aim to bring the greatest classical music to the widest possible audience. Beyond the concert hall, we offer the opportunity to participate, play alongside professional musicians and creatively explore the music featured in the Proms. Nurturing talent is central to this aim, and we continue to develop programmes around composition (BBC Proms Inspire), the voice (BBC Proms Youth Choir and Academy) and instrumental development (BBC Proms Youth Ensemble), creating exciting musical opportunities for young people.

For Families

Proms Family Workshops

At Imperial College Union. Family-friendly introductions to the music of the evening's Prom. Bring an instrument or just sit back and take it all in. (Suitable for ages 7-plus.)

Saturday 27 July, 5.45pm–6.30pm

Saturday 3 August, 5.45pm–6.30pm

Thursday 15 August, 5.15pm–6.00pm

Sunday 25 August, 3.30pm–4.30pm

Saturday 31 August, 5.45pm–6.30pm

No booking is necessary (except for 25 August, see booking details across). Entry is free and on a first-come, first-served basis. Doors open 30 minutes before the event begins; capacity is limited. Events end one hour before the start of the following Prom.

Proms Family Orchestra & Chorus

The Proms Family Orchestra & Chorus introduces families to making music together. Whatever your ability, the whole family can join in. Join professional musicians on the stage of the Royal Albert Hall to devise an environment-themed piece, inspired by Robert Macfarlane and Jackie Morris's book *The Lost Words* (Monday 26 August, 10.00am–1.00pm).

Entry is free. Suitable for all the family and open to all levels of ability (ages 7-plus). You don't need to be able to read music. Non-instrumentalists can join the chorus or the percussion section.

For Young Composers

BBC Proms Inspire

The BBC Proms Inspire scheme for young composers offers a friendly platform for 12- to 18-year-olds to meet other young music-makers, develop their musical creativity, share ideas and get their music heard. The scheme offers access to a thriving community of aspiring music-makers as well as opportunities to learn from leading composers at events throughout the year. Members of the scheme also receive exclusive ticket offers to BBC Orchestras and Choir concerts across the UK and to the Proms.

At the heart of the scheme is the **Inspire Competition.** Winners receive a professional performance of their composition at the Proms, a coveted BBC broadcast and a BBC commission. The **Inspire Day** – a day of workshops and events (13 August, 10.30am–4.00pm at Imperial College Union) – is followed by the Inspire Concert, where you can hear the winning pieces from this year's competition (5.00pm–6.00pm, BBC Maida Vale Studios).

The closing date for Inspire Competition entries is 5.00pm on 23 May; see bbc.co.uk/proms for terms and conditions.

For Proms Family Workshop (25 August only), Proms Family Orchestra & Chorus and Proms Inspire Day, places must be booked in advance at bbc.co.uk/proms. Booking opens at 10.00am on Friday 14 June.

For Young Performers

BBC Proms Youth Choir/Youth Choir Academy for singers aged 16 to 25 (see Prom 14)

BBC Proms Youth Ensemble for instrumentalists aged 16 to 25 (see Prom 70)

Proms CBeebies Choir for singers aged 10-plus (see Proms 3 & 5)

For more information about Proms Learning, email getinvolved@bbc.co.uk or call 020 7765 0557.

A Birthday 'Enigma'

Composer JOHN PICKARD introduces a 21st-century companion to Elgar's 'Enigma' Variations, in which 14 living composers join together to create a unique 60th-birthday present for British conductor Martyn Brabbins

When Edward Elgar completed his 'Enigma' Variations in 1899, he famously dedicated them 'to my friends pictured within'. The Variations are musical portraits of 13 friends, some of them close – such as Elgar's wife Alice, the subject of the first variation – some not so close; all rounded off by a self-portrait in the form of an extended Finale. The result, first performed on 19 June 1899, was an instant triumph, sealing Elgar's reputation as the leading British composer of his generation.

Now, 120 years later, the British conductor Martyn Brabbins, a popular figure at the Proms, has decided to revisit Elgar's scheme, but with a novel twist. He explains: 'My dear friend and agent, Susie Mcleod, had the idea of having a big project to mark my 60th birthday this year – and so I thought big! I concocted a way to combine two of my passions – British music and new music – by commissioning a new set of "Enigma" Variations.'

Brabbins decided to invert the idea of a single composer writing variations about several friends; instead he asked several composers to write, not so much about him, but certainly for him. 'So I approached an amazing clutch of composer friends, who instantly shared my enthusiasm. The BBC Scottish Symphony Orchestra [with whom Brabbins has a long-standing association] and Proms director David Pickard were also immediately enthusiastic.' The result is *Pictured Within: Birthday Variations for M. C. B.*, a BBC commission, which receives its world premiere on 13 August, conducted by its dedicatee – who turns 60 that same day.

◀ Elgar on a garden bench *(right)* with George Sinclair, who features in one of the 'Enigma' Variations; standing behind are musician friends Max Mossel *(left)* and Percy Hull

Multi-composer works are far more common than one might perhaps think. After all, one of the most famous of all choral works, Verdi's *Requiem*, began life as a composite work by 13 composers, a project designed to commemorate Rossini's death in 1868. Amazingly, even though every one of the composers involved delivered their allotted chunk (Verdi's was the *Libera me*), the first performance of the complete work did not take place until 1988.

In bringing together such a varied group of composers for this new project, overall stylistic inconsistency is guaranteed. You could say that this is the whole point and part of the fun. Nevertheless, one or two ground rules were deemed necessary in order to create some kind of coherence. First, the theme-and-variation structure determined that everyone would at least be working to the same theme. Then, as Brabbins points out, 'I was pretty firm with all the composers that I would choose which of Elgar's variations they were to model their contribution upon: this was to ensure variety within the piece as a whole. I was pretty clear in my mind which composer's style would fit the character enshrined in each Elgar variation.' On a practical note, Brabbins says, 'I didn't want the new piece to sprawl!' To this end, the composers were all asked to try to keep their allotted variation to the same duration as their Elgarian equivalent. British composer Colin Matthews reveals that, 'in discussing the project with Martyn, I said that I would like my variation to be modelled on one of Elgar's fast variations, and he offered me the fastest (and shortest) – the one depicting William Meath Baker (Variation 4), one of Elgar's friends who "expressed himself somewhat energetically".' Two composers – Sir Harrison Birtwistle (Variation 9, 'Nimrod') and myself (Variation 14, 'Finale: E. D. U.') – were given slightly longer time spans to fill.

A latter-day 'Enigma' Variations naturally required an'Enigma' of its own to provide intrigue and mystery. And at this point it is worth remembering that Elgar gave the name 'Enigma' only to the Theme, not to the whole piece, and that he did so only after having sent his finished score to his publisher. Why he did it no-one knows, but generations have assumed there was a puzzle there to be solved and have set about trying to solve it, with varying degrees of ingenuity (or, depending on your point of view, barminess).

Many Elgarian sleuths believe that the Theme is a counterpoint to another, hidden, tune. Everything from *Rule, Britannia!* to the hymn tune 'Now the day is over' has been posited, but nothing quite fits. As the musicologist J. P. E. Harper-Scott has trenchantly observed, 'Human nature guarantees that attempts to solve [the 'Enigma'] will never end until the Ark of the Covenant and the Holy Grail are on permanent display in the British Museum.'

In the new work, the 'enigma' is straightforward: the new Theme has been written by that venerable and prolific composer, 'Anon'. Brabbins reveals that the theme was 'a gift' but that is all he is

A Headful of Codes

The 'Enigma' was one of an array of ciphers and puzzles that occupied Elgar's thoughts

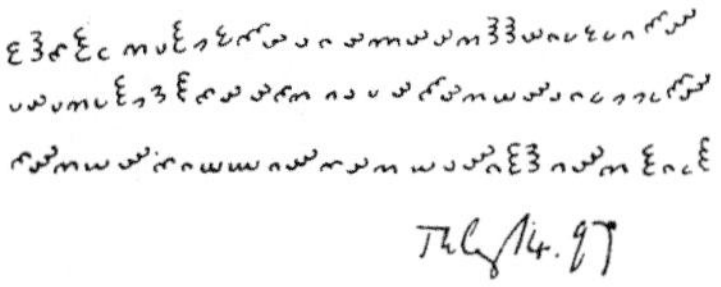

Although the 'Enigma' of Elgar's Variations remains unsolved and possibly never existed in the first place, there is abundant evidence elsewhere of Elgar's lifelong obsession with puzzles and codes.

As an eight-year-old, Elgar drew two intersecting five-line staves in a cruciform shape, placed a single note at the centre and added a different clef at the four compass points. By reading up, down, across and backwards, the central note spells out B–A–C–H ('H' being B in German musical spelling).

An inveterate puzzle-solver and crossword aficionado, Elgar kept musical sketchbooks that are littered with word and number games and substitution codes, doodlings between bursts of invention and striking evidence of a restless creative mind.

The most enduringly perplexing of all Elgar's puzzles is the so-called 'Dorabella' cipher *(above)*, which Elgar sent to Dora Penny ('Dorabella' of the 'Enigma' Variations) in 1897. Years later, Dora included a facsimile in her published memoir of Elgar. The cipher consists of three lines of 87 characters using 24 symbols. During 2007, the Elgar 150th-anniversary year, a cash prize was offered for its solution, but a convincing answer has yet to be found.

saying, so speculation as to its authorship will no doubt be rife. There are no obvious stylistic traits revealing it as the work of any particular composer and it is certainly not rehashed Elgar. But the closer one looks at this new Theme , the more apparent its kinship to Elgar's 'Enigma' Theme becomes. Both are tentative, introspective, provisional. Both have two subjects, the first with a kind of rocking motion in the leading line, the second using a rising and falling motion. Of more importance to the composers involved, though, the new Theme is a repository of different types of harmony: stacks of interlocking fifths, an angular atonal arc of melody, a series of regular, though unrelated, triads, even an unequivocal (though, in the context, highly enigmatic) C major chord at the end. In short, there is something there to suit most compositional voices among an extraordinarily diverse bunch of 'variationees'.

As of early January, about half the variations have been delivered. They reveal a range of approaches. According to Richard Blackford (Variation 8, 'W. N.'), 'the grace and gentle humour of Elgar's variation made me reflect on Martyn's own warmth and kindness. The movement is restrained and concise, but its expansive middle section leaves no doubt about the fire and passion its dedicatee brings to the concert platform.' Judith Weir (Variation 10, 'Dorabella') feels much the same way: she says that she 'hoped to endow the theme with some warmth and geniality, qualities which for me sum up Martyn's personality and disposition.'

Some of the pairings are truly intriguing. As a former violist in the Berlin Philharmonic, Brett Dean's response to Elgar's gently humorous evocation of an amateur violist's travails (Variation 6, 'Ysobel') is a fascinating prospect. Meanwhile, Gavin Bryars, master of the quietly contemplative, has the challenge of confronting the unruly antics of George Robertson Sinclair's bulldog, Dan (Variation 11, 'G. R. S').

As for my own contribution, I've had the honour, not to mention the alarming responsibility, of trying to round off the whole work with an extended Finale. I couldn't resist throwing in one or two enigmas of my own along the way. The subtitle of my Finale, 'The Art of Beginning', is a literary allusion that will easily be unravelled by devoted Elgarians (or by a quick internet search). Elsewhere, there are a couple of small musical jokes that are intended solely for Martyn's amusement.

How the whole piece will work out is anyone's guess. Maybe it will be a bit of a mess, but it is also possible that it will present fascinating snapshots of 14 contemporary composers (plus anonymous Theme-writer) attempting our own snapshots of our dear friend and colleague 'pictured within'. Colin Matthews sums up the project perfectly: 'It's typical of Martyn that he should give himself a birthday present that is at the same time a gift to all the composers involved in the form of a commission.' ●

John Pickard is a composer and musicologist. He is Professor of Composition and Applied Musicology at Bristol University and was General Editor of the *Elgar Complete Edition* from 2004 to 2016.

Pictured Within: Birthday Variations for M. C. B.; Elgar: 'Enigma' Variations

PROM 35 • 13 AUGUST

"PACKED WITH WIT, STORMING SONGS AND BEAUTIFUL COSTUMES."
The Guardian
WINNER! 100 MAJOR AWARDS
WICKED
THE UNTOLD STORY OF THE WITCHES OF OZ
WickedTheMusical.co.uk • #WickedUK
THE APOLLO VICTORIA THEATRE LONDON • SW1V 1LG
©WLPL

GEORGE ENESCU
FESTIVAL
The World in Harmony
31.08 - 22.09.2019
www.festivalenescu.ro

Festgesetzte Preise.
Cajetan del.

◀ Berlioz directs an orchestra featuring a smoking canon, timpani struck by mechanical wooden hammers and a sea of brass instruments; the caption for one version of this caricature (1846) reads: 'Fortunately the hall is solid … it can withstand the strain'

A Life with Berlioz

As Sir John Eliot Gardiner concludes his multi-year Proms series in the 150th-anniversary year of Berlioz's death, **JOHN ALLISON** talks to the conductor about a figure who has divided opinion, even in his native France, but who has come to be acknowledged as a revolutionary of vivid imagination

Given how many of the impulses in Hector Berlioz's music intersect with the wide-ranging interests of Sir John Eliot Gardiner, it is no surprise that the conductor should have enjoyed such a long-standing relationship with Berlioz's music. Berlioz was never afraid of thinking big and several of Gardiner's most notable *grands projets* have been based around his music. The bicentenary of the composer's birth, in 2003, saw Gardiner conducting the first-ever fully complete performances of his mammoth opera *The Trojans* in Paris, and trailblazing even further by doing so with period instruments.

Working towards this year's 150th anniversary of the French master's death, Gardiner has been presenting a five-year Berlioz odyssey at the Proms, which culminates this summer with the composer's first surviving opera, *Benvenuto Cellini* (1834–7). Last year's programme including *Harold in Italy* was preceded in 2017 by *The Damnation of Faust*, in 2016 by *Romeo and Juliet* (a personal favourite, as Gardiner reveals when pressed); the journey began in 2015 with the *Symphonie fantastique.*

It is no coincidence that Gardiner's career has unfolded in tandem with the modern re-evaluation of Berlioz's achievement – indeed, Gardiner has played a major role in it. He was just starting out half a century ago when London marked an earlier Berlioz anniversary with the famous 1969 Covent Garden staging of *The Trojans*, conducted by Colin Davis, the big *Berlioz and the Romantic Imagination* exhibition at the V&A (whose catalogue is still worth seeking out in second-hand shops) and the publication of David Cairns's groundbreaking English translation of the *Mémoires*. But since Gardiner was also still finding his own voice – notably through early performances of Monteverdi, Bach and Schütz – it is perhaps unsurprising that it was no single facet of Berlioz's art, except for his blazing genius, that most ignited his interest.

What, for instance, of the obvious connection with one of Gardiner's musical gods, Beethoven, of the neat coincidence of Berlioz's birth in the 'Eroica' year of 1803, and of the fact that his *Symphonie fantastique* can be seen as a 'Pastoral' Symphony gone nightmarishly wrong? 'These are fascinating connections, and it is incredible to think that the *Symphonie fantastique* came only three years after Beethoven's death in 1827. Berlioz's whole orchestral organism is founded entirely on Beethoven, but he takes it in different directions. He was more experimental than Beethoven. I see Berlioz and Schumann [another Gardiner speciality] together as the twin inheritors of Beethoven's legacy. They admired each other a great deal, and Schumann's critique of the *Symphonie fantastique* is one of the most sympathetic written by a composer of another composer's work – very unlike Wagner, who never had a good word to say about anyone! And it's interesting to me that Beethoven at one point seriously considered moving to Paris, because of his admiration for the Revolution and for Napoleon I.'

Symphonie fantastique (1830, rev. 1831–45)

If a single piece of music can stand as a document of the Romantic movement, Berlioz's *Symphonie fantastique* is that work. His first masterpiece, it has remained his best-known score and it was crucial in his development as a composer. Full of autobiographical meanings, it is the piece in which Berlioz's youthful passions all find a place, but it also shows how in Berlioz's hands the Beethovenian symphonic model became a branch of dramatic music.

Benvenuto Cellini (1834–7)

Reading the memoirs of the sculptor Benvenuto Cellini only after his return from an early sojourn in Italy, Berlioz found himself drawn back to the spirit of that country. More particularly, he was drawn to that 'bandit of genius', and Cellini's disordered life thus became the subject of Berlioz's first surviving opera. Its half-serious, half-comic spirit derives from the intersection of two stories – Cellini's love life and the casting of his great statue.

Should we see Berlioz, then, as a child of the Revolution? 'Well, in terms of when he was born, and of the size of his epic canvases, yes. But he admired Louis-Napoleon as well, even though he was less loyal in return, and open to the blandishments of Wagner.'

It is as an occasional theme of our conversation that Wagner emerges as one of the conductor's *bêtes noires*. 'A few years ago Sir Simon Rattle conducted a programme with the Orchestra of the Age of Enlightenment juxtaposing the love scene from *Romeo and Juliet*, which lasts just 17 minutes, with the whole second act of Wagner's *Tristan and Isolde*, and I just felt that Berlioz in those few minutes is more intense and more wonderful than the whole Wagner work.'

So is Gardiner, with his early-music pedigree, drawn more to Berlioz's Classical-period inheritance, and does he see Gluck as the Classical skeleton on which Berlioz hung his hyper-Romantic flesh? The lifelong love that Berlioz had for Gluck can be traced all the way from an early musical discovery (in the family library at home in La Côte-Saint-André) of a couple of *Orpheus and Eurydice* numbers arranged for guitar to his own version of the opera made for Pauline Viardot. And Gardiner's pioneering performances of Gluck, not least from the early 1970s onwards, and then during his stint (1983–8) as Music Director of Opéra de Lyon, must surely have informed his work on Berlioz. Gardiner acknowledges all these things, yet without nailing his colours to any particular mast.

'My main impulse was actually meeting the music as a singer and a player. While I was still at Cambridge I got involved in Colin Davis's Chelsea Opera Group performances, beginning by singing tenor in the chorus in *The Damnation of Faust*. These early events were all such intense experiences that they have merged a little in my mind, but I'm pretty sure that in *Romeo* I played violin and that, when we did *The Childhood of Christ*, I played viola. I went to Davis's *The Trojans* with the London Symphony Orchestra at the Festival Hall in 1966, and he became an inspiration to me.' Although Gardiner says that they were never especially close – 'I met him when I was 15 and knocked on his door saying I wanted to be a conductor, and he told me to go away and learn *The Rite of Spring*' – it was during Davis's tenure as Music Director at Covent Garden that Gardiner was invited to make his Royal Opera debut, conducting Gluck's *Iphigénie en Tauride* in 1973.

Together, Davis and Gardiner (with Beecham before them) embody that curious connection between British conductors and Berlioz, a phenomenon neither equalled nor fully understood across the Channel. 'It's one of those inexplicable things – why the French haven't revered two of their greatest composers, Rameau and Berlioz. Things are changing a little now, of course, and there's a new generation of French musicians and conductors who are really proud of French music, but it never used to be the case. When I was a student of Nadia Boulanger in the 1960s, it was damned difficult to hear any French music.' In the case of Berlioz, it's not that – as some have suggested – he's not French enough. 'No, Berlioz is quintessentially French. I think his past neglect has to do with the curious chauvinism of the French. They incline towards *haute cuisine*, of course – towards sculpture, painting and literature – but, thanks to the way in which the humanities are taught in France, music doesn't quite fit in. Historically they have felt a little insecure, drawn towards Germans and especially Italians. They brought Lully over early on, and later Paisiello, Pergolesi, Spontini, Cherubini, Rossini, Bellini and so on … This certainly made for a very rich fusion.'

Another problem the French seem to have had with Berlioz is not knowing where to place him and his journalistic activities. 'Yes, and I think that, for me, very much bound up with actually hearing and performing his music was that I was reading him. I love the *Mémoires*, but the letters are even more wonderful and especially the book that contains so much of his criticism, *À travers chants*. Berlioz has never been easy to pigeonhole.' Clearly, that's something that appeals to Gardiner, who understands the mystique around his music. 'You homogenise Berlioz at your peril. His music is graphic and explicit in a dramatic way. He had an overactive imagination. He managed to make a connection between his private emotional world and his strong literary sympathies – with Homer, Virgil, Shakespeare, Goethe and Schiller – and he had an incredible sense of theatre.

'It helped that his musical education was so unconventional, that he started off as a medical student in order to please his father and that he played the flute and the guitar. He was personally close to Chopin but musically the very antithesis – he was not a pianist, and his harmonies don't translate well to the piano. I'm not at all irritated about what people think of as his harmonic errors and gaffes – Boulez was incandescent about them – and I love the directness of his imagination. Somewhat like Janáček – they both wrote in blocks of sound – he assimilated folk music well and I think we hear an aural memory of his upbringing throughout his work. All the germs of his mature masterpieces are there in his early work.'

The humanity of the man is also very appealing. 'He was hugely opinionated, but he was incredibly collegial and genial. He would have been a wonderful person to share a bottle of wine with – though he'd first have placed his two pistols on the table. He was never without them! One has to feel sympathy for his disastrous love life, and for his tense relationship with his father: Louis didn't want Hector to be a musician, and that speaks to me in a way. My father wanted me to be anything but a professional musician – a farmer, perhaps, which I am, or an ecologist – and thought that you have to sell your soul to the Devil and enter a Faustian pact in this career. To him, music was all connected to the rituals of the seasons, and I suppose at least that has helped to shape my musical outlook.'

Much of Gardiner's career-defining work has been done with period instruments, and Berlioz was one of those composers who inspired him to set up his own orchestras. 'One reason I started the English Baroque Soloists was because modern woodwinds wouldn't have matched those very specific sounds we needed when we were doing a Rameau opera. And I feel very much the same with Berlioz when we perform him with the Orchestre Révolutionnaire et Romantique. He sounds brilliant on a modern orchestra – I've done

The Childhood of Christ (1850–54)

Though Berlioz rejected Christianity early on, he never lost his fascination with the theatrical potential of religion and its rituals. Yet the humanity and profound poignancy that inform *The Childhood of Christ* suggest something deeper at work, with the composer perhaps recalling the religious certainties of his childhood. So much of the music is in triple time (three beats to the bar), underlining the lyrical tenderness of the subject, and parts of the score find the mature composer coming close to sentimentality, without actually straying into it.

him with the Berlin Philharmonic – but even better with period instruments. It's got to do with the quality of sound and the fact that period instruments give a more visceral feel to the music. And, of course, modern orchestras no longer sound very French. I witnessed the birth of the Orchestre de Paris when I was a student in 1967. All of a sudden, there was a really good-quality, French-sounding orchestra. Charles Munch's opening concert was unforgettable. But then Munch died the following year, and the orchestra quickly became homogenised under his successors. The Frenchness drained out of it.'

Perhaps Gardiner's biggest triumph in the field of period performance has been his 2003 *Trojans* at the Théâtre du Châtelet in Paris. 'Berlioz had such an acute ear for instrumental colour – who else would combine bass clarinet, cor anglais and fourth horn for the death of Dido? He loved juxtaposing ancient instruments, like the natural trumpet, which hasn't changed since Monteverdi's day, with the latest things from Adolphe Sax's workshop. I was determined to find some saxhorns – Berlioz writes for nine of them in *The Trojans* – and was fortunate to come across a wonderful man, Bruno Kampmann, who works for the SNCF [French state railway] and collects instruments in his spare time. The walls of his flat near the Gare du Nord are lined with instruments. I took a couple of brass players along and we tried them out – at which point Madame Kampmann decided she had some shopping to do – and then he lent us his whole collection. There's something about the sonority of the saxhorn that is so plangent and individual. Hearing them on stage in the Trojan March, I just welled up.'

This season's *Benvenuto Cellini* is the culmination of Gardiner's Berlioz Proms odyssey, yet it is a relatively early work, one begun (in 1834) two years after the composer's return from his Italian sojourn as winner of the Prix de Rome. Gardiner sees it less as a paean to Italy than as 'yet another semi-autobiographical wish-fulfilment idea of the Romantic artist'. How does Gardiner position this thrilling yet problematic opera (existing in three versions) as the climax of his Proms journey through Berlioz? 'It's a little flawed, and I wouldn't call it a masterpiece, but it's galvanising and I can't think of another opera of the 19th century, except maybe Verdi's *Falstaff*, that has its exuberance, energy and sheer chutzpah. It's so cleverly constructed – orchestrally and chorally – and the whole of the Roman Carnival scene is a magical episode of organised chaos, a tour de force. It's great fun to conduct.' ●

South-African-born John Allison is Editor of *Opera* magazine and a music critic on *The Daily Telegraph*. From 2005 to 2015 he was Chief Music Critic of *The Sunday Telegraph*; he is the author of *The Pocket Companion to Opera* and a contributor to *BBC Music Magazine*.

Les nuits d'été
PROM 32 • 11 AUGUST

The Childhood of Christ
PROM 37 • 14 AUGUST

Benvenuto Cellini
PROM 59 • 2 SEPTEMBER

Symphonie fantastique
PROMS 72 & 73 • 12 SEPTEMBER

'You homogenise Berlioz at your peril. His music is graphic and explicit in a dramatic way': Sir John Eliot Gardiner conducting at the Proms in 2011

New Directions

With this year's Proms featuring new music from composers representing a wide range of musical influences and motivations – from nature and alchemy to film and electronica – ERROLLYN WALLEN traces her own varied and unconventional musical journey

The world that I inhabit involves negligible commercial gain but gives the creator the greatest opportunity for freedom of artistic expression. Those of us who have the opportunity to create have occasionally seen the mountain top – especially when our work reaches and moves an audience.

I remember, as an undergraduate, attending a concert of new music at the Queen Elizabeth Hall in London in which a person in the audience suddenly stood up and shouted, 'Music has taken the wrong turn!' before stamping out in disgust. I can't now remember the work being performed, but the passionate outrage of that person has stayed with me – listeners really *cared* about how things were going. Certainly, when I was studying composition there seemed to be a sense that the new music we were presented with, however dissonant and unfathomable to the average concert-goer, derived in a fairly orderly 'progression' from the lineage of Schoenberg, whose music was considered to belong to a direct succession of the Germanic tradition going back to Mozart, Haydn and Bach. Indeed, my own teacher, Nicola LeFanu, had studied with Egon Wellesz, who, in turn, had been a pupil of Schoenberg.

Fifty years ago it was a given that 'serious' contemporary classical composers were white, middle-class men, educated at a university or conservatory, and that their music would continue the unassailable lineage of the 'canon' and develop it way beyond Schoenberg's serialism. Many composers viewed their practice in scientific terms and, in the heroic quest to be avant-garde, music could no longer obey the dictates of conventional Western harmony – tunes were still out. The composer Iannis Xenakis (also an architect who had worked under Le Corbusier) used set theory, game theory and random processes in his compositions and, for a time at IRCAM (the computer-music research institute founded by Pierre Boulez in the 1970s), composers even donned lab coats. I was very excited by all this and immersed my ears in these men's music – Berio, Berg, Cage, Boulez, Stockhausen were on constant cassette shuffle. Even though I was studying for a Master's degree in Composition, I was never fully encouraged to believe that I, too, could be considered a 'composer' because, well, a young black woman born in Belize, Central America, didn't *quite* fit in. However, I greatly enjoyed my postgraduate studies, relishing the playing with numbers and pre-compositional techniques derived from the Second Viennese School – all in the service of trying to avoid tonality. Until the day I sat down and wrote a pop song.

While I was a student, the (Modernist) world continued to turn upon its axis until 'the veering winds shifted' (to paraphrase Byron) and Minimalism arrived on these shores, although it took nearly a decade for Britain to fully 'shift our sails'. Graduate composition students could be failed for forays into such radically different music, brought in on the breeze from Asia and Africa via the USA. As an undergraduate at Goldsmiths, I had already come across this music when fellow students, composers Andrew Poppy and Jeremy Peyton Jones, put on concerts of their Minimalist music and in 1978 Poppy's band put on a performance in the refectory of Terry Riley's *In C*, which starts in C major, uses short melodic fragments, aleatoric techniques and an indefinite number of performers. Poppy claimed that presenting this music in the refectory meant that everyone would hear it, not just music students. Later the work was performed in Goldsmiths' Art Department.

Although not a Minimalist myself, on completing my Master's at King's, I was asked to join a group called PULSE. This invitation was extended largely on account of my owning a Yamaha DX7 synthesiser – the first of its kind, developed by composer John Chowning at Stanford University. PULSE was formed by ex-students of Middlesex University, who quickly relegated me to the glockenspiel, while someone else played my DX7. Performing and eventually composing for this group, which mostly played on the comedy circuit of the 1980s, was a revelation to me at the end of my studies. Contemporary music could go anywhere, it could even be funny – context was the thing.

On leaving PULSE, as well as composing I continued to work as a keyboard player with bands ranging from heavy metal to jazz (despite my scant knowledge of popular music) and got a job in the 1990s in Manchester, as the music hostess on a 21-episode television game show presented by Tony Wilson – label boss of Factory Records and manager of The Haçienda nightclub, which was associated with the rise of acid and rave music. The requirements were to compose and play for the live show,

◀ Detail from a graphic score by Japanese experimental composer Makoto Nomura

Inspiring New Music

BBC Proms Inspire alumna **Sarah Jenkins**'s experience of the young composers' scheme

I applied to the BBC Proms Inspire Competition three times: the first time I attended a workshop on collaborative improvisation; the second I was Highly Commended; and the third time I won in the Senior Category. I have always loved exploring ideas, but Inspire has given me the confidence to believe in my own creative voice and not to feel that I need to conform to what other composers are doing. It has given me an incredible insight into the working lives of professional orchestral musicians, conductors and workshop practitioners, as well as radio broadcasters and producers.

Through Inspire I was commissioned to write a piece for the BBC Concert Orchestra. Working with conductor Bramwell Tovey and the orchestra taught me so much about writing for large ensemble and how to use rehearsal time effectively. It has cemented my love of composing and I want to work as hard as I can to try to forge a varied, dynamic career in music. I would recommend the workshops and Inspire days to any young composer – it feels like the most incredible melting pot of energy and creative ideas that you can all benefit from and share.

which featured comedians such as Caroline Aherne and Frank Sidebottom. I was working with samplers and programming keyboards with various sounds for the two shows that we filmed every day. This was only possible because of the rapid advances in music technology, some of which were made in places such as IRCAM, Columbia University and Stanford University. These advances, together with the arrival of MIDI (Musical Instrument Digital Interface), had a transformative effect on popular music production and performance. In turn, instruments such as the Hammond organ and electric guitar, invented in the 20th century and strongly associated with popular music, were used in works by contemporary classical composers seeking new timbres.

Fifty years ago, on 21 August 1969, Stockhausen's *Mikrophonie II*, a work for choir, Hammond organ and ring modulator, received its Proms premiere, but that same season did not include a single work by a woman composer nor by any composer of colour. Also 50 years ago the Afro-American Music Opportunities Association (AAMOA) was founded to support a range of activities related to black music and musicians. Its largest project was *The Black Composers Series 1974–1978*, released on vinyl in the 1970s and re-issued on disc this year. All the works are conducted by black conductor Paul Freeman, the architect of the project. The nine discs highlight two centuries of black composers (albeit solely male) performed by orchestras including the London Symphony Orchestra. The illustrious composers include William Grant Still (1895–1978), Pulitzer Prize-winning George Walker (1922–2018) and British composer Samuel Coleridge-Taylor (1875–1912). Still had been a pupil of Edgard Varèse and many had studied in Europe (including with Nadia Boulanger) only to return to the USA with limited opportunities for performances of their music. A year before George Walker died, Chineke! gave the Proms premiere of his moving *Lyric for Strings*. I had no idea of these composers' existence when I was studying contemporary music and had little idea of the contribution of black women composers such as Florence Price (1887–1953), who was the first African-American woman to have a symphonic work performed.

Modern state global colonialism or imperialism began in the 1500s and has meant that for centuries classical composers have come from many parts of the world, not just from Europe. Significant composers include José Maurício Nunes Garcia (1767–1830) from Brazil, Fela Sowande (1905–87) from Nigeria, Tania León (born 1943) from Cuba. The celebrated English composer of the Edwardian age, Samuel Coleridge-Taylor, was half Sierra Leonean.

Composers have always composed for the performers around them, whether that be within a church, a school, a film sound-stage or a university. Different genres and stylistic trends have had divergent histories. Many of these tributaries of music-making continue to be overlooked by academia and the establishment. It is clear that until a critical mass has formed around a particular trend, as in the case of Minimalism, much music has been ignored and ultimately languished, especially if it has not been documented in recordings, scores or written about by musicologists, music commentators or critics.

However, today, with so much information at their fingertips (for a laptop computer can access scores, recordings and performances, both live and historical, literally at the press of a button), many composers and listeners have begun to question the received idea of a single Western classical music narrative governed by progress and curated mostly by white European middle-class men. As they come across new music, telling new stories, they ask: What methodologies and criteria have been used to create the received canon? Who are the gatekeepers of the canon? What was the vernacular music, the street music that the 'greats' listened to?

While I was a student, the established British performing groups' repertoire didn't reflect the widest range of music being composed, yet some of these composers' works have now firmly entered the repertoire and can sell out any concert hall – Philip Glass, Steve Reich or Michael Nyman. In Europe the Dutch school of Minimalism spearheaded by Louis Andriessen (whose new work for vocalist and orchestra receives its UK premiere at this year's Proms) has had a significant and continuing effect on British composers – Steve Martland (who died in 2013) and Joe Cutler being among the most prominent. In their music the influence of jazz, pop and rock is especially significant.

Today, many composers, myself included, resist being part of any movement or 'ism' (or indeed 'wasm'), preferring to acknowledge that, with the vast history behind us and the various cultures and ideas swirling around us, it is more productive to stay alert, ever questioning of the techniques we use in our work. A pioneering curator such as Charles Amirkhanian, who founded the Other Minds festival in San Francisco, acknowledges the deep curiosity of the creator or audience to cross boundaries and genres and, together with Jim Newman, has formed a global new music community showcasing the work of composers from around the world.

Why compose in the first place? What is it that compels so many of us to commit our thoughts and experiences not into words, paint or film but into what can only be described as the experience of being human in time's continuum – musical sound?

As the obsession with progress in music abates, many composers are less interested in dogma than in trying to find means of re-connecting to a wider audience. For them this is true progress – to find a way of speaking to our time and plight in an authentic manner. With composers from a greater range of backgrounds being represented, the range of stories we tell is undeniably richer. We compose from where we find ourselves.

Earning a living as a composer is difficult for most of us and it is one of the reasons that has kept so many composers attached to academia. Educational institutions certainly offer significant resources – performing spaces, practice rooms, recording studios and libraries. The passing on of knowledge from one composer to another is mostly done here, and universities and conservatories are centres for discourse and debate. Today a PhD in Composition can be a passport to a career in teaching and full-time employment. Not all composers have followed this model, their aim being to earn a living from their artistic work. Collaboration with other

Composer Errollyn Wallen performing at the Tête à Tête Opera Festival, London

art forms – film, dance, theatre and visual arts – has opened up new avenues. This year's Proms features a number of living composers – including Sir Harrison Birtwistle, Zosha Di Castri, Wim Henderickx, David Sawer, Iris ter Schiphorst, Judith Weir and Hans Zimmer – who have collaborated widely and successfully.

Several years after leaving university, I sat down and composed a pop song. Then I composed another song, less categorisable. It marked a new freedom that I allowed myself. I opened a commercial recording studio, after which I formed my own group, Ensemble X, whose motto is 'we don't break down barriers in music … we don't see any'. Our concerts featured music that crossed the widest range of genres – from jazz-inspired compositions to works combining electronics with acoustic instruments and works that engaged with our time in direct ways. Although many advised us that 'this is not how you do things', I am pleased to say that I ignored this, rather in the same way I'd ignored the advice of my schoolteachers when I was a 9-year-old – 'little girl, classical music is not for you'.

The composers featured in this year's Proms range from sound artists to film-score writers and composers whose work ranges across a vividly broad spectrum, including popular music, jazz and improvised music. They go some way towards reflecting the true wealth of musical attitudes and styles that have always prevailed. Hopefully audiences will consider we are going in the right direction(s). ●

Errollyn Wallen's BBC commission *This Frame Is Part of the Painting* receives its world premiere in Prom 39 on 15 August.

Zosha Di Castri Long Is the Journey – Short Is the Memory *
PROM 1 • 19 JULY

Hans Zimmer Earth *
PROMS 3 & 5 • 21 & 22 JULY

Alexia Sloane Earthward *
PROMS AT … CADOGAN HALL 1 • 22 JULY

Anna Thorvaldsdottir Metacosmos ¥
PROM 6 • 22 JULY

Peter Eötvös Alhambra – violin concerto ‡
PROM 8 • 24 JULY

Tobias Broström Nigredo – Dark Night of the Soul ‡
PROM 9 • 25 JULY

Lera Auerbach Icarus #
PROM 12 • 27 JULY

Outi Tarkiainen Midnight Sun Variations *
PROM 22 • 4 AUGUST

Weinberg Cello Concerto #
PROM 25 • 6 AUGUST

Huw Watkins The Moon *
PROM 28 • 8 AUGUST

Detlev Glanert Weites Land ('Musik mit Brahms' for orchestra) ¥
PROM 33 • 11 AUGUST

Various Pictured Within: Birthday Variations for M. C. B. *
PROM 35 • 13 AUGUST

Errollyn Wallen This Frame Is Part of the Painting *
PROM 39 • 15 AUGUST

Joanna Lee At this man's hand *
PROMS AT … HOLY SEPULCHRE LONDON
17 AUGUST

Jonathan Dove new work †
PROM 43 • 19 AUGUST

Dieter Ammann Piano Concerto †
PROM 43 • 19 AUGUST

Weinberg Symphony No. 3 #
PROM 46 • 22 AUGUST

Alissa Firsova Red Fox *
in collaboration with Robert Macfarlane
PROM 49 • 25 AUGUST

Jörg Widmann Babylon Suite #
PROM 50 • 26 AUGUST

Ryan Wigglesworth Piano Concerto †
PROM 52 • 28 AUGUST

Dobrinka Tabakova new work *
PROM 56 • 31 AUGUST

Linda Catlin Smith new work *
PROM 58 • 1 SEPTEMBER

John Luther Adams In the Name of the Earth §
PROM 66 • 8 SEPTEMBER

Louis Andriessen The Only One ‡
PROM 67 • 8 SEPTEMBER

Freya Waley-Cohen new work *
PROMS AT … CADOGAN HALL 8
9 SEPTEMBER

Jonny Greenwood Horror vacui *
PROM 70 • 10 SEPTEMBER

Daniel Kidane Woke *
PROM 75 • 14 SEPTEMBER

** BBC commission: world premiere*
† BBC co-commission: world premiere
‡ BBC co-commission: UK premiere
§ European premiere
¥ UK premiere
 # London premiere

◀ Jackie Morris's painting for the hare – the subject of one of the 20 spells within *The Lost Words*

Lost Words in the Name of the Earth

PETROC TRELAWNY introduces two major family-friendly works that reflect environmental themes, linking them to a number of established pieces on the theme of nature and the world around us

The Lost Words is one of the most successful children's books of recent times. When writer Robert Macfarlane and artist Jackie Morris discovered that entries such as 'acorn', 'adder' and 'bramble' were being removed from the *Oxford Junior Dictionary* while more recent words – such as 'blog', 'broadband' and 'celebrity' – were added, they decided to create a book celebrating some of the vocabulary being cast onto a literary scrapheap. A rich collection of acrostic poems, called 'spells', sits alongside exquisite paintings in a book that has sold more than 100,000 copies to date. Jane Beaton, a bus driver from Stirling, decided to launch an appeal to buy the book for every school in Scotland; since then, more than a dozen crowdfunding campaigns have supplied copies to schools all around the country.

Television and arts producer Serena Cross immediately saw how the book could come to life on stage and is creating a family event that will put dancers, actors, a youth choir and a folk group alongside the young professional musicians of the Southbank Sinfonia, conducted by Jessica Cottis. 'The spells work brilliantly when you hear them sung or spoken,' she says. 'There is a sense of magic and mystery about them – a willow tree having a whispering inner voice, a glittering kingfisher foretelling the weather, the ghostly murmuration of swarming starlings, the mesmerising deep ocean hue of bluebells. Others are very funny – the meeting of a coot and a newt. And some are definitely dark – like the raven, stealing the eggs of other birds and pecking out eyes.'

With allusions to natural sounds, including water, wind and birdsong, along with man-made noises such as car alarms, ringtones and squeaking sneakers, many of the poems evoke music. There will be elements of folk, hip hop and classical in the music performed. While some of it will be specially commissioned, much will be drawn from the vast catalogue of works by composers inspired by the natural world. And items from that catalogue weave their way through a number of the concerts this season. 'Pleasant, cheerful feelings which awaken in one on arrival in the countryside' is how Beethoven described the first movement of his 'Pastoral' Symphony (No. 6); later comes a scene by a stream and a violent storm. Though Beethoven was reflecting a fashion for music rooted in nature when he wrote the work, there was nothing false about his love of a walk in the woods, where he would make notes as ideas came to him.

The giant, natural amphitheatres of Bryce Canyon in Utah inspired Messiaen's *Des canyons aux Étoiles …* ('From the Canyons to the Stars …'), while it was the Bavarian Alps that stirred Richard Strauss to write his huge *An Alpine Symphony*. He and friends hiked 12 hours up and down the Heimgarten Mountain, experiencing nature in all its fury: 'A terrible thunderstorm overtook us, which uprooted trees and threw stones in our faces.'

Smetana charts the path of the River Vltava in the most celebrated movement of his set

Lost and Found

Author **Robert Macfarlane** on how *The Lost Words* has taken wing in a variety of new guises

When Jackie Morris and I published *The Lost Words* in autumn 2017, we hoped we were planting an acorn. Even in our wildest imaginings we could not have foreseen the wildwood that has sprung up from our strange 'spell-book'. *The Lost Words* is a protest against the widening gap between everyday nature and childhood, and a celebration of the wondrous animals and plants with which we share our landscapes, from kingfishers and otters to bluebells and wrens. I wrote 20 'spells' to summon these creatures into children's mouths and minds, and Jackie conjured them onto the page with ink, water and gold-leaf.

Something about the book struck a powerful chord with readers. People began campaigns to place copies of it in schools and hospices. Others used it to work with refugees or those suffering from Alzheimer's disease (different kinds of 'lost words'). Tens of thousands of children have adopted it in outdoor teaching contexts, and it has been adapted for dance, radio, theatre, film. Now, it becomes a Proms concert at the Royal Albert Hall: a further magical flourishing of the *Lost Words* wildwood.

of symphonic poems *Má vlast* ('My Country'). In music that has become a symbol of Czech national identity, he paints the waterway as it flows from its source in Bohemian forests, through Prague, before merging with the Elbe. In her 1995 work *Forest* Judith Weir imagines intertwining lines of notes 'sprouting musical leaves'. Nearly everything in the piece grows 'from the tiny musical seeds encountered in the opening bars'.

It's hard to define the exact moment when we started to think seriously about the damage humankind was causing to much of our natural environment; the Clean Air Act that followed the Great Smog of 1952 was an early example of British action against pollution. Besides mourning the abandoned dictionary entries of its title, does *The Lost Words* also acknowledge the devastation we have wrought upon nature ? 'It's a work that brings things alive and shows us the wonder of them,' says Serena Cross. 'The spells rarely make direct reference to a species being under threat – but within them there is certainly a call to action.'

The Lost Words Prom will include one of the *songbirdsongs* by John Luther Adams. Two weeks later the American composer will return for the European premiere of his latest work, *In the Name of the Earth*. A piece for vast choral forces, its text is built from the names of North American mountain peaks, ranges, rivers and glaciers, in English, Spanish and indigenous languages. Agiocochook, Absaroka, Mojave and Tsalxhaan are among the place names that will be sung by eight choirs arranged around the Royal Albert Hall.

Adams was barely 20, and living in an old farmhouse in Georgia, when he became captivated by the song of the wood thrush. 'It led to my Opus 1, as well as the realisation that I had discovered something that could be worthy of a lifetime's devotion – nature.' For a while the composer became a full-time environmental campaigner, before concluding that making art could achieve more than activism. 'Politics is about power, whereas art concerns beauty and truth; creative thought, new ways of thinking, that's how change originates.' He admits that, when it comes to the environment and the untamed wild spaces of his homeland, he is still a political composer. 'But the music always comes first,' he insists. 'If it doesn't move you in musical terms, the other ideas mean nothing.'

In the Name of the Earth had its premiere last August as part of New York's Mostly Mozart Festival. It was due to be staged in Central Park, but bad weather saw it moved to the Cathedral of St John the Divine. 'The building has a very lush acoustic,' says Adams. 'It was so full that you got this gorgeous miasma of ravishing sound. But it's like I didn't quite hear the piece. Now I feel as though I will be hearing it clearly for the first time.' ●

Petroc Trelawny presents *Breakfast* on BBC Radio 3 and introduces the BBC Proms on radio and television.

The Lost Words
PROM 49 • 25 AUGUST

John Luther Adams In the Name of the Earth *European premiere*
PROM 66 • 8 SEPTEMBER

See Index of Works for nature-inspired pieces by Beethoven, Messiaen, Smetana, R. Strauss, Judith Weir and others

These Are the Breaks

Jules Buckley and the Heritage Orchestra have previously collaborated at the Proms with the likes of Jamie Cullum and Pete Tong, and last year explored the New York music scene. Now, as ANGUS BATEY discovers, they are amping up the dance element with a showcase of breaking, the beat-driven accidental hero of hip-hop culture

It's not a genre, not even a style; and it doesn't have a particular sound to speak of. Yet breakbeats have become one of the most influential and transformative forces in the past five decades of popular music.

The story of breakbeats begins in 1973, when a teenage DJ performed in public for the first time. Clive Campbell – whose nickname Hercules (given for his imposing stature) was soon remixed to form his professional moniker, DJ Kool Herc – made his debut in front of an audience on 11 August that year. The occasion was a back-to-school party thrown by his sister, Cindy, in the recreation room of their apartment block at 1520 Sedgwick Avenue in the New York borough of the Bronx. However, the real star of the show was not Herc, but his unique choice of records.

Before the Campbells moved to New York from Jamaica in 1970, Herc had absorbed the lessons of the island's sound-system culture and in his new home he built his own powerful rig: massive speakers giving him more volume, and far more bass, than other Bronx DJs. But the unique weapon in his DJ armoury was a collection of music unlike anyone else's. He guarded the identity of his records so fiercely he would often soak off the labels so that anyone leaning over his turntables wouldn't be able to discover what he was playing.

Herc noticed how revellers seemed to particularly enjoy the percussion-heavy middle sections of some of the records, so he worked out a way to prolong their dancefloor ecstasy. While the instrumental break was playing and the dancers were getting into the groove, he would cue up another copy of the same record on his second turntable, and, when the first record was about to go back to the melody, he switched to the other deck, and started playing the breakbeat again from the beginning, effectively extending the break, potentially indefinitely.

Other DJs were listening. Fellow Bronx resident Joseph Sadler, who DJ-ed under the name Grandmaster Flash, liked the innovation but thought it could be carried off with more precision. Flash understood electronics and liked to experiment. After building a device that allowed him to listen over headphones to one deck without the crowd hearing it and to switch the output instantly from one deck to the other, he was able to ensure the beat never faltered.

From these innovations, much of the popular music of the next four decades sprang. DJ equipment manufacturers developed turntables better suited to seamless beat-matching, and crossfaders became standard on all DJ consoles. As the phenomenon began to spread and become commercially successful, recording equipment suppliers began to cater for the types of composition that were emerging: sampling technology was developed, allowing music producers to take pieces of sound and loop them automatically. Hip-hop producers were far from the only ones to benefit. The techniques and tools went on to overhaul the way rock, pop and dance records were made, with entire genres – from techno to drum 'n' bass and grime – flowing from the same creative wellspring.

Herc's idiosyncratic collection is a mystery no longer, and the names of the key tracks he, Flash and other pioneers played across the Bronx in the mid-1970s are now well known. They include bombastic rock songs, uptempo disco hits, B-sides and album tracks by obscure funk and soul artists, experimental new-wave workouts, acerbic jazz cuts and even children's novelty songs. The one thing they all share is a moment somewhere when melody and lyrics cede the foreground to drums and percussion. These breakbeats are thunderous but never metronomic – commanding without becoming stentorian.

'What makes a great break? That's a hard question,' says conductor Jules Buckley, who, with his production partner and Heritage Orchestra co-founder, Chris Wheeler, is at the time of writing considering which breakbeat classics are going to feature in this year's Prom. 'Does it make you feel good? Does it make you want to dance? That's where this began.'

Which is indeed the case. Herc would never have spun two copies of the same record to prolong the breakbeat had it not been for seeing the reaction of dancers during a single play of the track. Once he'd pioneered his technique, and breaks could be extended from a few bars of music into minutes-long stretches, dancers were free to turn momentary explosions of movement into extended bursts of self-expression and to choreograph their performances in advance.

The dancers became known as 'break boys' or 'break girls', quickly abbreviated to b-boys/b-girls. Solo dancers could showcase their moves in front of rivals, who would then have a chance to respond.

◀ Street-smart street art: b-boys, with boombox, showing off their moves

Breaking battles became part of the Bronx-centred block-party scene, along with their party hosts – the masters of ceremony, or MCs, who began to deliver their shouts and chants as rhythmic rhymes over the microphone. Meanwhile, those whose creativity was visual rather than physical or aural were developing a new style of text-based street art, their pieces appearing on the blank canvases of the city – from the walls of burnt-out buildings to the exteriors of subway trains. The people of the Bronx had created a culture – soon known as 'hip hop'.

Buckley and Wheeler know, therefore, that any attempt to honour the world of the breaks needs to incorporate these different disciplines – what have become known as the four elements of hip-hop culture. Dance will be as prominent at the Prom as music, with top breaking crews taking centre-stage; MCs will perform alongside the Heritage Orchestra, complete with two drummers battling it out across the Royal Albert Hall stage, passing the beats from left to right and back again, just as a DJ would.

'No-one's ever attempted to explore and celebrate these breaks and play them live in this way. We're looking to demonstrate facets of the history of how it's all developed. It's taken ages to figure out how we could do this as legitimately as possible.'

At its heart, of course, the show will be about the music. Buckley and Wheeler are still whittling down their playlist, with the help of UK breaking guru DJ Renegade, and are aware of the challenges involved in providing a coherent and comprehensive overview of a sonic world that happily includes everything from UK prog-rock group Babe Ruth's bizarre excursion through 19th-century US border politics, 'The Mexican', the hectic pace of The Winstons' gospel-soul curio 'Amen, Brother', and Brick's disco monster 'Dazz'.

Yet the core of the repertoire that will make it into the evening's programme is obvious. 'In some ways, you could almost say there's just three or four tunes that provide the backbone to breakbeat culture,' Buckley says. He cites the Incredible Bongo Band's version of the late-1950s instrumental 'Apache', the Jimmy Castor Bunch's 1972 US hit 'It's Just Begun', and 'Give It Up or Turnit a Loose' – not the original version released as a single in 1969, but the harder, punchier reworking from 1970, included on James Brown's pseudo-live album, *Sex Machine*. 'And you can almost trace everything back to Clyde Stubblefield and "Funky Drummer",' he adds, highlighting the 1969 track that is often reckoned to have been sampled more times than any other release in the history of recorded music.

'We're going in on the music that's created a culture,' Buckley says, 'on music that's inspired millions of people worldwide, and continues to do so. Yet this world, the breaking world, is not that well known. Maybe we can help shed a bit of light on it, and educate ourselves as well.' ●

Angus Batey is a freelance journalist who has written about hip-hop culture since the 1980s. His work has appeared in most British national newspapers and many music magazines.

The Breaks

A celebration of breaking, with the Heritage Orchestra under Jules Buckley

PROM 64 • 6 SEPTEMBER

The daddy of the breaks: DJ Kool Herc (in Blackpool, UK, 2000), who pioneered the idea of prolonging dance-inducing percussion breaks by mixing between two turntables

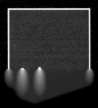

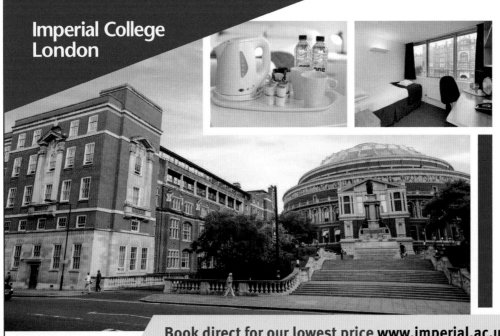

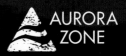

A Vehicle for Virtuosity?

Proms debut artist DANIEL PIORO surveys the variety of forms the violin concerto has adopted throughout history, and offers a personal perspective on its specific demands on the performer

In writing about the violin concerto, my words can only hope to be a messy window into my mind. I am at the very beginning of my understanding of this beautiful beast and, no matter how often I have experienced it, I realise that the next time I glimpse it in its natural habitat it will be both entirely the same and also a completely different animal. I am intrigued by the violin concerto, appalled by it, excited by it and finding ways of loving it.

Music, to me, is not something that can be dissected and labelled. On the surface the violin concerto is a vehicle for a soloist to command the concert space with their sound, often with hyper-realised skill, as an orchestra fills the harmonic spaces and lifts the solo line. Equally, it is a means for the composer to focus so intently on the timbre and character of the violin as to imbue the instrument with a charisma and vitality so potent that they leave their mark on musicians and non-musicians alike. And herein lies my own discomfort, the inconvenient truth that keeps me excited by the opportunity to perform a concerto and at the same time pushes me to play purely alone or – and this is my greatest joy in music – with others as musical equals.

Historically, the violin concerto is a vehicle for the soloist to show off. The violinist is the focus, any other musicians on stage are the supporting cast. Technical skill, finger dexterity and gymnastic use of the bow are given particular prominence and the undefinable divine that can be found in the greatest music is often pushed to the side. But music, in its truest form, should never come second, which is why Pekka Kuusisto's performance of Tchaikovsky's Violin Concerto with the BBC Scottish Symphony Orchestra at the BBC Proms in 2016 left such a profound mark. Not just on me, but also on everyone I know who heard it. The orchestra and the soloist played together in such a way that it didn't matter where the sound was coming from, who was the most important, or the least. It just *was*. It was a subversion of sorts, where the room was the resonator, the soloist was the orchestra and the orchestra was the soloist – the only thing of any importance in that moment was the music. This was the violin concerto transcending categories and becoming so much more than a sum of its parts.

So, if a violin concerto is simply a vehicle to show off the violin and the individual playing it, why did some of the great composers write them – and why do they continue to do so?

In my opinion the violin is a truly glorious instrument, for its closeness to the human voice and for the quality it has (that all bowed string instruments have) of evoking a thousand emotions in one bow stroke. But violin concertos are also ways of celebrating monumental events in history. They are fruits of friendship and collaboration between a composer and a soloist. They are works composed to satisfy the wishes of a wealthy patron. They are pieces that the composer needs to write, simply out of a love for the instrument and the call to compose, much as a writer needs to put

◀ An illuminating perspective from inside a violin

Joshua Bell

Dvořák Violin Concerto
PROM 2 • 20 JULY

'I am simply smitten with Dvořák's Violin Concerto. It is immediately appealing in so many ways – from the drama and virtuosity of the first movement to the magically long melodic lines of the slow movement (arguably the most beautiful in the entire repertoire!) and the playful and exciting Rondo which carries the listener to its thrilling conclusion.'

Nemanja Radulović

Barber Violin Concerto
PROM 4 • 21 JULY

'There is something light and innocent about Barber's Violin Concerto. There are many long phrases where it's important to find the right place to "breathe", particularly in the second movement. The third movement is probably one of the most virtuosic finales in the repertoire – it starts fast and finishes even faster, so it's a lot of fun to play!'

James Ehnes

Britten Violin Concerto
PROM 6 • 22 JULY

'Britten's Violin Concerto is a unique and powerful work – emotionally ambitious with an incredible weight behind it. It's a piece that has a profound impact on the audience, one that continues to live in the mind of the listener long after the last notes have sounded. It will be a great honour to perform this masterpiece at the Proms.'

Isabelle Faust

Peter Eötvös Alhambra
PROM 8 • 24 JULY

'The idea for Peter's new violin concerto came after Pablo Heras-Casado expressed the wish to add a new piece to his festival in Granada. When the first sketches of the piece arrived, I was immediately transfigured by their exotic lightness, dancing elegance and capricious temperament. The Alhambra has become music …'

words onto paper and follow some narrative known only to them.

When Beethoven wrote his Violin Concerto (a work that moves me to such extremes that I can barely listen to anyone play it for fear that it won't match the way I hear it in my head), it was not completed until just before the premiere. My own experiences of living composers changing pieces on the day of a concert are a good reminder of how that would have felt for both composer and soloist on that day in December 1806. I feel and hear a connection – transcending time – between Beethoven's concerto and Thomas Adès's concerto *Concentric Paths*, given its UK premiere at the Proms in 2005 by the brilliant Anthony Marwood.

Adès has constructed a piece, like Beethoven, where the solo part is both a stand-alone line and integral to the orchestral texture – there are solo passages that are barely distinguishable from those of the orchestra, like blinking lights from a satellite submerged in some cosmic mist. We see it, but barely. It doesn't matter that occasionally we lose sight of it, because the mist itself is so compelling. And then there is song. Vibrant. Profound. A call to prayer. The only moment this incredible unity changes is in the third movement, one that is sonically structured in such a traditional way (bringing to my mind the third movement of Sibelius's Violin Concerto) that it almost jars in comparison to what has come before it. A dance of sorts that, by its more conventional soloist-against-orchestra nature, reinforces the magic, majesty and cosmic beauty of the first two movements.

Some of the greatest violin concertos in Western classical history will be heard at this year's BBC Proms. Each work brings not just its own intensely beautiful music, but also deep technical challenges for the soloist and that extra challenge of looking at a frequently performed piece as if for the first time. Every soloist will bring their own truth, whether that is to Britten's superb work – three movements of beautiful writing for the violin that, in the first movement, calls to mind Beethoven's Classical masterpiece; in the second, the wild energy of Prokofiev; and in the final movement the rich dance tradition of Purcell – or Tchaikovsky's folk-song-in-three-parts that dances and flies in ways that would make Vaughan Williams's famous ascending lark furiously jealous in its idyllic English skies.

> “The violin is a truly glorious instrument, for its closeness to the human voice and for the quality it has … of evoking a thousand emotions in one bow stroke.”

The Proms also features a concerto by Korngold, that master whose film music has held him back from being lauded in our quite insular world, but who is increasingly gaining the recognition his compositions deserve. He composed a work so lyrical and refined that it has become a favourite piece among violinists, incorporating elements of his film music: a true gem. You will also be able to hear the sounds of Sibelius, with his concerto that most closely resembles an old Finnish fairy tale, ice and fire and gods and humankind, told by a roaring fire. And Barber. Barber's concerto, riddled and almost ruined in its creation by the kind of soloist-centric ego trip I have already touched upon. (Iso Briselli, the violinist for whom Barber was commissioned to compose his Violin Concerto, was reportedly disappointed by the 'lightweight' final movement of the work and asked Barber to rewrite it; when his request was declined, Briselli gave up any claim to the concerto, including its premiere.) It is a good example of the composer's rhapsodic sound-world and, at the last, a good example of the violinist's craving to impress.

Amid all this incredible history, there will also be two new violin concertos on display. One by Peter Eötvös (*Alhambra*, for Isabelle Faust); the other, in which I am the soloist, by Jonny Greenwood – which leads me on to my favourite part of what, for me, being a musician is. The process of creation.

Having a work created for me as a solo violinist is a process that I'm lucky to have already experienced a few times. It is not just an honour to have music written for you but, more interestingly, a real opportunity to inhabit someone else's mind, their own particular sound-world: the musical equivalent of reading those special books that stay with you for ever, living the lives of others through their eyes.

An example of this careful venturing into another's ideas can perhaps best be demonstrated by my work on an extraordinary piece called *Elsewhere*, which Edmund Finnis composed for me in 2015. Written for solo violin and reverb, it is a work that seems to be constructed from gossamer sounds, air, breath, the reflection of light on water and a succession of undulating noises that classical musicians are not trained to make or to desire.

Alone with the composer, this was when I felt intensely vulnerable, Edmund showing me the kind of unexpected sounds or overtones (ghostly 'half-notes') he wanted me to produce, using my violin purely as a tool. Not precious and not even particularly expressive, just practical and honest. And I struggled. This process of interpreting a composer's desires was something I had decided I should have been perfect at. Immediately. This was my first real lesson that immersion into someone else's creative process can be daunting. Scary, even. I was understanding his idea, and at the same time I was as far away from the truth of his idea as could possibly be.

The process of having a violin concerto written for you is much the same, but on an infinitely larger scale. At the moment I am working with two wonderful musicians, composers who come from very different places and who will tread very different paths. Two inspired minds playing with their own internal music, but also taking into consideration what I love most: sound exploration.

Both Jonny Greenwood (who is writing a concerto for me, the BBC National Orchestra of Wales and the Proms Youth Ensemble to perform at the Proms) and Tom Coult (who is writing a concerto for me and the BBC Philharmonic) listen to me. They watch how I move and how I play, in the literal sense, with the violin and its bow. How I dance freely and how I struggle when I play, what I am most drawn to and what I avoid. I am a very lucky person.

Nicola Benedetti

Tchaikovsky Violin Concerto
PROM 12 • 27 JULY

'Tchaikovsky's Violin Concerto is the quintessential virtuosic and romantic work: no other concerto comes close. It's a feat of stamina, it's open-hearted melodically and harmonically and it has all the hallmarks of an insatiable appetite that's never satisfied. The final movement should appear like a chase, a gallop, as if someone is lost in a maze and can't escape.'

Lisa Batiashvili

Prokofiev Violin Concerto No. 2
PROM 17 • 31 JULY

'It's nice to discover the different colours of Prokofiev and in his Second Violin Concerto he is very surprising. There is a connection between it and the work he wrote next – *Romeo and Juliet*. It is very clear to hear in the gorgeous second movement of the concerto, which is a love theme between Romeo and Juliet. I think that was the birth of that ballet, there.'

Pekka Kuusisto

Sibelius Violin Concerto
PROM 20 • 3 AUGUST

'In the first movement of Sibelius's Violin Concerto the soloist is a builder of entire imaginary worlds; in the second movement, suddenly, a Romantic exclaimer of her or his own emotions. All that matters in the third movement is virtuosity and a kind of dancing exorcism of the dark structures of the first movement and perhaps even of the intimacy of the second.'

Leonidas Kavakos

Korngold Violin Concerto
PROM 61 • 4 SEPTEMBER

'I've been playing Korngold's Violin Concerto for more than 20 years now. What fascinates me about the work is how he develops and orchestrates his melodies. He creates an amazing world around simple melodies. There's a purity about his tunes that just flowed out of him. For me, it is important to communicate that instead of putting too much sweetness into it.'

I do not just require this kind of deep contact and communication with the person writing the piece for me, but I have been given it.

Jonny Greenwood's piece is taking shape. I speak to him often, hearing his thoughts, reading through his ideas, delighting in a new mode here and a stubborn triple-stop there. We have sat together at his piano and I have played for him and I have seen ideas extinguish as he listens to me, as well as seeing new ideas appear. The orchestra will be an extension of my playing, an extraordinary and dramatic way of creating resonance using the timbre of string players overlapping each other, like one massive, breathing organism or a high priest and his choir. He has shown me moments of such beauty, where my sound is left alone in space, and moments of enchanting strangeness. I cannot wait to see how his music develops and, even as I share my own ideas of what I want as a violinist, I am aware of how resolutely individual to him this sound-world is.

And so I ask myself, should a soloist be so involved as a collaborator? I do bear this in mind when I'm making suggestions and cajoling the composer, but in the end the composer is the creator and I trust them with their vision. It may be a collaborative effort, but true collaboration does not equate to equality of vision and purpose. Trust is the key to it all. Much like in the violin concerto, the same is true for life. When there is trust, we can do anything. Trust is about the only thing that stops me from dying of stage-fright and also the thing that makes me thrill with happiness when I perform. The knowledge that I'm not just fulfilling a composer's instruction, or playing with a wonderful group of musicians, but that we trust each other and are making music together. That is the ultimate result of the creative process. It may be called a violin concerto, but in the end, for me, it's really just a magnified form of chamber music. ●

Daniel Pioro is a violinist and Artistic Director of the chamber ensemble Fibonacci Sequence.

Dvořák Violin Concerto
PROM 2 • 20 JULY

Barber Violin Concerto
PROM 4 • 21 JULY

Britten Violin Concerto
PROM 6 • 22 JULY

Peter Eötvös Alhambra (violin concerto)
BBC co-commission: UK premiere
PROM 8 • 24 JULY

Tchaikovsky Violin Concerto
PROM 12 • 27 JULY

Prokofiev Violin Concerto No. 2
PROM 17 • 31 JULY

Sibelius Violin Concerto
PROM 20 • 3 AUGUST

Korngold Violin Concerto
PROM 61 • 4 SEPTEMBER

Jonny Greenwood Horror vacui
BBC commission: world premiere
PROM 70 • 10 SEPTEMBER

WARNER BROS
ELECT
DEPT
14
TLANDT HOMES RENTAL HOUSING
STAGE 5
WARNER BROS
ELECT
DEPT
33

◀ Building the illusion: a crew on the set of the 1949 Warner Bros. film *The Fountainhead*, which featured a score by Max Steiner

Music for the Dream Factory

As John Wilson and his orchestra delve into the Warner Bros. archives, MERVYN COOKE surveys the wealth of composers that contributed to the studio's success in the Golden Age of Hollywood movies

During the heyday of the Hollywood studio system in the 1930s and 1940s, audiences flocked to see a seemingly endless stream of utopian romances, the exploits of dastardly but attractive villains (who always met their just deserts in the end), hilarious cartoon shorts and lavish musicals boasting spectacular song-and-dance routines. Lushly evocative film music, produced by the studios in enormous quantities, played a hugely significant role in the feel-good factor of movie attendance in those halcyon days, and not just in the area of song-and-dance.

During the era of silent film, music had already been a vitally important part of the cinema-going experience. When, in 1925, Warner Bros. purchased the Vitaphone sound system, which permitted recordings on disc to be synchronised with the projector, their principal aim was not to reproduce recorded dialogue but rather to ensure that standards of musical performance were uniformly high in every venue. The very first audience for a Vitaphone presentation was grandly informed that 'the motion picture is the most potent factor in the national appreciation of good music', and that the new technology 'will carry symphony orchestrations to the town halls of the hamlets'. Following the success of Warner's *The Jazz Singer* (1927), with its disc-synchronised songs and dialogue, the major Hollywood studios competed ferociously with one another in the race to produce film musicals as the more flexible sound-on-film technology quickly became the norm.

At Warner's, the 'backstage' musical flourished in the hands of Busby Berkeley, whose striking choreography for *Gold Diggers of 1933* included the opening number 'We're in the Money', performed by Ginger Rogers and a troupe of chorines cavorting with oversized coins. Symbolically, this routine marked the end of Depression-era austerity and an upturn in Hollywood's sometimes precarious fortunes. Original screen musicals continued to flourish for the following two decades, with highlights from the Warner stable including *Blues in the Night* (1941), Doris Day's debut feature *It's Magic* (1948) and *Calamity Jane* (1953). Transfers of stage shows to the silver screen were popular at Warner's, too, and these included no fewer than three films based on Romberg's *The Desert Song* (1929, 1943 and 1953). Occasionally, a dramatic feature might be turned into a screen musical, as in the Judy Garland vehicle *A Star Is Born* (1954). By the 1960s, when the film industry's fortunes slumped severely, transfers from popular stage musicals had become a far safer commercial bet than the risky business of commissioning original screen musicals, and Warner's well-known contributions towards this stage-derived catalogue came to include *The Music Man* (1962), *My Fair Lady* (1964) and *Camelot* (1967).

At the start of the 1930s, film music in other genres was restricted to featured songs and brief orchestral music for the opening and

Silver-Screen Glamour

John Wilson on the Warner films that sounded, as well as looked, a million dollars

In our Proms debut back in 2009 the John Wilson Orchestra and I honoured the MGM Film Musicals. Since then we've covered a whole range of music – from Hollywood to Broadway – including a tribute to Rodgers & Hammerstein. In 2019 we turn the spotlight on one particular Hollywood powerhouse.

Of all the major movie studios of Hollywood's 'Golden Age', none boasted a music department as illustrious and as versatile as that of Warner Bros. Max Steiner and Ray Heindorf produced some of their best work at Warner's and in his 16 scores for the studio, Erich Wolfgang Korngold furnished the movies of the 1930s and 1940s with an opulent sound and style that are imitated to this day and, for many, remain the high-water mark of music for motion pictures. Equally remarkable was the range of the studio's output: swashbuckling epics such as *The Sea Hawk*, Warner's signature dramas *Now, Voyager*, *The Old Man and the Sea*, *A Streetcar Named Desire*, *The Treasure of the Sierra Madre* and a host of glamorous musicals, including *My Fair Lady*, *The Music Man*, *A Star Is Born*, *Camelot* and *Calamity Jane*.

closing credit sequences. Naive though it may seem, it was felt that audiences would be perplexed by hearing music performed by an invisible orchestra on the soundtrack of a drama, unless there were a clear justification for its presence: if a scene required love music, for example, a gratuitous violinist might be visible in the background solely in order to explain the romantic music for strings soaring away on the soundtrack. All this changed after Max Steiner's substantial score for RKO's *King Kong* (1933) showed what well-crafted orchestral music could do to enhance a narrative and aid suspension of disbelief. Steiner was one of a clutch of immigrant composers from Europe who helped mould the distinctive style of Hollywood scoring in the Golden Age, and – along with Erich Wolfgang Korngold – one of two musicians from Vienna who made outstanding creative contributions to Warner Bros. productions.

Steiner was a veritable workaholic whose output of film scores totalled in excess of 300. Some 140 of these were written for Warner's, including the Spanish-flavoured *The Treasure of the Sierra Madre* (1948). By contrast, Korngold was a celebrity classical composer, a protégé of Richard Strauss, who cherry-picked his film assignments and was given much longer to work on them, completing only 16 in all. While both helped establish a late-Romantic orchestral idiom as the Hollywood norm, their compositional techniques and working methods were also distinct. Steiner had a literal-mindedness that resulted in a dogged adherence to Wagnerian leitmotifs ('every character must have a theme,' he once said), ironic quotations of pre-existing themes that the audience might enjoy spotting, and a liberal use of 'mickey-mousing' (in which musical gestures are synchronised to the on-screen action in the manner of cartoon scoring). Korngold's style was more flamboyant and proved especially well suited to Warner's swashbuckling adventures starring Errol Flynn, including *The Sea Hawk* (1940), whose swordfights cried out for miniature Straussian symphonic poems to underline their physical action.

Both Steiner and Korngold were cogs in the huge machine that was the typical Hollywood studio of the time. The five major studios (Warner Bros., MGM, Paramount, Twentieth Century–Fox and RKO) each housed a permanent music department, with contracted composers, arrangers, orchestrators, copyists, librarians and music editors, plus a resident orchestra, all working under a senior music director. At Warner's, long-serving music director Leo F. Forbstein helped negotiate the change from Vitaphone to sound-on-film and, as departmental head, personally collected the Oscar later earned by Korngold's score for *Anthony Adverse* (1936) at a time when these awards were made to the music department as a whole, not a named composer. Like many music directors, Forbstein served as a crucial intermediary between his hard-pressed department and the studio moguls. He was succeeded on his death in 1948 by Ray Heindorf, who had previously composed and conducted numerous scores for the studio. Among the best-known of the orchestrators was Hugo Friedhofer, who worked with both Steiner and Korngold on some of their highest-profile projects at Warner's and later became a celebrated film composer in his own right.

The influence of European Classical and Romantic music on Hollywood film scoring was obvious enough even without Dimitri Tiomkin's infamous televised Oscar acceptance speech in 1955, which began (as he transcribed it in his autobiography): 'I like to thank Johannes Brahms, Johann Strauss, Richard Strauss, Richard Wagner [laughter drowning out several other names], Beethoven, Rimsky-Korsakov [laughter drowning me out completely]'. (Tiomkin had not meant this tribute to his forebears as a joke: he was being utterly sincere, though in consequence incurred the wrath of other film composers who felt he had belittled their artistry.) But the mainstream orchestral style began to break down in the 1950s under the increasing influence of jazz and popular music on the output of a younger generation of American-born film composers. Alex North's landmark score for *A Streetcar Named Desire* (1951) infused Tennessee Williams's drama with a sultry jazziness so erotically suggestive that some of the music had to be replaced before the film could pass the censors. Jazz-influenced scores, almost always associated with modern urban settings and sleaze, became popular in the later 1950s, and the trend was continued by Henry Mancini, not only in the movies but also in TV dramas such as *Peter Gunn*. Mancini was a versatile composer, whose Oscar-winning title song to Warner's *Days of Wine and Roses* (1962) shows just one facet of his musical personality. Somewhat typecast as a romantic songwriter, he lamented that for commercial reasons his soundtrack albums (including that for *Days of Wine and Roses*) had to omit much of the dramatic underscoring, which he felt was his real forte.

Reflecting on his formative years in Hollywood during the 1950s, the late André Previn paid warm tribute to the exceptionally high standards of musicianship and tireless work ethic that prevailed in the studio music departments during the Golden Age. For apprentice composers, the chance to rehearse and record their music with superlative players within moments of completing it was a blessing unique to the film world, and the brilliant studio orchestrators (often unfairly dismissed as hacks) possessed 'the most enviable, sophisticated knowledge of what makes an orchestra sound'. 'All of us were expected to be total chameleons,' Previn remembers: '"I want this to sound like ..." Fill in the name of your preference: Ravel, Tchaikovsky, Strauss, Count Basie, a Broadway pit; that was an instruction we all heard.' This unashamedly nostalgic plundering of classical and popular styles to service clearly defined dramatic ends nevertheless produced some of the most enduringly memorable music of the 20th century. And this music is still very much with us. As John Williams once admitted: 'I'm a very lucky man ... If it weren't for the movies, no one would be able to write this kind of music any more.' ●

Mervyn Cooke is Professor of Music at the University of Nottingham and the author of *A History of Film Music* (2008). He edited *The Hollywood Film Music Reader* (2010) and co-edited *The Cambridge Companion to Film Music* (2016), and has also published several books on jazz and the life and works of Benjamin Britten.

The Warner Brothers Story

John Wilson conducts the John Wilson Orchestra

PROMS 29 & 30 • 9 AUGUST

A poster for the 1964 movie adaptation of *My Fair Lady*, featuring Audrey Hepburn and Rex Harrison; the movie won eight Oscars, including one for Best Scoring of Music, Adaptation or Treatment – awarded to the late André Previn

In Parlour and Palace

In the bicentenary year of Queen Victoria's birth, the Proms presents a concert featuring one of the monarch's own pianos, prompting MATTHEW SWEET to delve into her private and public musical pursuits, and the musical backdrop of her era

Florence, 1888. A recital is in progress. An Italian tenor, chestnut hair piled up like a generous serving of *stracci di castagne*, is mid-aria. When the last notes have faded, Queen Victoria expresses her approval. 'And where did you say it was from, Mr Puccini?' The composer pitches her the plot of *Manon Lescaut*: lovers separated by the class divide; an elopement; a tragic ending. 'I'm not sure we do like the sound of it after all,' she says. 'We prefer comic opera. Do you know any Gilbert and Sullivan?' And up she gets to murder 'I'm called Little Buttercup' from *HMS Pinafore*. 'I was taught by Mendelssohn, you know!' she trills, toasting herself with a flute of champagne.

It's a lovely scene; rich in humour, poignant, generous towards its participants. But it only happened when Judi Dench and Simon Callow dragged up as British queen and Italian composer to perform Lee Hall's screenplay for the 2017 film *Victoria and Abdul*. We shouldn't complain. The Golden Globe-nominated biopic begins with a caption confessing that its story is 'based on facts … mostly'. And the assumptions it makes about Victoria and her musical taste also tell a story about our relationship with the age that bears her name.

How musical was Queen Victoria? She employed a personal bagpiper to play under her window at breakfast time. (The enthusiasm was not shared by all members of her household.) She was an accomplished pianist who kept a keyboard at every residence, including on board the royal yacht. Music played an important role in her romantic life. On her first meeting with Albert in 1836, she was as much impressed by his talent for composition and his sweet singing voice as by his looks. Once they were married, the piano duet provided one of their rituals of intimacy – they had a particular fondness for arrangements of Beethoven's *Egmont* and *Leonore* overtures, and Mendelssohn's *Elijah* and *St Paul*.

Mendelssohn was in the monarch's close orbit and in June 1842 he made a strong first impression at Buckingham Palace – wowing Victoria with his 'fine intellectual forehead' and ability to play the Austrian national anthem with his right hand and *Rule, Britannia!* simultaneously with his left. On his second visit, one month later, the Queen sang for him – after first expelling her parrot, which had a habit of competitive screeching. In 1844 the record finds her gushing about sitting '10 steps away from Felix' at a concert performance of his *A Midsummer Night's Dream*. Six months before his death in 1847, the composer presented the royal couple with a selection of his *Songs without Words*, arranged for four hands. For Victoria, this became a way of evoking a lost friend: 'To feel,' she wrote, 'when one is playing his beautiful music, that he is no more, seems incomprehensible!'

Mendelssohn, however, wasn't Victoria's teacher. That job fell to Luigi Lablache, a Neapolitan bass who was a notable Leporello in *Don Giovanni*, a torchbearer at Beethoven's funeral and – deliciously – the great-great-grandfather of the 1940s film star Stewart Granger. Victoria took notes from Lablache until his death in 1858, and once made a pencil sketch that gave him two smudgy pink cheeks and a head emerging from his collar like a soufflé escaping a ramekin.

> “Six months before his death in 1847, Mendelssohn presented the royal couple with a selection of his *Songs without Words*, arranged for four hands. For Victoria, this became a way of evoking a lost friend: 'To feel,' she wrote, 'when one is playing his beautiful music, that he is no more, seems incomprehensible.'”

When Victoria was widowed in 1861, she asked her bagpiper to stand down. Albert's death, however, did not stop the music. The cultural quarter constructed in his memory included a 5,000-seater concert hall, which would become home to the Proms in 1941, and a new royal college that aimed to train up a new generation of orchestral players. On 24 November 1898 Henry Wood, founder-conductor of the Proms, gave a command performance at Windsor of music chosen by Victoria – from sheet music that nearly failed to appear, when the courier fell asleep on the train and was carried back to Waterloo. In white kid gloves that he felt made him look like a seaside

◀ Regal recital: Young Victoria (Jenna Coleman) displays her keyboard prowess in an episode from Season 1 of the UK television drama *Victoria*

Victoria's Piano

Pianist **Stephen Hough** looks ahead to playing a historic instrument at the Proms

Sometimes pianos are not glossy and black. This 1856 Erard, an extravagant creature with monkeys and cherubs capering all over its gilded, mahogany case, neither sounds nor looks like a contemporary piano but Chopin, Liszt and, indeed, Mendelssohn would have felt more at home playing it than any Steinway.

Erard was a cutting-edge company in the mid-Victorian years and their patented double-escapement action, later adopted by all piano-makers, allowed composers to let their most daring ideas take wing. But there is an intimacy, and human quality too, to this piano's reedy timbre which really does feel like something from another era. Its shallow action and smaller hammers require the pianist to play in a totally different, less muscular manner.

Of course, although it was not designed with the Royal Albert Hall's monumental size in mind, its luminous, singing tone works beautifully there. And, as it draws us into its circle, it isn't hard to imagine the queen and her consort, Prince Albert, seated at the same bench, playing a duet by candlelight or accompanying each other in song in one of Buckingham Palace's velvet-curtained rooms.

pier bandmaster, Wood led the orchestra through a programme that was five-eighths Richard Wagner. Ahead of popular taste, the Queen had championed Wagner since the 1850s: that night she asked for 'The Ride of the Valkyries' as an encore, which rattled the windows of the Long Gallery.

Gilbert and Sullivan also received the royal command. In 1891 the D'Oyly Carte Opera Company performed *The Gondoliers* at Windsor. The republican sentiments of Gilbert's libretto seem not to have caused offence – which is why one of the most-circulated stories about Victoria and *HMS Pinafore* should be treated with suspicion. A theatrical tradition, recorded down the years in reference works and programme notes, asserts that Victoria was so appalled by the opera's mockery of the Admiralty that it caused her to utter that famous catchphrase about not being amused. But the story seems to go no further back than a *New York Times* review of 1966. Like so many of those tenacious factoids about the 19th century, it is a 20th-century invention, calculated to mark the difference between the secretive, hypocritical and pompous Victorians and their laid-back, liberated successors.

A standard history book of the mid-20th century, T. K. Derry and T. L. Jarman's *The Making of Modern Britain* (1956), asks its readers to think of Victorian life as a zone of domestic boredom and repression. 'Outside amusements were few,' they wrote, 'hence the frequency with which the piano figured in the home.' If I were called in to choose an artefact to represent our enduringly weird and mixed-up relationship with the Victorians – an object that could reflect our collective sense of nostalgia, hostility, ambivalence and resentment – I would choose the piano. Not the sort you'll hear Stephen Hough tackling on 16 August – that great glittering slab of Erard bling that, visually at least, would not have disgraced a Liberace concert *(see panel left)*. Something more modest. The sort that Victorians encountered, ready for mass production, at the Great Exhibition of 1851.

We remember the Crystal Palace as a treasure house of the triumphs and eccentricities of 19th-century industry – a glittering flatpack showroom where hydraulic presses and steam-hammers thrummed beside wacky taxidermal tableaux of duelling dormice and ice-skating hedgehogs. But it was also a greenhouse under which a new musical culture thrived. The 1851 Exhibition put 1,800 musical instruments on display – including Britain's first sight of the saxophone. The piano, however, was present in the greatest numbers, and became an increasingly affordable object of middle-class desire. In the subsequent two decades, the cost of a new instrument fell from 40 guineas to 12, a downward curve encouraged by new manufacturing technology, hire-purchase schemes and a growing market for sheet music.

When the Palace was struck and rebuilt in Sydenham, its increased size allowed it to become a venue for the large-scale symphonic and choral works that were coming into vogue. In June 1854 Victoria and Albert heard a choir of 1,500 perform Handel's 'Hallelujah Chorus' under the glass. In 1872 Sullivan's festival *Te Deum*, written to mark the recent recovery of the

Prince of Wales from typhoid fever, was performed at the Palace with a 2,000-strong choir and orchestra and an audience of 30,000. In 1887 Sullivan was back to hear the Palace's musical director conduct an orchestra and choir of 3,500 as they performed his cantata *The Golden Legend*.

The Victorians were maximalists. They were uninterested in those ideas of restraint and taste later legislated by modernism, and then policed by its various institutions and groupuscules. The word 'monster' excited them like Bart Simpson at a truck show. The phrase 'Victorian monstrosity', customarily attached to structures such as the Albert Memorial, was a 20th-century reprimand for their love of bigness.

The same age also devised a punishment for the domestic culture of the Victorians. Between the 1950s and the 1980s, piano-smashing competitions were a common feature of rag weeks and village fêtes. The object was simple – to take a hammer to a Victorian upright and reduce it to fragments small enough to fit through a tyre or a toilet seat. In the 19th-century press, the image of the ruined piano is found most commonly in war reporting. The journalist George Augustus Sala documented the 'piano-smashing banditti' of the American Civil War. In 1900 the same act of vandalism was ascribed to the Boers. In post-war Britain it migrated to light-hearted local news stories – except when, on isolated occasions, the Victorian piano fought back. (At Bletchley carnival in 1966, 11 people were treated for splinter injuries.) 'Now, years later,' wrote one eyewitness, 'I think that it was possibly also a symbolic act, the ritual destruction of repressive Victorian values, embodied in the piano, which deserved to be taken out on to the village green by right-thinking English yeomen and smashed.'

Few today would rejoice at the sight of 19th-century piano wire bursting into tangled loops, or black and white keys spilt over the grass. A film such as *Victoria and Abdul* – the story of the Christian Queen's affectionate relationship with her Muslim secretary – is less a rebuke to the Victorian contemporaries of Puccini and Mendelssohnn than a reflection upon 21st-century Islamophobes. And yet our relationship with Victoria, her subjects, and the culture they produced, still retains a note of discord. It's the reason, I suspect, why, almost 12 decades after her death, we can't keep her off the screen – or stop her singing. ●

Matthew Sweet is the author of *Inventing the Victorians* (2001), *Shepperton Babylon* (2005), which spurred a television documentary series, and *The West End Front* (2011). He presents *Sound of Cinema* and *Free Thinking* for BBC Radio 3.

Elgar Sea Pictures
heard by Victoria at Balmoral Castle in 1899
PROM 39 • 15 AUGUST

Sullivan Victoria and Merrie England – suite

Mendelssohn Piano Concerto No. 1
performed by Stephen Hough on an Erard piano (1856) owned by Queen Victoria

Prince Albert of Saxe-Coburg and Gotha Songs

Mendelssohn Symphony No. 3, 'Scottish'

PROM 40 • 16 AUGUST

Berlioz Benvenuto Cellini
heard by Victoria at Covent Garden in 1853
PROM 59 • 2 SEPTEMBER

Gilt-y pleasure: the elaborately decorated 1856 grand piano by S. & P. Erard – a showpiece in itself – owned by Queen Victoria: Stephen Hough will perform Mendelssohn's First Piano Concerto on the instrument, which has been loaned by HM The Queen from the Royal Collection and normally resides in the White Drawing Room of Buckingham Palace

A History of Classical Music

As this year's Proms at … Cadogan Hall chamber-music concerts explore the history of classical music in eight concerts, KATE ROMANO takes us on a tour illustrating the periods represented

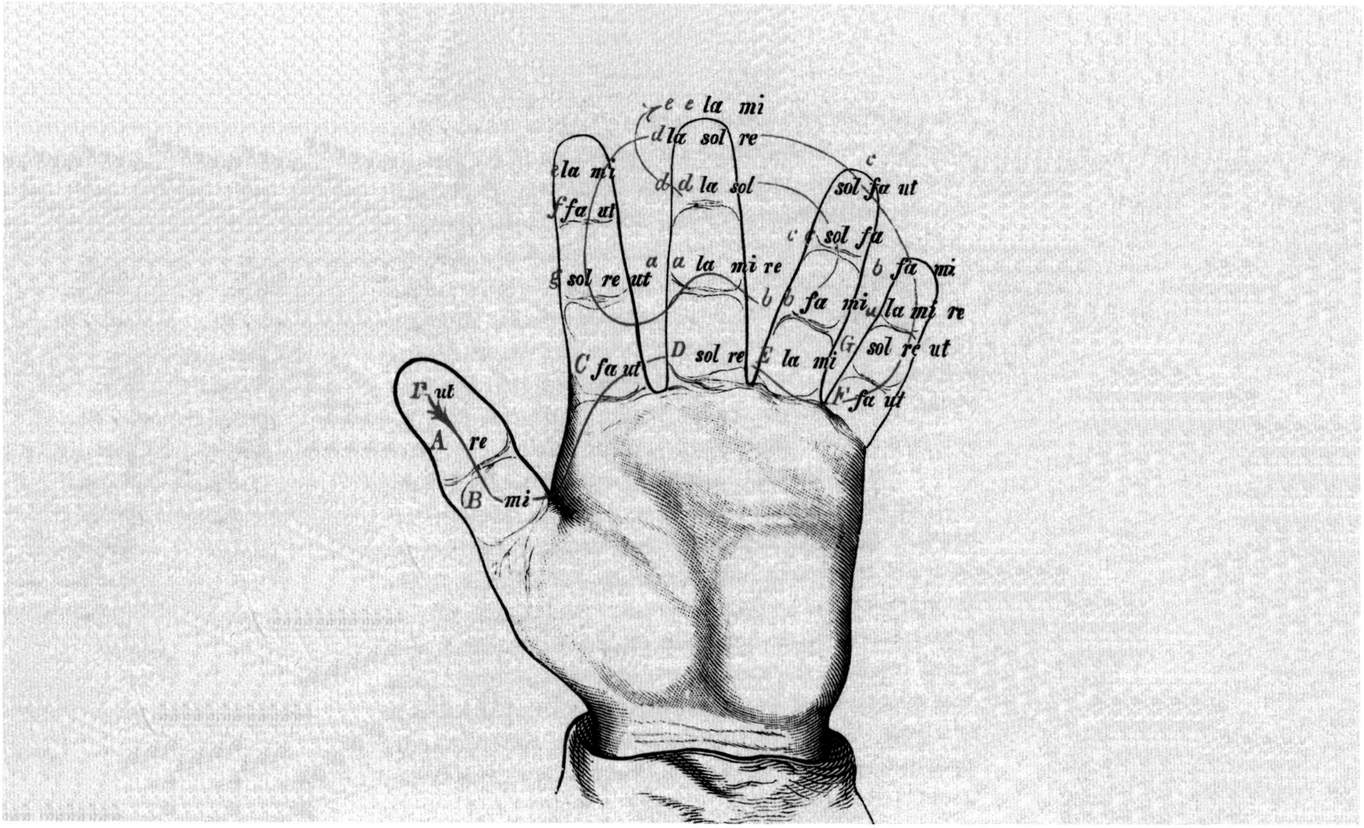

1 Medieval, 400–1400

In 1033 Guido d'Arezzo, a Benedictine monk, wrote a letter describing a method of learning chants that changed the course of music for ever. Guido explained how a chant could be sung at sight, rather than painstakingly learnt by rote, and without an instrument to provide the correct pitches.

Two things were needed: a system of notation and a device to help the singers. Guido's Hand is a mnemonic teaching aid where the syllables mark places (*'loca'*) associated with specific steps in the musical scale. Building on the theories of those before him, Guido gave names to pitches ('solmisation') and he reduced the seven-note scale to six to simplify interval patterns between notes. The innovation of the four-line music stave is often credited to Guido, although he only described it as 'a most excellent method of finding an unknown melody, recently given to us by God'.

2 Renaissance, 1400–1600

Inventor or improver, Guido's impact marked the point where musical repertoire became stabilised and Western society moved from reliance on memory towards dependency on written text. Four hundred years later, this cultural shift culminated in the glorious, mystical soundscape of the Renaissance – and there was no place better to experience it than among the aural architecture of Venice.

In ecclesiastical masterpieces such as St Mark's Basilica and Palladio's vast, sculptural Redentore, sound, set and image worked together like a Gothic theatrical drama. These grand temples with huge reverberant domes were the site of incredible polyphonic innovations by Adrian Willaert and Andrea and Giovanni Gabrieli. Choirs were divided (*cori spezzati*), hidden in raised galleries or behind iron grilles, and carefully positioned for optimum clarity, beauty and mystery. This potent synergy inspired devotion in congregations and impressed the Doge; seated upon his throne, the powerful ruler of the Venetian Republic would have been treated to the first use of a spatial 'surround-sound' system in Western music.

3 Baroque, 1600–1750

Music broke free from the gilded cage of the Church in the 17th and 18th centuries, taking to the open air and public spaces. There were no concert halls, but musical gatherings started to take place in unlikely venues. In 1678 Thomas Britton, a coal merchant with a sprightly intellect, initiated an astonishingly successful and long-running series of concerts in a tiny attic above his Clerkenwell coal yard. Audiences chatted, ate and drank, and boundaries between amateur and professional musicians were cheerfully blurred.

Then there were the pleasure gardens – intoxicating dream-lands with woody paths and twinkling lamps, where fine art met high fashion, where princes danced with prostitutes and music by Handel and his peers could be heard by thousands. The elegant octagonal bandstand built at Vauxhall in 1735 was possibly the first building in London designed solely for the performance of music. London's pleasure

◀ **1 Medieval** Guido's Hand – a mnemonic device used during the medieval period to assist sight-singing

2 Renaissance The opulent gold interior of St Mark's Basilica in Venice

3 Baroque 'Promenading' around the octagonal bandstand at the Vauxhall Pleasure Gardens

gardens defined the city's nightlife and created the first true mass audience for high-quality music and popular songs – a model for the 'promenade' concerts that were to be reimagined by Henry Wood over a century later.

4 Classical, 1750–1800

By the end of the 18th century, the Baroque instrumental collectives had evolved into the orchestra as we know it today. The keyboard continuo had gone, wind instruments appeared in pairs, first violin leadership was gradually replaced by a conductor and most orchestral musicians were specialists on their instruments.

What was it like to be a professional orchestral musician in 1800? German musicians were usually part of a church or court ensemble. Members of Haydn's orchestra had luxurious lodgings at Prince Esterházy's palace. Their instruments, food and job security were provided in exchange for serving the tastes of their patron.

London musicians had more freedom; they juggled jobs with numerous orchestras and were well paid. To address the lack of long-term security they created mutual assistance societies, the foundation of the 20th century's musicians' unions. The 19th century sowed the seeds of employment patterns that resonate today and established a spectacular orchestral sound that was to inspire some of the greatest music ever written.

4 Classical The concert hall at the Esterházy Palace in Austria, where Haydn conducted the orchestra while in service to the Prince

5 Early Romantic, 1800–1850

In 1813 a small mechanical device with a clock-ticking function – Johann Maelzel's metronome – was introduced to the orchestras and skilled musicians of the 19th century. Reactions were mixed. Beethoven started to label his works with metronome marks, as did his editors. But many musicians found the idea of the metronome 'disagreeable to those who have a real feeling for music … too mechanically uniform'. A time-keeping machine, it was widely felt, was the antithesis of good musical performance. Maelzel was an inventor, showman and entrepreneur – could he have known that the metronome was a solution to a problem that didn't really exist?

ABOVE **5 Early Romantic** A decorated metronome – Johann Maelzel's 'Instrument for the Improvement of all Musical Performance'

RIGHT **6 Late Romantic** Siegfried Wagner conducting in the recessed orchestra pit at the Bayreuth Festspielhaus

But the metronome was ahead of its time. No-one could have predicted how much relevance it would have in our fast-paced, synchronised, regulated world. Today, values and habits built on accuracy and precision are ingrained in our musical performances. The simple tick-tock time-keeping of the metronome belies its role as a powerful mirror of changing musical and cultural tastes.

6 Late Romantic, 1850–1900

In the late 19th century musical and cultural tastes turned towards the act – or art – of listening. As composers became more esteemed, audiences were kept at a greater distance and listening in worshipful silence was expected.

The Bayreuth Festspielhaus, built by Richard Wagner for the performance of his *Ring* cycle, opened in 1876, encapsulating this new reverence. Theodor Adorno used the term 'phantasmagorical' to describe the perfect unity of musical, dramatic and artistic elements in Wagner's operas. One could say the same about the Bayreuth architecture; the acousmatic sound emerging from the 'invisible orchestra' under the stage, the dousing of the lights and the simple décor spawned an entire concert reform movement. Singers were

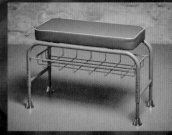

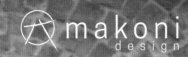

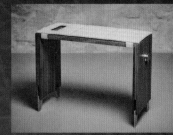

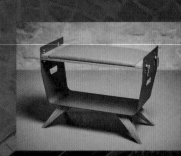

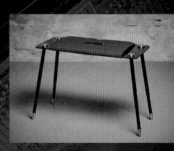

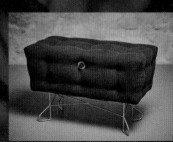

obscured by veils or floral screens, while lights and scent were used to make the experience of listening ever more spiritual and transcendent.

But listening like this was hard work. It drove a barrier between devoted followers and those who missed being able to enjoy music on their own terms, who were drawn to the music halls. It's far easier to put up walls than to remove them and the legacy of this cultural divide remains apparent today.

7 Early 20th Century, 1900–1950

What might Wagner have made of a 1924 experiment when *Die Walküre* was broadcast from the Bavarian State Opera … over the telephone? Bound (at least figuratively) to the music, committed subscribers to the 'Opera-Telephone' could devote themselves fully to the work in the privacy of their own homes. But it was radio, with its more relaxed approach and technical advances, that became the dominant force for experiencing music in the early 20th century.

BBC Radio was founded in October 1922 and, with characteristic vim and vigour, produced an ambitious live broadcast from the Royal Opera House just three months later. The BBC claimed that the wireless was 'the magical agent that has made available the finest things there are to hear in music. All may – in spirit – sit side by side with the patrons of the stalls and hear some of the best performances in the world.'

'Listening in' (as it was known) became part of everyday life, shaping our musical tastes and bringing a huge variety of classical music to a new radio audience.

8 Contemporary, 1950–2019

Historically, Western Classical music has moved towards permanence, stability and finding ways of harnessing the repertoire so that it can be collected, treasured and debated. Yet around the periphery of this museum of sound, a mid-20th-century experimental revolution was taking place.

Composers such as John Cage, Pauline Oliveros and Cornelius Cardew wrenched music out of the museum and put it back in people's minds. Notation struggled to express radical new ideas about how and what music was for. Scores expanded into beautiful graphic landscapes or transformed into complex and thrilling journeys, with notation set free of the suffocating systems of before.

There is no Guido's Hand to help performers navigate the many landscapes of the music of our own time. A chambered nautilus was used as a cover image in 1974 for Italo Calvino's novel *Invisible Cities*. It combines the idea of patterns with limitless imagination. Just like Calvino's fantasy travelogue, there is a disorientating thrill in traversing the musical paths, places and 'thought experiments' of our own time as performer or listener – and in knowing that we are part of the next chapter of classical musical history. ●

Kate Romano is a producer, clarinettist and writer. Previously a senior member of academic staff at the Guildhall School of Music & Drama, she is currently the Artistic Director of Goldfield Productions.

This year's Monday-lunchtime Proms at … Cadogan Hall series explores the history of classical music across its eight concerts, with works spanning the 12th century to the present day, from Hildegard of Bingen and Barbara Strozzi to Oliver Knussen and Sir Harrison Birtwistle. See Listings (pages 124–160).

7 Early 20th Century A BBC microphone – the first radio broadcasts on the wireless in the 1920s brought 'the finest things … in music' into people's homes

8 Contemporary The patterns of the chambered nautilus evoke the limitless imagination of the 21st century

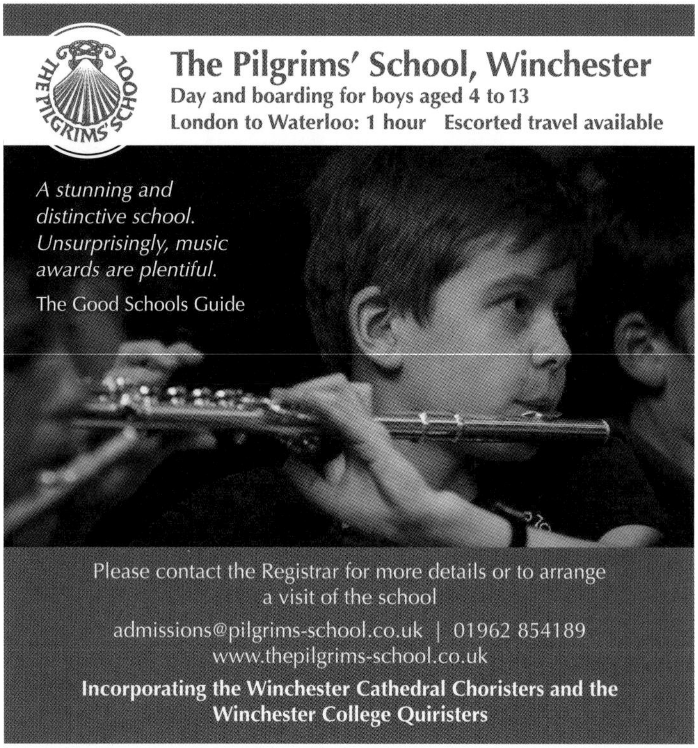
THE PILGRIMS' SCHOOL
The Pilgrims' School, Winchester
Day and boarding for boys aged 4 to 13
London to Waterloo: 1 hour   Escorted travel available
A stunning and distinctive school. Unsurprisingly, music awards are plentiful.
The Good Schools Guide
Please contact the Registrar for more details or to arrange a visit of the school
admissions@pilgrims-school.co.uk | 01962 854189
www.thepilgrims-school.co.uk
Incorporating the Winchester Cathedral Choristers and the Winchester College Quiristers

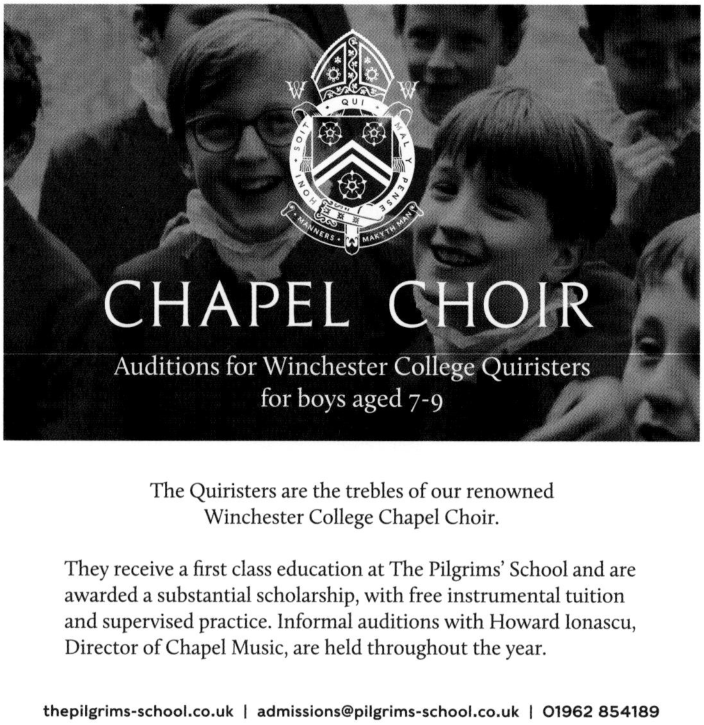
MANNERS MAKYTH MAN
CHAPEL CHOIR
Auditions for Winchester College Quiristers for boys aged 7-9
The Quiristers are the trebles of our renowned Winchester College Chapel Choir.
They receive a first class education at The Pilgrims' School and are awarded a substantial scholarship, with free instrumental tuition and supervised practice. Informal auditions with Howard Ionascu, Director of Chapel Music, are held throughout the year.
thepilgrims-school.co.uk | admissions@pilgrims-school.co.uk | 01962 854189

OXFORD LIEDER FESTIVAL
TALES OF BEYOND
MAGIC, MYTHS AND MORTALS
11–26 OCTOBER 2019
Louise Alder
Benjamin Appl
Ilker Arcayürek
Eugene Asti
BBC National Orchestra of Wales
Brodsky Quartet
Imogen Cooper
Neal Davies
Stéphane Degout
Doric String Quartet
Christopher Glynn
Hartmut Höll
Graham Johnson
Sophie Karthäuser
Stephan Loges
Malcolm Martineau
Owen-Apekisheva Duo
Christoph Prégardien
Gweneth-Ann Rand
Dorothea Röschmann
Carolyn Sampson
Cédric Tiberghien
Camilla Tilling
Jac van Steen
Roger Vignoles
Roderick Williams
and many others...
Oxford Lieder
Celebrating Song
www.oxfordlieder.co.uk

CANTERBURY FESTIVAL 2019
Kent's International Arts Festival
19 OCTOBER - 2 NOVEMBER
CANTERBURY FESTIVAL
Featuring:
The Sixteen | The Tallis Scholars |
Finghin Collins (piano) |
'The Keys of Canterbury' by John Harle (world premiere) with Jess Gillam (sax)
On sale from 15 July
SALON PERDU
For more information visit canterburyfestival.co.uk or call 01227 452 853
Partner and Principal Sponsor
Canterbury Christ Church University

Sun 7 July
The Bridgewater Hall
THE ANVIL
AN ELEGY FOR PETER
A major new work
Composed by Emily Howard
Libretto by Michael Symmons Roberts
Performed by the BBC Philharmonic,
the BBC Singers and the Hallé choirs
Commissioned by Manchester International Festival, the BBC Philharmonic and BBC Radio 3.
Produced by Manchester International Festival and the BBC Philharmonic.
Thur 11 July
The Bridgewater Hall
LENIN GRAD
THE HALLÉ
Shostakovich's Symphony No.7
Conducted by Sir Mark Elder
Produced by Manchester International Festival and the Hallé.
Mon 15 – Sat 20 July
Royal Exchange Theatre
TAO OF GLASS
PHILIP GLASS & PHELIM MCDERMOTT
Commissioned by Manchester International Festival, Improbable, Perth Festival and Ruhrfestspiele Recklinghausen.
Produced by Manchester International Festival, Improbable and the Royal Exchange Theatre.
MIF Manchester International Festival 2019
MIF Manchester International Festival 2019
MIF Manchester International Festival 2019
4 – 21 July
mif.co.uk
bruntwood
MAG Manchester Airport
NCP
MANCHESTER CITY COUNCIL
Supported using public funding by ARTS COUNCIL ENGLAND
BBC
The Guardian
Manchester Evening News

Chinese Revolutions

Western classical music in China is enjoying an unparalleled renaissance. As the Shanghai Symphony Orchestra – 140 this year – makes its Proms debut, JINDONG CAI and SHEILA MELVIN review the scene and place it in the frame of 400 years of rich but turbulent history

The home of the Shanghai Symphony Orchestra (SSO) is in an elegant, tree-lined enclave, once Shanghai's French Concession, but nowadays a microcosm of China's thriving classical-music world. The SSO holds pride of place in a serene, custom-built complex that includes its offices, archives, rehearsal space and 1,200-seat concert hall that opened in 2014. Around the corner is the Shanghai Conservatory of Music, founded in 1927, whose post-2000 building spree has seen it sprout high-rises and expand its student body to 2,500. Currently, it is building an opera theatre with a 1,230-seat auditorium and rehearsal halls for orchestra, chorus, Chinese traditional ensembles and ballet.

Clustered between the SSO and the Conservatory are dozens of stores selling pianos and string instruments, off-the-shelf or made to order. China is now the world's biggest producer and exporter of musical instruments, accounting for more than 70 per cent of the world's pianos and 85 per cent of string-instrument production in 2017. Estimates of the number of piano students in China vary between 30 and 60 million: whatever the real figure, it is big.

A similar picture exists in other big Chinese cities. Suzhou, Shanghai's neighbour, has one of China's youngest orchestras, with more than half its musicians recruited globally. Chengdu, in south-western Sichuan, is home to four orchestras and the Sichuan Conservatory, which claims 14,000 students. Harbin, in north-eastern Heilongjiang, is a UNESCO-designated City of Music. It opened a stunning Grand Theatre in 2015 and a massive conservatory in 2016 that is partnered with the St Petersburg Conservatory. Zhejiang Province also opened a new conservatory in 2016, bringing China's total number of stand-alone conservatories to 11.

And classical music isn't just for urban elites. On 1 January, millions gather around TVs to watch the live Vienna Philharmonic New Year's Day concert. China's own orchestras give New Year concerts over the same period, some for the public and others for large companies and government departments. They also regularly tour to smaller cities, which are increasingly growing their own orchestras; in 2014, 40-plus professional orchestras were registered with the China Symphony Orchestra Foundation and by 2018 there were 82.

This passion for music runs deep. 'Music is the unifying centre of the world,' argued Xunzi (312–230 BCE), 'the key to peace and harmony.' The Chinese government appears to agree. In September last year China's Ministry of Culture and Tourism declared the start of a 'Symphonic Era' and a 'China symphonic music creation support programme' for works that reflect the nation's 'great achievements' since 1979. The programme is billed as part of the ongoing effort to create a transformative and innovative society – one that must include 'excellent symphonic and national orchestra works'.

Opera in the space age: detail of the Grand Theatre (opened 2016) in Harbin, Heilongjiang Province – part of a new arts hub set by the Songhua River

East Meets West

Conductor **Long Yu** on the increasing irrelevance of traditional boundaries

I belong to a very special generation in China's history. Growing up, we were not allowed to perform or listen to Western music; and, as a classical-music student, I was among the first musicians to study abroad. This was transformative for me and, as China opened up to Western classical music again, our enthusiasm has made China one of the largest centres for classical music in the world. To witness this history has been quite remarkable.

I grew up in Shanghai and, like the Shanghai Symphony Orchestra's repertoire for the Proms, this vibrant city has many cultural influences. Musicians often separate Eastern and Western music but, to me, music is music, and I do not feel the divide is necessary.

Our Proms programme reflects how East and West can complement and enrich each other, with Qigang Chen's *Wu Xing* ('The Five Elements') alongside Mozart – a piano concerto featuring the young Chinese-American winner of the Leeds International Piano Competition 2018 – and Rachmaninov. I hope this programme will inspire more musicians to put the two cultures alongside each other in conversation.

The path by which symphonic music became part of China's cultural patrimony is a meandering one. In 1601 the Jesuit priest Matteo Ricci gave the Wan Li emperor a clavichord; subsequent missionaries followed suit, gifting successive emperors with European instruments. The Kangxi emperor was fascinated by staff notation and learnt to play several songs on the harpsichord. By the time his grandson, Qianlong, came to power, the palace had enough Western instruments to create an ensemble of 18 eunuchs who performed while wearing Western-style suits, shoes and powdered wigs!

In the aftermath of the First Opium War (1839–42), a growing number of Europeans and Americans settled in port cities, such as Shanghai, forcing China to open up. Many wanted to hear their own music. So, in 1879, China's very first orchestra – now the Shanghai Symphony Orchestra – was established by the city's foreign residents. The musicians in the ensemble were all recruited from Manila, a Spanish outpost for centuries that had a Western music tradition, and the audience was almost exclusively foreign.

By the early 20th century, however, interest in Western music was growing. A handful of intellectuals went abroad to study music, including Xiao Youmei, who obtained a doctorate at the Leipzig Conservatory, and Huang Zi, who received a BA in composition at Yale. Upon their return, both men were drawn to Shanghai because of its orchestra, which had been dubbed 'the best orchestra in the Far East'. Xiao decided Shanghai was the best place to put a national conservatory because he could recruit Shanghai Symphony musicians as teachers or, as he put it, 'borrow foreign chickens to produce Chinese eggs'.

In the 1920s and 1930s, Shanghai became the crucible of symphonic music development in China. The Russian Revolution caused a massive exodus of intellectuals and artists to the East. Some settled in Harbin, which had a thriving Russian Jewish community, an orchestra and many music schools, while others made their way to Shanghai. 'The port was swarming with musical artists by this time,' wrote R. B. Hurry, then choirmaster of Shanghai's English Cathedral, 'all eager to play, teach, sing, act or lecture anywhere, if only an audience and pupils could be attracted.' With the rise of Hitler, more than 18,000 European Jews also sought safety in Shanghai, among them many musicians. These musical refugees found eager Chinese pupils and contributed to the blossoming of a truly cosmopolitan music world. Global stars such as Fritz Kreisler and Jascha Heifetz performed with the Shanghai Symphony, as did budding Chinese musicians such as Ma Sicong.

The outbreak of the Second World War altered the trajectory of musical development, causing many Chinese to see pure classical music as a 'dead end' and to direct their efforts towards patriotic music. Some, such as He Luting (who would later head the Shanghai Conservatory), Li Delun (who would lead the Central Philharmonic) and Xian Xinghai (who composed the *Yellow River Cantata*), left Shanghai for the Communist base camp at Yan'an and founded an orchestra there, performing on a hotchpotch of instruments that included Standard Oil barrels. When Yan'an was abandoned, the orchestra started walking north. They stopped each evening to perform land-reform propaganda and play pieces such as Schubert's *Marche militaire*, a Mozart Serenade, even a 'Liberated Don Quixote' (a spoken drama with incidental music). After three full years of walking and playing, they reached Beijing just in time to help liberate the city from nationalist Kuomintang control.

The founding of the People's Republic of China in 1949 opened up a long-lasting debate between those who thought classical music was bourgeois, and should be forbidden, and those who argued that it could serve workers, peasants and soldiers. In the 1950s orchestras, ballet companies, opera houses and conservatories were founded with the help of Soviet and East German experts. Composers were encouraged to write symphonic music with Chinese themes, such as the 1959 violin concerto *Butterfly Lovers* by He Zhanhao and Chen Gang. Celebrations of the 10th anniversary of the People's Republic of China even included a performance of Beethoven's Ninth Symphony, with the choral finale sung in Chinese.

In the 1960s the political pendulum swung ever further left, culminating in the Cultural Revolution (1966–76). Gangs of teenaged Red Guards sought to destroy the 'Four Olds' – customs, culture, habits and ideas: Western music was banned. Prominent classical musicians were humiliated, beaten, locked up and forced to criticise themselves. The terror was such that 17 teachers at the Shanghai Conservatory took their own lives, as did the Shanghai Symphony's pianist Gu Shengying. Shanghai Symphony conductor Lu Hongen refused to criticise his teachers and vocally defended classical music. He was jailed and condemned to death – and went to his execution, on 27 April 1968, humming Beethoven's *Missa solemnis*.

When the turmoil ended and China opened up, a tremendous interest in symphonic music was unleashed. The Central Conservatory reopened in 1978, receiving 18,000 applicants for 100 places. Its first class included composers Tan Dun, Zhou Long, Chen Yi and Ye Xiaogang, all of whose works are performed around the world. The following decades brought high periods – 'piano fever' and 'Beethoven fever' – and low periods, as orchestras and conservatories struggled to rebuild in challenging economic circumstances.

But, then, in the post-2000 economic boom, classical music was finally able to obtain adequate support over a sustained period. The result is that orchestras such as the Shanghai Symphony, for the past decade under the baton of Long Yu, have become world-class organisations. There can be few countries where musicians have struggled harder or sacrificed more – China has earned its newfound status as a global centre of classical music performance and production, and its musicians, composers and orchestras are ready, as the old saying goes, to shake the world. ●

Born in Beijing, Jindong Cai is a professor of music and arts at Bard College, New York State, and director of the school's US-China Music Institute. Sheila Melvin writes about business and culture in China. She is the author of *The Little Red Book of China Business* and the co-author, with Cai, of *Rhapsody in Red: How Western Classical Music Became Chinese* and *Beethoven in China: How the Great Composer Became an Icon in the People's Republic*.

Shanghai Symphony Orchestra/Long Yu

PROM 57, 1 SEPTEMBER

Many hands unite as 2,008 musicians play the fou, an ancient Chinese percussion instrument, at the Opening Ceremony of the 2008 Olympic Games in Beijing

Lost Legacies

This year the Proms marks the anniversaries of Barbara Strozzi and Clara Schumann, composers born 200 years apart. ANNA BEER contrasts their respective careers with the reception of women composers today

Venice 1619: a baby girl is christened Barbara Valle in the church of Santa Sofia, Cannaregio. Her mother is, perhaps, a courtesan. Her father, the documents say, is *incerto*: unknown. We do know that Giulio Strozzi, a leading figure in the musical and literary life of Venice, raises the child. By the time Barbara is 18, Giulio has ensured not only that she has received a fine musical education, but that she has a platform for her exceptional talent, his own academy, the Unisoni. A virtuoso singer, Barbara is also a composer, for she lives and works in an era in which performance and composition go hand in hand. Her *First Book of Madrigals* is published in 1644, the year in which Barbara Strozzi (now with Giulio's name, for she is after all his product) gives birth to her third child by Giovanni Vidman, one of Giulio's patrons.

Had she been born a man, of course, the options open to Barbara would have been very different. Consider Francesco Caletti, born in Crema in 1602. Like Barbara, Francesco showed early musical talent. Unlike her, he was adopted by Federico Cavalli, the Venetian governor of Crema, and under his patronage joined St Mark's Choir as a boy soprano. Aided by noble patrons and a rich wife, Francesco would become crucial to the formation of Venetian opera, as investor and composer. As Francesco Cavalli he would be the most performed composer of opera in the quarter-century after Monteverdi's death.

This brave new world of Venetian opera was closed to Strozzi – at least as a composer – but she nevertheless took her own remarkable musical journey. (Singers were emerging as the most important force in the Venetian music industry, whether on stage, in private, or even in church. These performers were certainly paid far better than the composers of their music, so Strozzi's commitment to composition is telling.) Pushed to explore different ways to be heard as a composer, Strozzi produced seven further volumes of music between 1651 and 1664, characterised by 'sheer music' or 'pure voice' (an unusually large proportion of her music does not articulate any word at all), pungent chromaticism and relentless syncopation. She plays equally sophisticated games with gender and sexuality, her music often both erotic and unsettling. Confident and innovative to the last, Strozzi insisted on a high level of performance indications in her printed works. The composer was striving to ensure as precise, and as authentic, a legacy of her art as she could.

Two hundred years later, Clara Wieck's early life was equally dominated by an ambitious father. Friedrich, piano seller and music teacher of Leipzig, turned his daughter, born in 1819, into a performing phenomenon. Clara was her father's best pupil, a walking advertisement for his abilities. At the age of 5, she could play by ear, transpose, improvise, all before she could read music. At 10, formal harmony, counterpoint and composition classes began. Like Strozzi, Clara's development as a composer was inextricably linked to her life as a performer. In order to improvise brilliantly, she needed to understand harmony and form, while audiences expected performers to play their own compositions at recitals. Clara Wieck was a child-prodigy pianist. She therefore became a child-prodigy *composer* for the piano.

Outstanding among the words of Wieck's adolescence is her Piano Concerto, Op. 7. Dramatic and innovative, it reveals the teenage composer's virtuosity and independent thinking. It is also a vehicle for display, well-structured but infused with a sense of improvisation. Clara would develop as a composer in the early months of her marriage to Robert Schumann, as the new couple studied counterpoint together and collaborated on song-writing, and she continued to compose despite the demands of marriage and motherhood. Her superb Piano Trio (written over a summer when Robert was sick in mind and body, Clara had given birth to her fourth child in February and then suffered a miscarriage) is, said critic Joan Chissell, a work of 'contrapuntal cunning', showing what *Grove Music Online* terms a 'mastery of sonata form and polyphonic techniques'. Schumann herself acknowledged her pleasure in its composition, despite or because of the crises surrounding her: 'There is nothing better than the pleasure of composing something oneself, than hearing it played. There are some nice sections in the Trio and I believe that its form is also rather well executed.'

It was a fleeting moment of satisfaction. As soon as Robert wrote his own Piano Trio, the doubts crept in. 'Of course', Clara wrote, her trio 'remains the work of a woman', lacking 'force' and 'invention'. Her self-assessment is hardly surprising given contemporary

◀ FAR LEFT *The Viola da Gamba Player* by Bernardo Strozzi (1581–1644), believed to depict Barbara Strozzi

LEFT Clara Schumann at the piano, c1880s

attitudes. As one reviewer said of her concerto: 'If the name of the female composer were not above the title, one would never think it were written by a woman.'

It is well known that Clara Schumann, composer, fell silent when Robert died. Significantly, however, she continued performing even while Robert was slowly dying in an asylum, taking on the most punishing of touring schedules, spending months on the road away from her young family. It was not external factors that silenced Clara Schumann, it was her internalisation of the beliefs of her society: 'I once thought that I possessed creative talent, but I have given up this idea; a woman must not desire to compose – nor has one been able to do it, and why should I expect to?' She chose to stop composing, working tirelessly instead to promote her husband's work and creating the (male) canon that would, ironically, exclude her.

The weight of patriarchal beliefs that silenced Clara Schumann in her lifetime mean that we still do not hear the work of the many women who did compose. The perpetuation of the male canon has meant that, although a composer might be celebrated in her own lifetime as 'exceptional', she is quickly dismissed and forgotten. The next generation has to fight the battle for acceptance all over again.

Women composers themselves have always wanted to take gender out of the equation. Back in 1644, with her first publication, Strozzi feared the 'swords of slander' and with good reason, given the relentless attacks upon her reputation. Her next work talked of 'the lowly mine of a woman's poor imagination' and she continued to be preoccupied by 'feminine weaknesses', while claiming to be free of them. But, in her remarkable final three works, Strozzi did not even mention being a woman, attempting to place herself beyond gender. It is an impossible dream.

Virginia Woolf wrote, famously and contentiously, that 'a woman must have money and a room of her own if she is to write fiction'. But a composing woman needs even more: a community that not only values her art but enables it to be heard beyond the traditional spaces for women's music, whether nunnery or home. This is why initiatives that invest in female talent, such as Keychange, driven by the PRS Foundation, are so crucial. Forty-five international music festivals, including the BBC Proms, have pledged to achieve a 50/50 gender split in aspects of their events, such as live music acts, conference talks or commissions, by 2022, in an effort to bring about a more balanced industry. As we commemorate the births of Strozzi and Schumann, we should not only celebrate what they achieved – against the odds – but continue to work towards a world in which it is just that little bit easier to be a woman and a composer. We will all be the richer. ●

A Fellow of Kellogg College, Oxford, Anna Beer is the author of *Sounds and Sweet Airs: The Forgotten Women of Classical Music* (Oneworld Publications, 2016).

Barbara Strozzi Vocal works
PROMS AT ... CADOGAN HALL 2 • 29 JULY

Clara Schumann Piano Concerto
PROM 42 • 18 AUGUST

Clara Schumann Piano Trio
PROMS AT ... CADOGAN HALL 6
26 AUGUST

> “The composer demonstrates in all her work that gentle, poetic nature that marked her out, on her entry into the artistic world, as more than a virtuoso, and brought her many friends. However, at the same time the old adage that the female sex is more suited to imitation than to original creativity in the artistic realm, can also be applied to her in some measure … However, in Clara Schumann's writing there is many an original feature.

A mixed review of Clara Schumann's talents as a composer in the *Allgemeine Musikalische Zeitung* in 1845

I Put a Spell on You

Singer, pianist and social activist, Nina Simone was one of the 20th century's most extraordinary artists. Ahead of a Prom dedicated to the 'High Priestess of Soul', COURTNEY PATTERSON-FAYE explores her troubled background and enduring influence

When Nina Simone stepped onto a stage, audience members, even her devout followers, never knew exactly what to expect. Her skill at crossing musical genres continues to astonish anyone who truly listens to her music. Her ability to move effortlessly between jazz, pop, gospel, soul and the more-than-occasional show tune seems to reflect the artist's wide-ranging interests, which also embraced social activism, as well as her turbulent personal life. Her defiant, insistent and captivating presence continues to beguile audiences, both old and new, who enter into her musical world and swiftly become amazed at all of its offerings, from her ability to fuse classical techniques with soulful rhythms to her improvisational skills, which left jazz legends dazed and confused.

Born Eunice Kathleen Waymon in Tryon, North Carolina, Simone began playing piano at the age of 3 and, under her mother's tutelage, became a regular pianist at her family's church by the age of 6. In her autobiography, *I Put a Spell on You*, she described how music enveloped the entire family. Simone's parents, her all-round 'entertainer' father John Divine Waymon, and piano-playing mother Mary Kate, embedded a love of music into their children. Simone and all seven of her siblings played piano and sang around the house and in church. However, little Eunice's virtuoso piano playing caught the attention of the woman who employed her mother as a housemaid, leading to the start of more formal classical training.

◂ Nina Simone commanding attention in the studio, *c*1967

Lessons with Muriel Mazzanovich, or 'Miz Mazzy', helped Eunice gain the technique to match her abilities and she gradually moved from performing alongside her mother at various churches throughout North Carolina to enrolling at the Allen High School for Girls and taking lessons with Carl Friedberg in New York City. During the summer of 1950, she worked hard with Friedberg to prepare for an audition to become the first black classical pianist to enter Philadelphia's Curtis Institute of Music, but was denied acceptance into the programme. Devastated and heartbroken, Simone would later conclude that racial bias, not lack of ability, kept her from matriculating into the Curtis Institute. Now taxed with supporting herself and her family, which had moved to Philadelphia in support of her dreams, she had to chart a new course through life.

In 1954 Eunice Waymon walked into the Midtown Bar and Grill in Atlantic City, New Jersey, and walked out with her new stage name: Nina Simone. Not wanting her (Methodist preacher) mother to find out about her job as a pianist there (a 'sinful' activity), Waymon picked Nina – derived from 'niña', a term of affection her beau at the time bestowed upon her – and Simone – the first name of acclaimed French actress Simone Signoret. There, at the Midtown Bar and Grill, Nina Simone became a musical couturier and created the musical formulae that made listeners fall at her feet. Instructed by the bar's owner to sing as well as play during her sets if she wanted to keep her job, Simone would merge threads belonging to pop and show tunes with jazz, soul and funk with shiny, silky gossamers from her classical music sewing kit. She was an artful weaver, constructing musical garments with what she called 'classical motifs', trendy bass lines and supernatural powers. In turn, her sets drew plenty of people to Atlantic City, especially those from the music industry.

Between 1958 and 1993, Simone recorded over 40 original albums, which included live performances and covers of some prominent artists, especially Billie Holiday. Her debut album with Bethlehem Records, *Little Girl Blue*, contained her only Top 20 hit, 'I Loves You, Porgy', written by George and Ira Gershwin. Her time at Bethlehem became representative of her tumultuous relationship with the music industry, which worked hard to syphon what it could from Simone. At Bethlehem she signed a contract without reading it, giving away the rights to her music – a move that would cost her over a million dollars. This was especially egregious given that songs from her first recording session for Bethlehem were released on another album without her consent after she left the label. She never received any payment for it and had to fight in court against its continued distribution.

However, as turbulent as her recording career was, her talent never wavered. She performed 'I Loves You, Porgy' alongside blues and jazz standards such as 'Nobody Knows You When You're Down and Out', 'My Baby Just Cares For Me' and 'Don't Let Me Be Misunderstood'. Combined with her musical mastery, her relationships with cultural, social and political figures such as Lorraine Hansberry, Langston Hughes, James Baldwin, Miriam Makeba, Stokely

when performance counts
Bird College
Conservatoire for
dance and musical theatre
OVER 70 YEARS
OF OUTSTANDING PERFORMANCE
birdcollege.co.uk

Carmichael and Amiri Baraka solidified Simone's place in both professional and intellectual circles that broadened not only her reach, but also her impact on the lives of black people. This is most deftly revealed in Simone's recording of the protest song 'Mississippi Goddam' on her 1964 album *Nina Simone in Concert*. Simone, responding to the cruelty of the Southern states' discriminatory Jim Crow laws, penned the song after civil rights activist Medgar Evers's assassination in Jackson, Mississippi, and the bombing of the 16th Street Baptist Church in Birmingham, Alabama, both in 1963. Her once silky, shiny threads were now spun coalmine black as she began to grapple with social injustice and inequality.

Simone's music was imbued with struggle, empowerment and self-determination. She often sang about racial and gender disparity, with particular attention to how black women had to carve out their own place in the world. She covered and gave new voice to *Hair*'s 'Ain't Got No/I Got Life', while she gut-wrenchingly told stories in 'Four Women' and between refrains in 'See-Line Woman' that highlighted the past and present battles of black women with racism, sexism and classism. In 1969 Simone's love for the playwright Lorraine Hansberry led her and longtime co-composer and friend Weldon Irvine to write 'To Be Young, Gifted and Black' as a tribute to Hansberry. The song, inspired by Hansberry's play of the same name, became such a popular beacon for black liberation that the Congress of Racial Equality (CORE) declared it the 'Anthem of Black America'. Simone herself, sharing the title of her 1967 album, was dubbed 'The High Priestess of Soul'.

Pushed to keep a busy performance schedule, Simone often struggled with mental illness (she was diagnosed with bipolar disorder in the late 1980s) and faced familial, financial and personal conflict at home. While she may have never reached the zenith of success she constantly pursued, her catalogue of work and social activism has impacted and influenced artists across genres and international boundaries. In particular, Lauryn Hill seems to embody and reflect Nina Simone's musical, personal and social justice legacy. Her 2014 song 'Black Rage' eerily mimics Simone's 'Mississippi Goddam' in purpose and execution, while artists such as Aretha Franklin, Elton John, Beyoncé, David Bowie, Emeli Sandé, Sade, Janis Joplin, Common, Nick Cave, Lykke Li, Kanye West, Jeff Buckley and Meshell Ndegeocello have all demonstrated just how much she shaped their creative output.

Nina Simone's induction into America's Rock & Roll Hall of Fame in 2018 has similarly ushered in a new wave of admirers. These newcomers to her couture boutique of classical rhythms join in with the rest of us to catch a glimpse of the artist at work. Her compositions and arrangements are still unmatched. Whether in life or in the afterlife, Nina Simone continues to spin musical tapestries that dazzle our minds, hearts and souls. ●

Courtney Patterson-Faye is an Assistant Professor of Sociology at Wesleyan University, Connecticut, USA. Her research, writing and teaching centres on the intersections of Black Studies, Sociology, Fat Studies and Gender and Women's Studies.

Mississippi Goddam: A Homage to Nina Simone

Metropole Orkest/Jules Buckley

PROM 45 • 21 AUGUST

Nina Simone *(left)* at New York's Madison Square Garden Jazz Festival in 1959 with Duke Ellington *(centre)* and Buddy Rich

◀ Granny, Major and Mother Clanger watching the lunar eclipse from their small planet far, far away

A Musical Trip to the Moon

Get ready to become a musical astronaut and blast off to the Moon at this year's CBeebies Proms!

Music can take us places beyond our wildest dreams, but have you ever imagined going to the Moon? At this year's CBeebies Proms, children will have the chance to travel through space, with help from CBeebies friends and presenters YolanDa Brown, Justin Fletcher, Chris Jarvis, Maddie Moate and Cat Sandion.

Europe's first majority BME orchestra, Chineke!, under conductor Kwamé Ryan, will be on hand to provide budding musical astronauts with the special musical powers they need to go on an exciting journey far beyond the Royal Albert Hall.

These Proms will introduce your children to the wonders of orchestral music with excerpts from Benjamin Britten's *The Young Person's Guide to the Orchestra* and works by Copland and Puccini. Watch as they lift off into the universe, taking John Adams's *Short Ride in a Fast Machine* to fly through the stars and follow in the footsteps of Neil Armstrong and Buzz Aldrin by walking on the Moon.

And, to help your musical astronauts explore what our home planet looks like from space, Chineke! will be joined by the CBeebies Prom Choir for the world premiere of *Earth* by film composer Hans Zimmer, just announced as one of this year's exciting Ten Pieces Trailblazers. BBC Ten Pieces opens up the world of classical music to young people, this year focusing on works from pioneering composers that expand our musical horizons, with something for every curious listener.

With special on-screen appearances by favourite CBeebies characters, get set to bring your young travellers on an unforgettable musical journey through the universe at the CBeebies Proms. ●

CBeebies Proms: A Musical Trip to the Moon

PROMS 3 & 5 • 21 & 22 JULY, 11.00am–*c*12.15pm

Proms for families

Bring the whole family on a musical adventure at this year's Proms. Family-friendly concerts include the Relaxed Prom (Prom 24, 6 August) and The Lost Words (Prom 49, 25 August). There are matinee performances and Proms with favourite works by composers including Brahms, Elgar, Holst and Sibelius, as well as new pieces to discover in our selection below.

PROM 12 • 27 JULY, 7.30pm–*c*9.55pm

PROM 20 • 3 AUGUST, 7.30pm–*c*9.50pm

PROM 24 • 6 AUGUST, 11.30am–*c*12.45pm

PROM 29 • 9 AUGUST, 3.00pm–*c*5.30pm

PROM 32 • 11 AUGUST, 11.00am–*c*1.10pm

PROM 49 • 25 AUGUST, 5.30pm–*c*7.30pm

PROM 57 • 1 SEPTEMBER, 11.00am–*c*1.00pm

Proms on Radio, TV, Online

> “The spirit of broadcasting – its widespread democratic appeal – is in complete harmony with the spirit of the Proms.

Proms programme writer Rosa Newmarch (1857–1940) on the BBC's running of the Proms

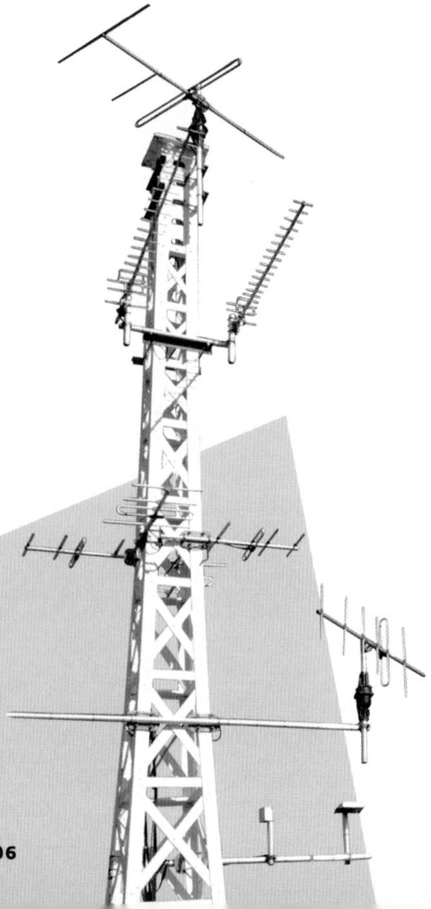

When the BBC took over the Proms in 1927 and began to broadcast concerts on radio, the primary aim of the Proms – to give audiences from all backgrounds and musical experience the opportunity to become familiar with orchestral music – was extended on a national scale. The BBC's involvement has transformed the reach of the festival, extending the audience from around 125,000 people in its early years to the millions who now enjoy the Proms on radio, television and online, with every concert broadcast live on Radio 3.

On Radio

Hear every Prom live on BBC Radio 3 on your radio, on your computer, tablet or mobile in HD Sound via the Radio 3 and BBC Proms websites, or on your digital TV service.

Listen out for Proms-themed special editions of *In Tune*, *Record Review* and *Composer of the Week*, as well as coverage of pre-Prom talks and events.

BBC Sounds brings together radio, music and podcasts in a personalised app and website. With BBC Sounds you can take the Proms with you and listen anytime, anywhere.

On TV

With 24 Proms broadcast on TV this year, Jan Younghusband, Head of Commissioning for BBC Music TV, says, ‘Once again the Proms season celebrates the greatest new and established talent from across the world and this year's TV broadcasts will highlight these outstanding composers, conductors and performers both on the concert platform and through interviews and discussions with experts. Our aim for our TV audiences has always been to put artists centre-screen and this year promises to be very exciting with such a powerful and inspiring breadth of talent and music on stage.’

Online

Visit bbc.co.uk/proms for everything you need to know about the Proms, including all the audio and video from the festival. ●

Free Events

> “The arts matter because they express … the soul of a civilisation. A nation without arts would be a nation that had … lost interest in the past and lacked curiosity about the future.

Sir John Tusa, one of this year's Proms Plus Talk contributors, in his book *Art Matters*

The BBC Proms has long enjoyed a reputation for presenting the broadest range of classical music to the widest possible audience, and for over a decade it has also added a comprehensive series of talks and introductions given by a plethora of musicians, composers and musical experts – truly a festival within a festival. These events – all of them free – are designed to offer a lively and engaging insight into the works being performed, often also placing them in their historical and social contexts.

Highlights include a three-part series honouring Proms founder-conductor Henry Wood, born 150 years ago; an introduction to Smetana's *Má vlast* from Czech-born former managing director of the BBC World Service, Sir John Tusa; an exploration of witches, witchcraft and witch trials; and writers and broadcasters Matthew Sweet and David Benedict discussing the colourful sound-world of Warner Bros. film scores.

There are events marking anniversaries for composers Sir James MacMillan (60 this year) and Mieczysław Weinberg (born 100 years ago), plus contribitions from a selection of BBC Radio 3's New Generation Thinkers.

You can be in the audience for special editions of popular BBC Radio programmes such as *In Tune*, *The Listening Service*, *The Verb* and *Front Row*, and hear dynamic young acts discovered by BBC Music Introducing.

Just as Radio 3's microphones are 'always on' at the Royal Albert Hall, so the station's production teams are on hand to cover these revealing events – most of which are broadcast in edited form during the interval of the following Prom. ●

All pre-Prom events are free and most are unticketed; start-times vary. Places for some participatory events must be booked in advance. Most events take place at Imperial College Union, close to the Royal Albert Hall. *For more details, see Listings (pages 124–160).*

Concerts
2019–20
BBC SINGERS
Join the BBC Singers and Chief Conductor Sofi Jeannin for a vibrant season of concerts.
Glorious court music from the 17th and 18th centuries, striking new works pushing at the boundaries, swinging big band vocal classics from the 1940s and 1950s and more …
To find out more and to book tickets:
bbc.co.uk/singers
BBC RADIO 3
T: @bbcsingers
F: /bbcsingers
I: @bbc_singers

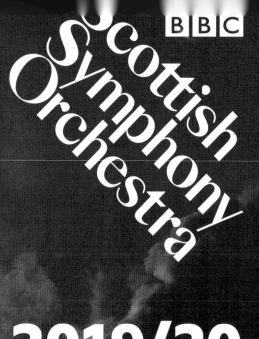

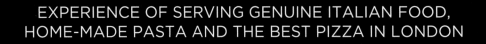

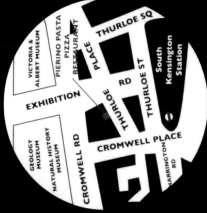

Concert Listings

Full details of all the 2019 BBC Proms concerts are in this section *(pages 124–161)*, as well as an at-a-glance calendar *(overleaf)*, Spotlight interviews with selected artists and details of the free pre-concert Proms Plus Talks and other events *(see also page 107)*.

Items marked 'Henry Wood Novelties' indicate works given their UK or world premiere by Proms founder-conductor Henry Wood, whether at the Proms or elsewhere.

Please note: concert start-times vary – check before you book.

Booking

Online
bbc.co.uk/proms or royalalberthall.com

By phone
on 020 7070 4441†

General booking
opens at 9.00am on Saturday 11 May. For booking, venue and access information, see pages 163–170.

On Radio, on TV, Online

Every Prom is broadcast live on BBC Radio 3; Proms 30 and 45 are recorded for future broadcast on BBC Radio 2

24 Proms are broadcast on BBC Four, BBC Two or BBC One – look out for this symbol

All Proms are also available for 30 days after broadcast via the BBC Proms website and can be downloaded onto your mobile or tablet via the BBC Sounds app.

Concert details were correct at the time of going to press. Please check the BBC Proms website for the latest information. The BBC reserves the right to alter artists or programmes as necessary.

† CALL COSTS
Standard geographic charges from landlines and mobiles will apply. All calls may be recorded and monitored for training and quality-control purposes

Monday	Tuesday	Wednesday	Thursday
22 July **Prom 5, P@CH 1, Prom 6** **11.00am • CBeebies (see Prom 3)** **1.00pm • Medieval/Renaissance choral music** VOCES8 **7.30pm •** Ehnes; RAM, *etc.*/Gardner	23 July **Prom 7** **7.30pm • Mozart, Ben-Haim Schoenberg, R. Schumann** Son, BBC Philharmonic/Wellber	24 July **Prom 8** **7.30pm • Debussy, P. Eötvös, Bartók, Stravinsky** Faust, BBC SO/Eötvös	25 July **Proms 9 & 10** **7.00pm • R. Strauss, T. Broström, Brahms** Hardenberger, Berwaerts, BBC NOW/Stenz ☽ **10.15pm • The Race for Space**
29 July **P@CH 2 & Prom 14** **1.00pm • Baroque choral music** Flores, Cappella Mediterranea/Alarcón **7.30pm • Haydn: The Creation** soloists, BBC Philharmonic/Wellber	30 July **Proms 15 & 16** **7.00pm • Beethoven, Shostakovich** Bavarian Radio SO/Jansons ☽ **10.15pm •** Angélique Kidjo	31 July **Prom 17** **7.30pm • Sibelius, Prokofiev, R. Strauss** Batiashvili, Bavarian Radio SO/Jansons	1 August **Prom 18** **7.30pm • Britten, Mahler** Andsnes, Mahnke, Skelton, BBC SO/Gardner
5 August **P@CH 3 & Prom 23** **1.00pm • Baroque instrumental** Bezuidenhout/The English Concert **7.30pm • Arnold, Rachmaninov, *etc.*** Gavrylyuk, BBC Philharmonic/Gernon	6 August **Proms 24 & 25** **11.30am • Relaxed Prom** Gavrylyuk, BBC Philharmonic/Gernon **7.30pm • Sibelius, Weinberg, *etc.*** Gabetta, BBC SO/Stasevska	7 August **Proms 26 & 27** **7.00pm • Brahms, Wagner, Mozart** soloists, BBC NOW/Stutzmann ☽ **10.15pm • The Sound of Space: Sci-Fi Film Music** LCO/Ames	8 August **Prom 28** **7.00pm • Takemitsu, H. Watkins, Borodin, Rachmaninov** Romaniw, BBC NOW/Otaka
12 August **P@CH 4 & Prom 34** **1.00pm • Schubert, Sirmen, Haydn** Aris Quartett **7.30pm • Schubert, Tchaikovsky, Lutosławski** Argerich, WEDO/Barenboim	13 August **Proms 35 & 36** **7.00pm • Various, Vaughan Williams, Brahms, Elgar** BBC Scottish SO/ Brabbins ☽ **10.15pm • Late-Night Mixtape**	14 August **Proms 37 & 38** **7.00pm • Berlioz: The Childhood of Christ** Hallé/Elder ☽ **10.15pm • Bach cantatas** Solomon's Knot	15 August **Prom 39** **7.00pm • Mendelssohn, Elgar, E. Wallen, Mussorgsky orch. Ravel** Morison, BBC NOW/Chan
19 August **P@CH 5 & Prom 43** **1.00pm •** Alder/Matthewman **7.30pm • J. Dove, D. Ammann, Beethoven** BBC SO/Oramo, Ferris	20 August **Prom 44** **7.30pm • Koechlin, Varèse, Walton** Finley, LSO/Rattle	21 August **Prom 45** **7.30pm • Mississippi Goddam: A Homage to Nina Simone** Ledisi, Metropole Orkest/Buckley	22 August **Prom 46** **7.30pm • Howell, Elgar, Knussen, Weinberg** Kanneh-Mason, CBSO/ Gražinytė-Tyla
26 August **P@CH 6 & Prom 50** **1.00pm • R. Schumann, C. Schumann** Amatis Piano Trio **7.30pm • R. Schumann, J. Widmann, Beethoven** Orchestre de Paris/Harding	27 August **Prom 51** **7.00pm • Mozart: The Magic Flute (Glyndebourne)** OAE/Manacorda	28 August **Prom 52** **7.30pm • Mozart, Tchaikovsky, R. Wigglesworth, Stravinsky** Lewis, Britten Sinfonia/R. Wigglesworth	29 August **Proms 53 & 54** **7.00pm • Vaughan Williams, H. Wood, Elgar** soloists, BBC SO/Davis ☽ **10.15pm • Duke Ellington's Sacred Music** Nu Civilisation Orchestra/ P. Edwards
2 September **P@CH 7 & Prom 59** **1.00pm • Weinberg, Bacewicz** Świtała, Silesian String Quartet **7.00pm • Berlioz: Benvenuto Cellini** ORR/Gardiner	3 September **Prom 60** **7.30pm • Beethoven, Bruckner** Perahia, Vienna Philharmonic/Haitink	4 September **Proms 61 & 62** **7.00pm • Dvořák, Korngold** Kavakos, Vienna Phiharmonic/Orozco-Estrada ☽ **10.15pm •** Canzioniere Grecanico Salentino	5 September **Prom 63** **7.30pm • Rachmaninov, Brahms** Wang, Staatskapelle Dresden/Chung
9 September **P@CH 8 & Prom 68** **1.00pm •** Knussen CO/R. Wigglesworth **7.30pm • Wagner Night** Goerke RPO/ Albrecht	10 September **Proms 69 & 70** **7.00pm • Smetana, Tchaikovsky, Shostakovich** Czech Phil/Bychkov ☽ **10.15pm •** Pioro, BBC NOW/Brunt	11 September **Prom 71** **7.30pm • Bach Night** Dunedin Consort/Butt	12 September **Proms 72 & 73** **7.00pm & ☽ 10.15pm • Berlioz: Symphonie fantastique** Baynton, Aurora Orchestra/Collon

Friday	Saturday	Sunday
19 July **Prom 1** **7.30pm • Z. Di Castri, Dvořák, Janáček** BBC SO/Canellakis	20 July **Prom 2** **7.30pm • Dvořák, Smetana** Bell, Bamberg SO/Hrůša	21 July **Proms 3 & 4** **11.00am • CBeebies Prom: A Musical Trip to the Moon** Chineke!/Ryan **7.30pm • J. Adams, Barber, Holst** Radulović, Bournemouth SO/Karabits
26 July **Prom 11** **7.30pm • 1969: The Sound of a Summer** BBC Concert Orchestra/Bell	27 July **P@BAC & Prom 12** **3.00pm • Contemporary experiments** **7.30pm • L. Auerbach, Tchaikovsky, Prokofiev** Benedetti, NYOGB/M. Wigglesworth	28 July **Prom 13** **7.30pm • Messiaen: Des canyons aux étoiles …** Owen, Hockings, Neal, Hodges, BBC SO/Oramo
2 August **Prom 19** **7.30pm • R. Strauss, R. Schumann, J. MacMillan** Melnikov, BBC Scottish SO/Dausgaard	3 August **Prom 20** **7.30pm • Sibelius** Kuusisto, folk musicians, BBC Scottish SO/Dausgaard	4 August **Proms 21 & 22** **11.00am • Organ recital** Latry **7.30pm • Rachmaninov, O. Tarkiainen, Shostakovich** BBC Philharmonic/Storgårds
9 August **Proms 29 & 30** **3.00pm & 7.30pm • The Warner Brothers Story** John Wilson Orchestra/Wilson	10 August **Prom 31** **7.30pm • Brahms, R. Strauss, Bruckner** Davidsen, Philharmonia Orchestra/Salonen	11 August **Proms 32 & 33** **11.00am • Berlioz, R. Strauss** DiDonato, Brass of the NYOGB, NYO USA/Pappano **8.00pm • D. Glanert, Schubert/Glanert, Mahler** Gansch, BBC SO/Bychkov
16 August **Prom 40** **7.30pm • Sullivan, Mendelssohn, Prince Albert of Saxe-Coburg and Gotha** Fisher, Hough, Orchestra of the Age of Enlightenment/A. Fischer	17 August **P@HSL & Prom 41** **3.00pm •** BBC Singers/Jeannin **7.30pm • Rimsky-Korsakov, Rachmaninov, Lyadov, Glazunov** Ghindin, LPO/Jurowski	18 August **Prom 42** **7.30pm • Beethoven, C. Schumann, S. Gubaidulina, Shostakovich** Batsashvili, Ulster Orchestra/Payare
23 August **Prom 47** **7.30pm • Bach, Bruckner** Schönheit, Gewandhausorkester Leipzig/Nelsons	24 August **Prom 48** **7.30pm • Silvestri, Prokofiev, Rachmaninov** Cho, BBC SO/Măcelaru	25 August **Prom 49** **5.30pm • The Lost Words** Childress, Singh, Southbank Sinfonia/Cottis
30 August **Prom 55** **7.00pm • Handel: Jephtha** soloists, Scottish Chamber Orchestra/Egarr	31 August **Prom 56** **7.30pm • Ravel, Ireland, D. Tabakova, Debussy (orch. Wood), Granados (orch. Wood), Wagner (orch. Wood), Grainger (arr. Wood)** Anderson-Frank, McCawley, BBC Concert Orchestra/Tovey	1 September **Proms 57 & 58** **11.00am • Chen, Mozart, Rachmaninov** Lu, Shanghai SO/Yu **7.30pm • L. C. Smith, Janáček, Szymanowski, Tchaikovsky** Jarman, BBC Scottish SO/Volkov
6 September **Prom 64** **8.00pm • The Breaks** Heritage Orchestra/Buckley	7 September **Prom 65** **7.30pm • Mozart, R. Strauss, Beethoven** Kontora, Deutsche Kammerphilharmonie Bremen/Carydis	8 September **Proms 66 & 67** **11.00am • J. L. Adams: In the Name of the Earth** choruses **7.30pm • Mussorgsky, Andriessen, J. Weir, Sibelius** Fischer, BBC SO/Oramo
13 September **Prom 74** **7.30pm • Beethoven Night** Watts, NDR Radiophilharmonie Hannover/Manze	14 September **Prom 75** **5.00pm • Proms in the Park** **7.15pm • Last Night of the Proms** Barton, BBC SO/Oramo	

Key

☽ Late Night Prom

P@CH Proms at … Cadogan Hall

P@BAC Proms at … Battersea Arts Centre

P@HSL Proms at … Holy Sepulchre London

Friday 19 July

PROM 1
7.30pm–c9.35pm • Royal Albert Hall

PRICE BAND C
WEEKEND PROMMING PASS *see bbc.co.uk/proms*

KARINA CANELLAKIS

First Night of the Proms 2019

Zosha Di Castri Long Is the Journey – Short Is the Memory *c15'*
BBC commission: world premiere

Dvořák The Golden Spinning Wheel *28'*

INTERVAL

Janáček Glagolitic Mass (final version, 1928) *43'*
Henry Wood Novelties: UK premiere, 1930

Asmik Grigorian *soprano*
Jennifer Johnston *mezzo-soprano*
Ladislav Elgr *tenor*
Eric Owens *bass-baritone*
Peter Holder *organ*

BBC Singers
BBC Symphony Chorus
BBC Symphony Orchestra
Karina Canellakis *conductor*

The BBC's *Our Classical Century* series concludes with a new work that marks the 50th anniversary of *Apollo 11*'s mission to the Moon. Janáček's monumental *Glagolitic Mass*, steeped in Moravian rhythms, is heard alongside Dvořák's fairy-tale tone-poem. *See 'Beyond the Bust', pages 8–13; 'New Directions', pages 42–47; Spotlight on Asmik Grigorian, page 125.*

First half live on BBC Two, second half live on BBC Four

IN TUNE
5.00pm–7.00pm • Imperial College Union A live Proms edition of BBC Radio 3's *In Tune*, presented by Sean Rafferty. *Tickets available from BBC Studio Audiences: bbc.co.uk/showsandtours/shows. Broadcast live on BBC Radio 3*

Saturday 20 July

PROM 2
7.30pm–c10.00pm • Royal Albert Hall

PRICE BAND B
WEEKEND PROMMING PASS *see bbc.co.uk/proms*

JOSHUA BELL

Dvořák Violin Concerto in A minor *32'*

INTERVAL

Smetana Má vlast *75'*

Joshua Bell *violin*

Bamberg Symphony Orchestra
Jakub Hrůša *conductor*

Following his thrilling Proms debut in 2017, Czech conductor Jakub Hrůša returns with two popular masterpieces from his homeland. With its song-like slow movement and irrepressible, folk-infused finale, Dvořák's Violin Concerto is one of the best-loved in the repertoire. American virtuoso Joshua Bell joins the Bamberg Symphony Orchestra as soloist. Journey through the Czech countryside in the second half with Smetana's symphonic suite *Má vlast* ('My Country') – a colourful celebration of a nation's landscape, castles and warriors, with the sweeping melody of 'Vltava' at its heart. *See 'A Vehicle for Virtuosity?', pages 64–69.*

Broadcast on BBC Four on Sunday 21 July

PROMS PLUS TALK
5.45pm–6.25pm • Imperial College Union An introduction to Smetana's *Má vlast* with Czech-born former manager of the BBC World Service, Sir John Tusa.
Edited version broadcast on BBC Radio 3 during tonight's interval

Sunday 21 July

PROM 3
11.00am–c12.15pm • Royal Albert Hall

PRICE BAND H

CLANGERS

CBeebies Prom: A Musical Trip to the Moon

Join favourite CBeebies presenters for a family Prom designed to fire youthful imaginations and demonstrate the power of dreaming big. Young musical astronauts can follow in the footsteps of the *Apollo 11* mission, experiencing new adventures along the way – including a meeting with the Clangers. The concert also features a new BBC Ten Pieces Trailblazers commission by film music's living legend Hans Zimmer, which imagines how our Earth appears as seen from the Moon. The orchestra is Chineke! – Europe's first majority Black and Minority Ethnic orchestra. *See 'The Sound of Space', pages 14–19; 'Music, Inspiration … Education', pages 20–23; 'A Musical Trip to the Moon', pages 104–105.*

There will be no interval

British Sign Language-interpreted performance

This concert will be repeated on Monday 22 July at 11.00am; for concert listing, see Prom 5

Recorded for future broadcast on CBeebies

Every Prom broadcast live on BBC Radio 3

Sunday 21 July

PROM 4
7.30pm–c9.30pm • Royal Albert Hall

PRICE BAND B
WEEKEND PROMMING PASS *see bbc.co.uk/proms*

NEMANJA RADULOVIĆ

John Adams Short Ride in a Fast Machine *4'*

Barber Violin Concerto *23'*

INTERVAL

Holst The Planets *50'*

Nemanja Radulović *violin*

Trinity Boys Choir
Bournemouth Symphony Orchestra
Kirill Karabits *conductor*

A concert of 20th-century classics from Kirill Karabits and the Bournemouth Symphony Orchestra continues a weekend marking the 50th anniversary of the first manned mission to land on the Moon. Space travel has never been more richly imagined than in Holst's suite *The Planets*, but in order to get there you'll need to take a *Short Ride in a Fast Machine*, courtesy of John Adams's exhilarating, propulsive Minimalist masterpiece. The lyrical beauty of Samuel Barber's Violin Concerto, with its exquisite slow movement, offers a contrasting moment of contemplation. Dynamic Franco-Serbian violinist Nemanja Radulović makes his Proms debut as soloist.
See 'The Sound of Space', pages 14–19; 'A Vehicle for Virtuosity?', pages 64–69.

PROMS PLUS TALK
5.45pm–6.25pm • Imperial College Union Fifty years after we first walked on the Moon, Richard Wiseman reflects on the long footprint of those small steps.
Edited version broadcast on BBC Radio 3 during tonight's interval

Spotlight on ... Proms Debut Artists

Asmik Grigorian • Prom 1
soprano

'I always think I'm a drama queen,' laughs Asmik Grigorian, the Lithuanian soprano who will be singing at this year's First Night of the Proms. 'I love full, big orchestral pieces and of course my strength is music by composers such as Puccini, Tchaikovsky and Strauss.'

She's about to add Janáček to her list of musical loves: as well as the demanding soprano role in the *Glagolitic Mass* at the Royal Albert Hall, she'll be making her debut this year in the title-role of the opera *Jenůfa*. 'I've never done any Janáček before, so this is Janáček year,' Grigorian explains. 'It's extremely beautiful. I have a feeling my voice will like his music very much.'

'I love almost everything I do,' she adds, perhaps pinpointing an important ingredient of her success. Born in Vilnius, in a country packed with choirs, Grigorian says that since she was 5 'all my life has been in music'. But it was an appearance in 2004, in Mozart's *Don Giovanni*, that made her understand that 'I was in the place that I am supposed to be'. Since then, Grigorian's career has taken her to the great opera houses and festivals, with major roles in operas including Tchaikovsky's *The Queen of Spades*, Berg's *Wozzeck* and Strauss's *Salome*: 'Every single role I've done feels so true to me. Everything happens step by step by step.'

Angélique Kidjo • Prom 16
singer

'We have to acknowledge our common ancestry: we are all Africans!' Beninese Afropop superstar Angélique Kidjo is looking way back to the origins of humanity to shed light on her own musical forays between genres. 'I don't like labels and classifications. I've always mixed genres and styles. I began this year as the soloist in Philip Glass's new Symphony No. 12, then I played a few concerts in my Talking Heads *Remain in Light* project, I released an album dedicated to Celia Cruz and I'm curating four concerts in Carnegie Hall's new season. My whole life has been about creating bridges between musicians from all over the world.'

Kidjo makes her Proms debut in a Late Night Prom on 30 July, and marks the occasion with a tribute to Cuban diva Celia Cruz, who died in 2003. 'I grew up in Benin listening to salsa and Celia struck me because she was the only great female singer in a world of male Latin musicians. Since then, I discovered that much of her early music was inspired by Yoruba songs that had come to the Americas from Benin during the slave trade. I feel she's like a musical sister from another continent that 400 years of history has separated. I wanted to pay homage to her by reinventing those Yoruba-infused songs in the West-African Afrobeat and juju styles, from which they originally came.'

Monday 22 July

PROM 5
11.00am–c12.15pm • Royal Albert Hall

PRICE BAND H

MADDIE MOATE

CBeebies Prom: A Musical Trip to the Moon

Programme to include:

John Adams Short Ride in a Fast Machine *4'*

Britten The Young Person's Guide to the Orchestra – Fugue (finale) *4'*

Copland Fanfare for the Common Man *3'*

Puccini Madam Butterfly – Humming Chorus *4'*

Hans Zimmer Earth *c6'*
BBC commission: world premiere

YolanDa Brown *(from 'YolanDa's Band Jam')*
Justin Fletcher *(from 'Something Special', 'Justin's House' and 'Gigglebiz')*
Chris Jarvis *(from 'CBeebies Stargazing' and 'Show Me, Show Me')*
Maddie Moate *(from 'Do You Know?')*
Cat Sandion *(from 'CBeebies House' and 'Magic Door')*
Angie Newman *British Sign Language interpreter*

CBeebies Prom Choir
Chineke!
Kwamé Ryan *conductor*

There will be no interval

British Sign Language-interpreted performance

For concert description, see Prom 3

This concert, a repeat of Prom 3, will not be broadcast by BBC Radio 3

Recorded for future broadcast on CBeebies

Monday 22 July

PROMS AT … CADOGAN HALL 1
1.00pm–c2.00pm • Cadogan Hall

For ticket prices, see page 165

VOCES8

Hildegard of Bingen Spiritus sanctus vivificans *3'*

Pérotin Viderunt omnes – excerpt *3'*

Josquin des Prez Ave Maria … Virgo serena *5'*

Mouton Nesciens mater virgo virum *5'*

Victoria Regina coeli a 8 *4'*

Jonathan Dove Vadam et circuibo civitatem *9'*

Lassus Missa 'Bell'Amfitrit'altera' – Gloria *6'*

Palestrina Magnificat primi toni *5'*

Byrd Sing joyfully *3'*

Alexia Sloane Earthward *c4'*
BBC commission: world premiere

Gibbons O clap your hands *5'*

VOCES8

There will be no interval

This year's Monday-lunchtime Proms at … Cadogan Hall series takes listeners through over 800 years of musical history over the course of just eight concerts. Proms debut artists VOCES8 launch the series in a programme ranging from the supple chant melodies of Hildegard of Bingen to the sophisticated choral polyphony of Palestrina, Lassus and William Byrd. *See 'A History of Classical Music', pages 78–83.*

Monday 22 July

PROM 6
7.30pm–c9.35pm • Royal Albert Hall

PRICE BAND B

JAMES EHNES

Anna Thorvaldsdottir
Metacosmos *14'*
UK premiere

Britten Violin Concerto *32'*

INTERVAL

Stravinsky The Rite of Spring *35'*

James Ehnes *violin*

Orchestra of the Royal Academy of Music and The Juilliard School
Edward Gardner *conductor*

Earthy, pagan dances meet the Music of the Spheres in this concert of 20th- and 21st-century orchestral works. Stravinsky's infamous ballet score *The Rite of Spring* pulses with rhythmic energy and urgency, while Icelandic composer Anna Thorvaldsdottir's luminous and intricately textured *Metacosmos* travels deep into space. At the centre of the programme is Britten's elegiac Violin Concerto, written on the cusp of the Second World War. Violinist James Ehnes joins Edward Gardner and musicians from both London's Royal Academy of Music and New York's Juilliard School. *See 'The Sound of Space', pages 14–19; 'A Vehicle for Virtuosity?', pages 64–69.*

PROMS PLUS TALK
5.45pm–6.25pm • Imperial College Union In the first of a series of talks focusing on Proms founder-conductor Henry Wood, musicologist and broadcaster Hannah French explores his relationship with the Royal Academy of Music.
Edited version broadcast on BBC Radio 3 during tonight's interval

Tuesday 23 July

PROM 7
7.30pm–c10.00pm • Royal Albert Hall

PRICE BAND A

OMER MEIR WELLBER

Mozart Piano Concerto No. 15 in B flat major *25'*

Ben-Haim Symphony No. 1 *30'*

INTERVAL

Schoenberg Five Orchestral Pieces *16'*
Henry Wood Novelties: world premiere, 1912

R. Schumann Symphony No. 4 in D minor (revised version, 1851) *26'*

Yeol Eum Son *piano*

BBC Philharmonic
Omer Meir Wellber *conductor*

Omer Meir Wellber makes his Proms debut as the BBC Philharmonic's newly appointed Chief Conductor Designate. South Korean pianist Yeol Eum Son joins them as soloist in Mozart's Piano Concerto No. 15 in B flat major – with its intricate wind writing and lively hunting-horn finale. Schumann's mould-breaking Fourth Symphony, with its opening journey from darkness to blazing light, is paired with Schoenberg's revolutionary *Five Orchestral Pieces* and Paul Ben-Haim's 1940 Symphony No. 1 – an emotive musical statement at a time of international conflict.
See 'Beyond the Bust', pages 8–13; Spotlights on Yeol Eum Son, page 134, and Omer Meir Wellber, page 140.

Broadcast on BBC Four on Friday 26 July

PROMS PLUS TALK
5.45pm–6.25pm • Imperial College Union BBC Radio 3 New Generation Thinker Daisy Fancourt asks if music can heal the mind and body.
Edited version broadcast on BBC Radio 3 during tonight's interval

Spotlight on ... BBC Radio 3 New Generation Artists

Catriona Morison • Prom 39
BBC Radio 3 New Generation Artist, 2017–19

Edinburgh-born mezzo-soprano Catriona Morison won BBC Cardiff Singer of the World, arguably the world's most prestigious vocal contest, two years ago. Not surprisingly, her life has changed immeasurably as a result. 'At the time it was really quite overwhelming – in a positive way, of course,' she remembers. 'But I didn't want to jump into anything – I needed some time to work things out.'

Her position as a BBC Radio 3 New Generation Artist has offered her similar opportunities: 'It's given me lots of contact with the BBC orchestras and the opportunity to record in the Maida Vale Studios.'

It's with the BBC National Orchestra of Wales that Morison makes her BBC Proms debut, with two contrasting works that place her voice firmly in the spotlight. Elgar's *Sea Pictures* is, Morison says, 'one of the most wonderful pieces written for mezzo – they have such beautiful, lyrical lines to sing'. Continuing the concert's image-related theme, Morison's second outing is in composer Errollyn Wallen's Howard Hodgkin-inspired *This Frame Is Part of the Painting*, a new work written specifically for her. 'I've been speaking to Errollyn quite a bit about it – she really wants to hear what's going to work best for me and I've benefited from hearing about her inspirations. It's amazing to be able to work so closely with a composer like that.'

Fatma Said • Prom 26
BBC Radio 3 New Generation Artist, 2016–18

'My Egyptian identity is not only important to me – it *is* me!' Soprano Fatma Said is describing how her background feeds into her performances. 'Egypt is the Middle East, it's Africa, it's part of the Arab countries and it's part of the Mediterranean – all these different impulses affect my interpretations and musical understanding.'

This breadth of vision is one of the things that marks Said out as a distinctive figure among her generation of singers. As a BBC New Generation Artist from 2016 to 2018, she broadened her outlook even further, she says: 'It was one of the most beautiful experiences, and gave me a great deal of studio recording practice – there's so much to learn about oneself in that area. It also gave me the opportunity to sing in many venues across the UK, not only in London.'

Mozart's *Requiem* on 7 August offers Said more than one first. 'I've never actually attended a BBC Proms concert, although I used to watch the concert broadcasts and dream of being there one day. I've never performed the *Requiem* before, either. Mozart's music is as sacred as the text, and he treats the voice like a holy instrument. His way of composing for soprano teaches us about the voice and how to use it. The more I indulge in Mozart's music, the more I learn about my own vocal technique.'

Wednesday 24 July

PROM 8
7.30pm–*c*9.25pm • Royal Albert Hall

PRICE BAND A

ISABELLE FAUST

Debussy Prélude à l'après-midi d'un faune *10'*
Henry Wood Novelties: UK premiere, 1904

Peter Eötvös Alhambra (violin concerto) *20'*
BBC co-commission with Festival Internacional de Música y Danza de Granada, Orchestre de Paris and Stiftung Berliner Philharmoniker: UK premiere

INTERVAL

Bartók Dance Suite *17'*
Henry Wood Novelties: UK premiere, 1925

Stravinsky The Firebird – suite (1919) *23'*
Henry Wood Novelties: UK premiere, 1913

Isabelle Faust *violin*

BBC Symphony Orchestra
Peter Eötvös *conductor*

Dance – whether in the exotic pulse of Bartók's *Dance Suite*, the insistent Russian folk rhythms of Stravinsky's *The Firebird* or the languorous ballet of Debussy's faun – runs right through tonight's Prom. Peter Eötvös conducts his new violin concerto *Alhambra* – performed here by the work's original soloist, award-winning German violinist Isabelle Faust. *See 'Beyond the Bust', pages 8–13; 'New Directions', pages 42–47; 'A Vehicle for Virtuosity?', pages 64–69.*

PROMS PLUS TALK
5.45pm–6.25pm • Imperial College Union A discussion about Bartók with musicologist and broadcaster Erik Levi.
Edited version broadcast on BBC Radio 3 during tonight's interval

Thursday 25 July

PROM 9
7.00pm–*c*9.05pm • Royal Albert Hall

PRICE BAND A

HÅKAN HARDENBERGER

R. Strauss Till Eulenspiegels lustige Streiche *15'*

Tobias Broström Nigredo – Dark Night of the Soul (concerto for two trumpets and orchestra) *28'*
BBC co-commission with Malmö Symphony Orchestra: UK premiere

INTERVAL

Brahms Symphony No. 1 in C minor *45'*

Jeroen Berwaerts *trumpet*
Håkan Hardenberger *trumpet*

BBC National Orchestra of Wales
Markus Stenz *conductor*

The mischievous escapades of the irrepressible Till Eulenspiegel – Germany's beloved folk-hero – introduce a concert that celebrates the dramatic power of the orchestra. Markus Stenz conducts the BBC NOW in its first concert of the season, pairing Strauss's lively tone-poem with Brahms's turbulent Symphony No. 1 – the work that announced him as the 'heir to Beethoven'. Trumpeters Håkan Hardenberger and Jeroen Berwaerts are rival soloists in a rhythmically charged new double concerto by Swedish composer Tobias Broström. *See 'New Directions', pages 42–47; Spotlight on Jeroen Berwaerts, page 132.*

PROMS PLUS TALK
5.15pm–5.55pm • Imperial College Union An introduction to the music in tonight's Prom with researcher, writer and presenter Katy Hamilton.
Edited version broadcast on BBC Radio 3 during tonight's interval

Thursday 25 July

PROM 10 • LATE NIGHT
10.15pm–*c*11.30pm • Royal Albert Hall

PRICE BAND F

PUBLIC SERVICE BROADCASTING

The Race for Space

Public Service Broadcasting
The Multi-Story Orchestra
Christopher Stark *conductor*

There will be no interval

Cult London band Public Service Broadcasting makes its Proms debut in a special Late Night Prom to mark the 50th anniversary of the first manned mission to the Moon. The electronics/instrumental outfit is joined by The Multi-Story Orchestra to perform an orchestral arrangement of their 2015 studio album *The Race for Space*. Blending both acoustic and electronic performance and archive audio samples, the album explores the highs and lows of the US–Soviet space race of the 1960s, and is heard here for the first time in this specially commissioned new version. *See 'The Sound of Space', pages 14–19.*

Broadcast on BBC Four on Friday 26 July

Friday 26 July

PROM 11
7.30pm–c9.45pm • Royal Albert Hall

PRICE BAND B
WEEKEND PROMMING PASS *see bbc.co.uk/proms*

STEPHEN BELL

1969: The Sound of a Summer

Will Gregory Moog Ensemble

BBC Concert Orchestra
Stephen Bell *conductor*

There will be one interval

Woodstock, the *Apollo 11* mission to the Moon, the ongoing Vietnam War, The Beatles' final album (*Abbey Road*) – 1969 was a pivotal year. This Prom explores the film and popular music of 1969 to recreate the soundtrack of a special summer. The BBC Concert Orchestra under Stephen Bell presents a typically wide-angled view, taking in music inspired by the era-defining Woodstock festival, excerpts from the films *Battle of Britain*, *The Italian Job*, *Butch Cassidy and the Sundance Kid* and *Midnight Cowboy*, and 'Here Comes the Sun' from The Beatles' final album *Abbey Road*. As the USA's victory in the space race inspired new music to match the emerging digital era, the Moog synthesizer broke into the mainstream with the album *Switched-on Bach*. A concert evoking the end of the Swinging Sixties, with a cross-generational appeal that offers both a sunburst of nostalgia and iconic revivals.

PROMS PLUS TALK
5.45pm–6.25pm • Imperial College Union Poets Jacob Polley and Rachael Allen read from their work and respond to themes in the music of tonight's concert.
Edited version broadcast on BBC Radio 3 during tonight's interval

Saturday 27 July

PROMS AT … BATTERSEA ARTS CENTRE
3.00pm–c4.30pm *For ticket prices, see bbc.co.uk/proms*

CREWDSON & CEVANNE

Artists to include:

Oliver Coates
Crewdson & Cevanne
Jennifer Walshe

The BBC Proms takes over the newly refurbished Battersea Arts Centre for a showcase of provocative, witty and boundary-crossing composer-performers who have been driving new music in previously unimagined directions. In this Promenade-only (standing) event, expect to discover artists experimenting with found sounds, new instruments, electronics and the outer limits of the human voice.

There will be no interval

Every Prom broadcast live on BBC Radio 3

Saturday 27 July

PROM 12
7.30pm–c9.55pm • Royal Albert Hall

PRICE BAND B
WEEKEND PROMMING PASS *see bbc.co.uk/proms*

NICOLA BENEDETTI

Lera Auerbach Icarus *12'*
London premiere

Tchaikovsky Violin Concerto in D major *35'*

INTERVAL

Prokofiev Romeo and Juliet – suite *50'*

Nicola Benedetti *violin*

National Youth Orchestra of Great Britain
Mark Wigglesworth *conductor*

Explosive energy and enthusiasm are the hallmarks of every performance by the National Youth Orchestra of Great Britain, made up of the UK's most talented musicians aged from 13 to 18. The ensemble's annual visit to the Proms is always a festival highlight. This year Mark Wigglesworth conducts NYOGB in a suite from Prokofiev's passionate ballet *Romeo and Juliet* and they are joined by violinist Nicola Benedetti for Tchaikovsky's warmly lyrical Violin Concerto. The concert opens with Lera Auerbach's bracing symphonic poem *Icarus*, inspired by the myth of the heroic but ill-fated son of Daedalus who flew too close to the sun. *See 'A Vehicle for Virtuosity?', pages 64–69.*

Broadcast on BBC Four on Sunday 28 July

PROMS FAMILY WORKSHOP
5.45pm–6.30pm • Imperial College Union Join professional musicians for a family-friendly introduction to tonight's Prom. Bring an instrument or just sit back and take it all in! *Suitable for ages 7-plus.* *See page 23 for details.*

28 | 31 JULY

Sunday 28 July

PROM 13

7.30pm–c9.25pm • Royal Albert Hall

PRICE BAND A

WEEKEND PROMMING PASS *see bbc.co.uk/proms*

SAKARI ORAMO

Messiaen Des canyons aux étoiles ... *105'*

Martin Owen *horn*
David Hockings, Alex Neal *percussion*
Nicolas Hodges *piano*

BBC Symphony Orchestra
Sakari Oramo *conductor*

There will be no interval

The 'wild and colourful beauty' of Utah and Arizona was the inspiration for one of the 20th century's most singular and extraordinary works, a musical act of 'praise and contemplation' painted in the brightest and most vivid of sounds. Olivier Messiaen's mighty *Des canyons aux étoiles* ... ('From the Canyons to the Stars ...') is a sonic meditation in which birdsong mingles with desert winds, and the rustling of sand. Sakari Oramo conducts the BBC SO, with pianist Nicolas Hodges and horn player Martin Owen taking the demanding solo parts. *See 'The Sound of Space', pages 14–19.*

THE LISTENING SERVICE

5.55pm–6.25pm • Imperial College Union In a live edition of *The Listening Service*, Tom Service responds to Messiaen's 'Interstellar Call' – join us on the launch pad! *Tickets available from BBC Studio Audiences: bbc.co.uk/showsandtours/shows. Broadcast on BBC Radio 3 tonight at 7.00pm*

Monday 29 July

PROMS AT ... CADOGAN HALL 2

1.00pm–c2.00pm • Cadogan Hall

For ticket prices, see page 165

LEONARDO GARCÍA ALARCÓN

Strozzi L'amante segreto *8'*

Bembo Ercole amante – 'Mingannasti in verità' *3'*

Strozzi Che si può fare *10'*

Bembo Ercole amante – 'Volgete altrove il guardo' *4'*

Strozzi Sino alla morte *12'*

Cavalli Ercole amante – 'E vuol dunque Ciprigna' *3'*

Strozzi Lagrime mie *9'*

Mariana Flores *soprano*

Cappella Mediterranea
Leonardo García Alarcón *harpsichord/organ/director*

There will be no interval

Few composers paint human emotion as vividly or with greater insight, wit and poignancy than Barbara Strozzi – the pioneering Venetian composer, born 400 years ago, whose songs and madrigals stand alongside Monteverdi's as some of the greatest of the age. Argentine soprano Mariana Flores and period-instrument ensemble Cappella Mediterranea celebrate Strozzi's anniversary with a selection of love songs by the composer and her contemporaries, including the arresting 'Lagrime mie' and the touching 'Che si può fare'. *See 'A History of Classical Music', pages 78–83; 'Lost Legacies', pages 96–99; Spotlight on Leonardo García Alarcón, page 155.*

Monday 29 July

PROM 14

7.30pm–c9.55pm • Royal Albert Hall

PRICE BAND B

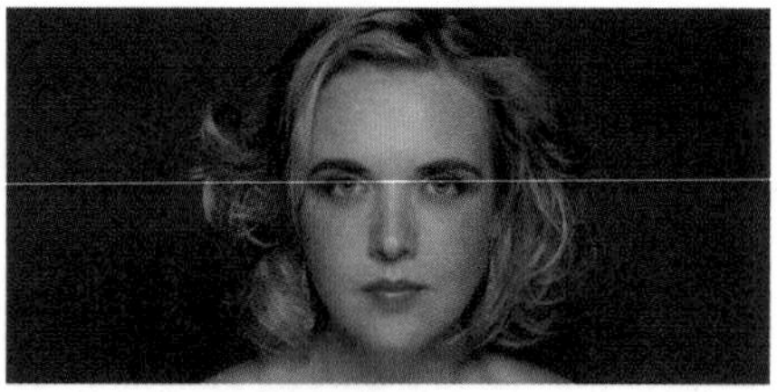

SARAH-JANE BRANDON

Haydn The Creation *105'*
(sung in German)

Sarah-Jane Brandon *soprano*
Benjamin Hulett *tenor*
Christoph Pohl *baritone*

BBC Proms Youth Choir
BBC Philharmonic
Omer Meir Wellber *conductor*

There will be one interval

Haydn's colourful oratorio returns to the Proms for the first time in a decade. The BBC Philharmonic is joined by the BBC Proms Youth Choir to perform the composer's late masterpiece. From its opening Representation of Chaos, through the creation of stars, seas and storms, a magnificent musical sunrise and of course every animal from whales to eagles and even a worm, *The Creation* is one of the great musical dramas, teeming with life and detail. *See 'The Sound of Space', pages 14–19; Spotlight on Omer Meir Wellber, page 140, and Benjamin Hulett, page 150.*

PROMS PLUS TALK

5.45pm–6.25pm • Imperial College Union An introduction to *The Creation* with Revd Lucy Winkett.
Edited version broadcast on BBC Radio 3 during tonight's interval

Tuesday 30 July

PROM 15
7.00pm–c9.05pm • Royal Albert Hall

PRICE BAND C

MARISS JANSONS

Beethoven Symphony No. 2 in D major *32'*

INTERVAL

Shostakovich Symphony No. 10 in E minor *55'*

Bavarian Radio Symphony Orchestra
Mariss Jansons *conductor*

One of Europe's greatest orchestras, the Bavarian Radio Symphony Orchestra, returns to the Proms under Chief Conductor Mariss Jansons. In the first of two concerts *(see also Prom 17)* they pair two contrasting symphonies in a programme that moves from sunshine to bitterness. 'This symphony is smiling throughout,' wrote Berlioz of Beethoven's Second Symphony – a work in which seemingly sunny moods conceal personal tragedy and loss. Loss and anger move to the foreground in Shostakovich's 10th Symphony, a work in which brutality and anguish speak emotively of life in Stalin's Russia.

PROMS PLUS TALK
5.15pm–5.55pm • Imperial College Union Musicologist Marina Frolova-Walker discusses Shostakovich and his Symphony No. 10.
Edited version broadcast on BBC Radio 3 during tonight's interval

Tuesday 30 July

PROM 16 • LATE NIGHT
10.15pm–c11.30pm • Royal Albert Hall

PRICE BAND E

ANGÉLIQUE KIDJO

Angélique Kidjo

Described as 'the undisputed queen of African music', three-time Grammy Award-winner Angélique Kidjo makes her Proms debut with her nine-piece band in a late-night tribute to the celebrated salsa songstress Celia Cruz. Kidjo grew up in Benin, West Africa, listening to salsa and found Celia Cruz a huge inspiration. She later discovered that much of Cruz's music was inspired by Yoruba traditional songs that migrated from Benin to the Americas with the slave workers. Kidjo here reinvents these songs in the Afrobeat and juju styles of West Africa, reflecting their true origins. *See Spotlight on Angélique Kidjo, page 125.*

There will be no interval

Broadcast on BBC Four on Friday 2 August

Every Prom broadcast live on BBC Radio 3

Wednesday 31 July

PROM 17
7.30pm–c9.45pm • Royal Albert Hall

PRICE BAND D

LISA BATIASHVILI

Sibelius Symphony No. 1 in E minor *38'*
Henry Wood Novelties: UK premiere, 1903

INTERVAL

Prokofiev Violin Concerto No. 2 in G minor *26'*
Henry Wood Novelties: UK premiere, 1936

R. Strauss Der Rosenkavalier – suite *24'*

Lisa Batiashvili *violin*

Bavarian Radio Symphony Orchestra
Mariss Jansons *conductor*

The second concert from Mariss Jansons and the Bavarian Radio Symphony Orchestra pays tribute to the 150th anniversary of the birth of Proms founder-conductor Henry Wood. A passionate champion of new music, Wood gave the UK premieres of many major works featured this season, including both Sibelius's turbulent Symphony No. 1 and Prokofiev's Second Violin Concerto – played here by Georgian soloist Lisa Batiashvili – whose initial simplicity and directness give way to spiky virtuosity in the finale. The concert closes in Vienna, with the waltz-filled and lushly orchestrated suite from Richard Strauss's popular opera *Der Rosenkavalier. See 'Beyond the Bust', pages 8–13; 'A Vehicle for Virtuosity?', pages 64–69.*

Broadcast on BBC Four on Friday 30 August

PROMS PLUS TALK
5.45pm–6.25pm • Imperial College Union Journalist and string-instrument expert Ariane Todes explores Prokofiev's Violin Concerto No. 2 and the Russian school of violin-playing.
Edited version broadcast on BBC Radio 3 during tonight's interval

Spotlight on … Premiere Soloists

Jeroen Berwaerts • Prom 9

Tobias Broström: Nigredo – Dark Night of the Soul

'A perfect month for me would be: premiering a new trumpet concerto; a few concerts with some Jacques Brel songs; and a discussion with my students about John Cage's *Ten Rules for Students, Teachers and Life*.' Belgian trumpeter Jeroen Berwaerts's wide-ranging tastes encompass jazz, period performance, contemporary music, core classical repertoire and plenty more. 'I can't do just one thing,' he explains. 'I need that variety to keep things interesting.'

It's with a brand-new piece that he makes his BBC Proms debut as a soloist or, more correctly, co-soloist in Swedish composer Tobias Broström's double trumpet concerto *Nigredo – Dark Night of the Soul*, alongside fellow trumpeter Håkan Hardenberger. 'Tobias knows the trumpet very well,' Berwaerts continues. 'His writing is very melodic, full of tension and colours.' How does Berwaerts feel about sharing the stage with Hardenberger? 'He was my idol. When I was younger, I bought Håkan's CDs and practised until I could play along with them. We met three years ago in Sweden, where I played a recital including Ligeti's *Mysteries of the Macabre*, which was written for Håkan. You can imagine how that felt. Now, working with him is about sharing and learning on a professional basis – but, at the same time, it's a dream come true.'

Andreas Haefliger • Prom 43

Dieter Ammann: Piano Concerto

Pianists aren't short of great concertos to play, so a new one has to be special. When Andreas Haefliger first heard Dieter Ammann's music seven years ago, he was immediately fascinated. 'I found that in all the complexity of his music there were unexpected touches of colour and beauty,' recalls Haefliger. 'I thought it would be brilliant if he could write a concerto.' Now the Swiss composer – a modernist at heart with a background in jazz – has done just that. Ammann's Piano Concerto will be premiered at this year's Proms and then Haefliger will take it on tour around the world.

Convincing Ammann took some persistence. He works on one piece at a time, and gave '50 nos' before finally saying yes. Haefliger then played some of his favourite repertoire to the composer, including Mussorgsky, Brahms and Beethoven. 'I showed him what I like about the piano, the myriad sounds it can make,' explains Haefliger. 'He's composed a really modern concerto with the piano as a strong protagonist. I love that.'

When the score arrived, Haefliger was faced with the small matter of learning this incredibly difficult piece. 'Five pages a month!' says Haefliger. He performs it with the BBC Symphony Orchestra: 'They're scarily good! One of the best at this repertoire. It'll be an enormous pleasure.'

Thursday 1 August

PROM 18

7.30pm–c9.50pm • Royal Albert Hall

PRICE BAND A

CLAUDIA MAHNKE

Britten Piano Concerto (revised version, 1945) *35'*

Henry Wood Novelties: world premiere, 1938

INTERVAL

Mahler Das Lied von der Erde *64'*

Henry Wood Novelties: UK premiere, 1914

Leif Ove Andsnes *piano*
Claudia Mahnke *mezzo-soprano*
Stuart Skelton *tenor*

BBC Symphony Orchestra
Edward Gardner *conductor*

Claudia Mahnke and Stuart Skelton are the soloists in Mahler's *Das Lied von der Erde*. This sweeping orchestral song-cycle is a powerful, personal statement of loss, orchestrated with infinite variety and skill. It's paired with another mould-breaking work – Britten's Piano Concerto. Premiered at the Proms in 1938 with the 24-year-old composer as soloist, the work is as much a celebration of orchestral texture as pianistic bravura, bursting with youthful energy and invention. Norwegian pianist and Proms regular Leif Ove Andsnes is the soloist.
See 'Beyond the Bust', pages 8–13; Spotlight on Leif Ove Andsnes, page 157.

Broadcast on BBC Four on Friday 2 August

PROMS PLUS TALK

5.45pm–6.25pm • Imperial College Union Hannah French and former Proms Controller Sir Nicholas Kenyon discuss Henry Wood's relationship with 20th-century music in the second of three events celebrating the 150th anniversary of Wood's birth.

Edited version broadcast on BBC Radio 3 during tonight's interval

Friday 2 August

PROM 19
7.30pm–c9.45pm • Royal Albert Hall

PRICE BAND (A)
WEEKEND PROMMING PASS *see bbc.co.uk/proms*

ALEXANDER MELNIKOV

R. Strauss Also sprach Zarathustra *34'*

INTERVAL

R. Schumann Piano Concerto in A minor *32'*

Sir James MacMillan The Confession of Isobel Gowdie *26'*

Alexander Melnikov *piano*

BBC Scottish Symphony Orchestra
Thomas Dausgaard *conductor*

'I always wanted a great bravura piece by him,' wrote Clara Schumann of her husband. Her hope was answered in Robert Schumann's Piano Concerto – a work whose broad, symphonic scope explores and tests the relationship between soloist and orchestra. Russian pianist Alexander Melnikov joins the BBC Scottish SO and its Chief Conductor Thomas Dausgaard for a programme that also includes the sweeping drama of Strauss's tone-poem *Also sprach Zarathustra*, with its memorable opening sunrise (heard on the soundtrack for Stanley Kubrick's *2001: A Space Odyssey*) and the violence and compassion of Sir James MacMillan's early masterpiece *The Confession of Isobel Gowdie*, inspired by the execution of a 17th-century 'witch' and premiered at the Proms in 1990. *See 'The Sound of Space', pages 14–19.*

PROMS PLUS TALK
5.45pm–6.25pm • Imperial College Union Composer Sir James MacMillan, 60 this year, discusses *The Confession of Isobel Gowdie* and talks about his inspiration and ideas.
Edited version broadcast on BBC Radio 3 during tonight's interval

Saturday 3 August

PROM 20
7.30pm–c9.50pm • Royal Albert Hall

PRICE BAND (A)
WEEKEND PROMMING PASS *see bbc.co.uk/proms*

Programme to include:

Sibelius Violin Concerto in D minor *34'*
Henry Wood Novelties: UK premiere, 1907

INTERVAL

Sibelius Symphony No. 5 in E flat major (original version, 1915) *36'*

Pekka Kuusisto *violin*
Taito Hoffrén *singer*
Ilona Korhonen *singer*
Minna-Liisa Tammela *singer*
Vilma Timonen *kantele*
Timo Alakotila *harmonium*

BBC Scottish Symphony Orchestra
Thomas Dausgaard *conductor*

Violinist Pekka Kuusisto memorably set the entire Proms audience singing a Finnish folk song in 2016. Now he returns for a Prom joined by fellow Finnish folk musicians, which sprinkles rustic Finnish folk music among two pinnacles of Finnish orchestral sophistication: Sibelius's great Romantic Violin Concerto (with Kuusisto as soloist) and his Fifth Symphony – a work suffused with light and autumnal warmth. Thomas Dausgaard conducts the symphony's original, four-movement version, allowing a glimpse into the creative process of a work that Sibelius revised over a period of four years. *See 'Beyond the Bust', pages 8–13; 'A Vehicle for Virtuosity?', pages 64–69.*

PROMS PLUS TALK
5.45pm–6.25pm • Imperial College Union (Concert Hall)
An introduction to the music of tonight's Prom with BBC Radio 3 New Generation Thinker Leah Broad.
Edited version broadcast on BBC Radio 3 during tonight's interval

PROMS FAMILY WORKSHOP
5.45pm–6.30pm • Imperial College Union (Dining Hall)
Join professional musicians for a family-friendly introduction to tonight's Prom. Bring an instrument or just sit back and take it all in! *Suitable for ages 7-plus. See page 23 for details.*

Sunday 4 August

PROM 21
11.00am–c12.15pm • Royal Albert Hall

PRICE BAND (A)
WEEKEND PROMMING PASS *see bbc.co.uk/proms*

Khachaturian, transcr. Kiviniemi Gayane – Sabre Dance *3'*

Falla, transcr. Latry El amor brujo – Ritual Fire Dance *5'*

Beethoven Adagio in F major (for mechanical clock) *5'*

J. S. Bach Toccata and Fugue in D minor, BWV 565 *10'*

Gigout Air célèbre de la Pentecôte *3'*

Liszt, arr. Guillou Prelude and Fugue on BACH *14'*

Widor Bach's Memento – No. 4: Marche du veilleur de nuit *4'*

Saint-Saëns, arr. Lemare Danse macabre *8'*

Improvisation *c10'*

Olivier Latry *organ*

There will be no interval

Celebrated French organist Olivier Latry returns to the Proms for the first time in over a decade for a programme centred around transcriptions and arrangements for the 'King of Instruments'. The organist of Paris's Notre-Dame Cathedral roams through 250 years of music in a wide-ranging recital programme that stretches from Bach to Falla. There's a rhythmic charge to the recital, which includes virtuosic transcriptions of Khachaturian's frenzied *Sabre Dance*, Falla's hypnotic *Ritual Fire Dance* and Saint-Saëns's devilish *Danse macabre*, as well as Bach's dramatic Toccata and Fugue in D minor, and Bach arrangements by French organist-composers Widor and Gigout.

Every Prom broadcast live on BBC Radio 3

Spotlight on … Pianists

Eric Lu • Prom 57

Yeol Eum Son • Prom 7

'Winning the Leeds International Piano Competition was a dream come true for me.' US pianist Eric Lu, still just 21, is looking back with understandable pride to his 2018 triumph. 'It was an honour to have played there – many of the pianists I most admire are among the competition's previous winners. My life has changed tremendously since then, and the win has helped open the doors to many amazing stages – such as London's Wigmore Hall and Amsterdam's Royal Concertgebouw, and of course the BBC Proms.'

Lu makes his Proms debut with a work that's particularly close to his heart. 'I only started working formally on Mozart's Piano Concerto No. 23 a few years back, but it's a piece I grew up with, listening to countless recordings and concerts. Mozart is one of the composers I feel most close to. His keyboard writing has such transparency, and an operatic sense of lyricism.'

What does he enjoy about this specific concerto? 'The whole piece is centred around its famous second movement, which is filled with loneliness and an intimate pathos. Whenever Mozart writes in a minor key, we're shown a completely different side to him. In a way, it reminds me of the last piece he worked on, the *Requiem*. It's a jewel among Mozart's concertos.'

Born in South Korean but now resident in Hanover, Yeol Eum Son first came to wide prominence following awards at the 2011 Tchaikovsky Competition and the 2009 Van Cliburn Competition, two of the world's most prestigious keyboard contests. 'They opened many doors for me,' she explains. 'They still do, actually. I still get invitations from some organisations who remember me fondly from those competitions.'

Those successes, however, came after keyboard studies from a remarkably early age. 'I don't remember the moment when I first decided to become a musician – there was probably never such a moment,' she says. 'But I remember very clearly being three and a half when I first started piano. I was an extremely shy kid, but I felt so comfortable on stage. By the age of 18, she appeared with the New York Philharmonic and recorded her first CD.

She makes her BBC Proms debut with a concerto by a musician especially close to her heart. 'Mozart has been my favourite composer for a long time – both as a player and as a listener. His music is so contradictory – fresh yet elegant, complex yet simple.' She performs Mozart's Piano Concerto No. 15: 'I think I first heard it in the movie *Amadeus*. I've adored it ever since, but I first played it only in 2016.'

Sunday 4 August

PROM 22
7.30pm–c9.35pm • Royal Albert Hall

PRICE BAND (A)
WEEKEND PROMMING PASS *see bbc.co.uk/proms*

JOHN STORGÅRDS

Rachmaninov The Isle of the Dead *21'*
Henry Wood Novelties: UK premiere, 1915

Outi Tarkiainen Midnight Sun Variations *c10'*
BBC commission: world premiere

INTERVAL

Shostakovich Symphony No. 11 in G minor, 'The Year 1905' *58'*

BBC Philharmonic
John Storgårds *conductor*

Death and darkness encounter light and new life in this Prom given by the BBC Philharmonic and its Chief Guest Conductor John Storgårds. Two Russian classics brood on death and loss; Rachmaninov's atmospheric *The Isle of the Dead* conjures an ominous scene – a ghostly ferryman transporting the souls of the dead to rest – while Shostakovich's bitterly passionate Symphony No. 11 takes inspiration from the 'Bloody Sunday' massacre of 1905. But there's light and hope in Outi Tarkiainen's *Midnight Sun Variations* – a celebration of rebirth in the perpetual day of an Arctic summer. *See 'Beyond the Bust', pages 8–13; 'New Directions', pages 42–47.*

Broadcast on BBC Four tonight

PROMS PLUS TALK
5.45pm–6.25pm • Imperial College Union Fairy-tales expert Nicole Schmidt and BBC Radio 3 New Generation Thinker Leah Broad explore Nordic legends.
Edited version broadcast on BBC Radio 3 during tonight's interval

Monday 5 August

PROMS AT … CADOGAN HALL 3
1.00pm–c2.00pm • Cadogan Hall

For ticket prices, see page 165

KRISTIAN BEZUIDENHOUT

Purcell
The Virtuous Wife – overture *3'*
The Fairy Queen – Hornpipe *2'*
The Virtuous Wife – Second Music; First Act Tune *4'*
The Indian Queen – Rondeau *2'*
Chacony *4'*

Marchand Pièces de clavecin, Book 1 – Allemande *3'*

Jacquet de la Guerre
Violin Sonata in D minor *10'*

Telemann Sonata in A minor, TWV 43:a 5 *10'*

Handel Trio Sonata in G major *13'*

Kristian Bezuidenhout *harpsichord*
The English Concert

There will be no interval

Celebrated keyboard player Kristian Bezuidenhout and period-instrument ensemble The English Concert present a Baroque journey around Europe. England's lively restoration theatre scene is represented by Purcell dances, while harpsichord music by Élisabeth Jacquet de la Guerre and Louis Marchand conjures up the splendour of the French court of Louis XIV. Chamber music by Telemann and Handel completes the programme. *See 'A History of Classical Music', pages 78–83.*

Monday 5 August

PROM 23
7.30pm–c9.40pm • Royal Albert Hall

PRICE BAND (A)

ALEXANDER GAVRYLYUK

Arnold Peterloo Overture *10'*

Rachmaninov Rhapsody on a Theme of Paganini *23'*

INTERVAL

Tchaikovsky Swan Lake – excerpts *50'*
Henry Wood Novelties: UK premiere (suite), 1901

Alexander Gavrylyuk *piano*

BBC Philharmonic
Ben Gernon *conductor*

The BBC Philharmonic and Principal Guest Conductor Ben Gernon open with Malcolm Arnold's dramatic *Peterloo Overture* in the 200th anniversary of the Peterloo Massacre at St Peter's Fields in the orchestra's hometown of Manchester. Excerpts from *Swan Lake*, the first of Tchaikovsky's great ballet scores, include the colourful sequence of national dances and the heartbreaking final scene in which Odette and her beloved Siegfried are united for ever in death, breaking the spell of the sorcerer Rothbart. Russian virtuoso Alexander Gavrylyuk returns, following his Proms debut in 2017, as soloist in Rachmaninov's *Rhapsody on a Theme of Paganini*, with its famous lyrical 18th Variation. *See 'Beyond the Bust', pages 8–13.*

This concert (except Arnold) will be repeated on Tuesday 6 August as our Relaxed Prom, see Prom 24

PROMS PLUS TALK
5.45pm–6.25pm • Imperial College Union A look beneath the surface of swans – in nature and culture – with 'Human Swan' Sacha Dench and arts journalist Sarah Crompton. *Edited version broadcast on BBC Radio 3 during tonight's interval*

Tuesday 6 August

PROM 24
11.30am–c12.45pm • Royal Albert Hall

For ticket prices, see page 164

BEN GERNON

Relaxed Prom

Rachmaninov Rhapsody on a Theme of Paganini *23'*

Tchaikovsky Swan Lake – excerpts *35'*

Alexander Gavrylyuk *piano*

BBC Philharmonic
Ben Gernon *conductor*

There will be no interval

The BBC Philharmonic performs Russian classics by Rachmaninov and Tchaikovsky in a more relaxed environment – suitable for children and adults with autism, sensory and communication impairments and learning disabilities, as well as individuals who are Deaf, hard-of-hearing, blind and partially sighted. There is a relaxed attitude to movement and noise in the auditorium, plus 'chill-out' spaces outside the auditorium. You can move about, dance, sing or just listen. Produced in partnership with Royal Albert Hall Education & Outreach and Proms Learning, the Relaxed Prom features audio description and British Sign Language interpretation.

Audio-described and British Sign Language-interpreted performance

This concert, which repeats works from Prom 23, will not be broadcast by BBC Radio 3

Marco Borggreve (Bezuidenhout, Gavrylyuk); Simon Annand (Gernon)

Tuesday 6 August

PROM 25
7.30pm–c9.50pm • Royal Albert Hall

PRICE BAND B

SOL GABETTA

Sibelius Karelia – suite *15'*
Henry Wood Novelties: UK premiere, 1906

Weinberg Cello Concerto *31'*
London premiere

INTERVAL

Tchaikovsky Symphony No. 6 in B minor, 'Pathétique' *51'*

Sol Gabetta *cello*

BBC Symphony Orchestra
Dalia Stasevska *conductor*

Dalia Stasevska makes her Proms debut as the BBC Symphony Orchestra's newly appointed Principal Guest Conductor. Cellist Sol Gabetta joins them to celebrate the centenary of one of the 20th century's great unsung heroes, Mieczysław Weinberg, whose Cello Concerto – premiered by Rostropovich in 1957, a decade after it was written – deserves a place alongside those of his great friend and colleague Shostakovich. The programme also includes Tchaikovsky's much-loved 'Pathétique' Symphony, with its thrilling Scherzo, and Sibelius's suite *Karelia* – a stirring celebration of Finland's proud history. *See 'Beyond the Bust', pages 8–13; Spotlight on Dalia Stasevska, page 137.*

PROMS READING
5.45pm–6.25pm • Imperial College Union An exploration of Tchaikovsky's letters with discussion and readings.
Edited version broadcast on BBC Radio 3 during tonight's interval

Wednesday 7 August

PROM 26
7.00pm–c9.00pm • Royal Albert Hall

PRICE BAND B

SUNNYBOY DLADLA

Brahms Tragic Overture *14'*

Wagner Tristan and Isolde – Prelude and Liebestod (orchestral version) *17'*

INTERVAL

Mozart, compl. Süssmayr Requiem in D minor *50'*

Fatma Said *soprano*
Kathryn Rudge *mezzo-soprano*
Sunnyboy Dladla *tenor*
David Shipley *bass*

BBC National Chorus of Wales
BBC National Orchestra of Wales
Nathalie Stutzmann *conductor*

Love and loss, life and death collide in an emotionally charged concert given by Nathalie Stutzmann and the BBC National Orchestra and Chorus of Wales. Turbulent shifts of mood characterise Brahms's *Tragic Overture*, and their ripples continue through the Prelude and Liebestod from Wagner's powerful operatic exploration of forbidden love, *Tristan and Isolde*. At the heart of the programme is Mozart's *Requiem* – the composer's final work, left unfinished at his early death, and his own musical epitaph. Soloists include former BBC Radio 3 New Generation Artists Fatma Said and Kathryn Rudge. *See Spotlight on Fatma Said, page 127.*

Broadcast on BBC Four on Sunday 11 August

PROMS PLUS TALK
5.15pm–5.55pm • Imperial College Union Poet Clare Pollard and Jennifer Wallace discuss the power of tragic tales.
Edited version broadcast on BBC Radio 3 during tonight's interval

Wednesday 7 August

PROM 27 • LATE NIGHT
10.15pm–c11.30pm • Royal Albert Hall

PRICE BAND F

LONDON CONTEMPORARY ORCHESTRA

The Sound of Space: Sci-Fi Film Music

Music from sci-fi film and TV scores, including excerpts from:

Jed Kurzel Alien: Covenant
Hans Zimmer Interstellar
Mica Levi Under the Skin
Clint Mansell Moon
Steven Price Gravity
John Murphy Sunshine
Carly Paradis The Innocents

London Contemporary Orchestra
Robert Ames *conductor*

There will be no interval

A Late Night Prom with a futuristic spin brings together some of the best sci-fi film music. Excerpts from cult soundtracks come together with recent works by Hans Zimmer and Mica Levi. The award-winning London Contemporary Orchestra – whose collaborators include Radiohead, Goldfrapp and Steve Reich – perform music from *Under the Skin, Interstellar* and the recent Netflix series *The Innocents*, among other titles, as well as from *Alien: Covenant*, whose soundtrack the LCO recorded. *See 'The Sound of Space', pages 14–19.*

Broadcast on BBC Four on Friday 9 August

Julia Wesely (Gabetta); Simon Pauly (Dladla); Sarah Jeynes/BBC (London Contemporary Orchestra)

Thursday 8 August

PROM 28
7.00pm–*c*9.05pm • Royal Albert Hall

PRICE BAND (A)

NATALYA ROMANIW

Takemitsu Twill by Twilight *13'*

Huw Watkins The Moon *c20'*
BBC commission: world premiere

INTERVAL

Rachmaninov The Bells *37'*
Henry Wood Novelties: UK premiere, 1921

Borodin Prince Igor – Polovtsian Dances *14'*
Henry Wood Novelties: UK premiere, 1897

Natalya Romaniw *soprano*
Oleg Dolgov *tenor*

BBC National Chorus of Wales
Philharmonia Chorus
BBC National Orchestra of Wales
Tadaaki Otaka *conductor*

Sleigh bells, wedding bells, warning bells and mourning bells all peal through Rachmaninov's choral symphony *The Bells* – which sets a text by Edgar Allan Poe with broad brushstrokes and bright colours. Borodin's exotically seductive *Polovtsian Dances* also features, alongside a world premiere by Huw Watkins inspired by the 50th anniversary of the first manned mission to the Moon. See *'Beyond the Bust', pages 8–13; 'The Sound of Space', pages 14–19; 'New Directions', pages 42–47; Spotlight on Tadaaki Otaka, right.*

PROMS PLUS TALK
5.15pm–5.55pm • Imperial College Union Authors Laura Purcell and Iain Sinclair join Matthew Sweet to discuss American gothic and horror writer Edgar Allan Poe, whose poetry inspired Rachmaninov's *The Bells*.
Edited version broadcast on BBC Radio 3 during tonight's interval

Spotlight on … BBC Conductors

Tadaaki Otaka • Prom 28
BBC National Orchestra of Wales

'My favourite music festival!' Tadaaki Otaka has plenty of experience to draw on in his huge enthusiasm for the BBC Proms – he's been appearing at the festival since the 1980s. 'I find the Proms audiences help the musicians give their best performances – they encourage us very much.' This year he directs the BBC National Orchestra of Wales, of which he became Principal Conductor in 1987 and Conductor Laureate in 1996. 'We have worked together for over 30 years,' he explains. 'We're like very good old friends. When I started working with them, it was a small orchestra, but the great thing is that the players really love music.'

Rachmaninov has long been a particular passion for Otaka and the composer's grand, Poe-inspired choral symphony *The Bells* forms the centrepiece of his concert. 'I always very much enjoy Rachmaninov's romantic, rhythmical side,' he observes. There's also the world premiere of Welsh composer Huw Watkins's *The Moon* and music from Otaka's own country: Takemitsu's delicate *Twill by Twilight*. 'For every musician, the most important music comes from his or her own country,' says Otaka. 'For the orchestra, that means Wales. For me, Japan. Takemitsu was a fantastic composer and a wonderful person. I liked him and I love his beautiful music. He is the pride of the Japanese.'

Dalia Stasevska • Prom 25
BBC Symphony Orchestra

As a teenager, her greatest idol was Leonard Bernstein and she played along to Wilhelm Furtwängler's Beethoven symphony recordings on her violin. Yet it wasn't until Dalia Stasevska went to Helsinki's Sibelius Academy to study the violin that she discovered conducting. 'You didn't see many women conductors, so it never came into my mind that I could do it,' she says. 'Then I saw a female conducting student, and within three months I was in a conducting class.'

The Finnish conductor has just been appointed Principal Guest Conductor of the BBC Symphony Orchestra, a position previously held by David Robertson. She makes her debut in that role at the Proms this summer, with Tchaikovsky ('His music is dear to me'), Sibelius ('I wanted to bring something Finnish to the Proms') and Weinberg ('His Cello Concerto is full of intimacy').

Sibelius premiered his *Karelia* suite in 1893, the same year that Tchaikovsky first aired the Sixth Symphony, just nine days before his death. 'I'm happy there's a small connection,' Stasevska says. 'They are totally different composers, but they have a similar energy. You often hear that Tchaikovsky's "Pathétique" Symphony is the testimony of a man who knew he was going to die. I feel the opposite – he's passionate to live. From the moment it starts, it's unstoppable.'

Friday 9 August

PROMS 29 & 30 • 3.00pm–c5.30pm & 7.30pm–c10.00pm • Royal Albert Hall

PRICE BAND D
WEEKEND PROMMING PASS *see bbc.co.uk/proms*

FILMING OF 'THE FOUNTAINHEAD'

The Warner Brothers Story

Music from one of the leading studios of Hollywood's Golden Age of cinema, including excerpts from:

Arlen Blues in the Night

Korngold The Constant Nymph; The Sea Hawk

Loewe My Fair Lady; Camelot

North A Streetcar Named Desire

Steiner Now, Voyager; The Treasure of the Sierra Madre

Styne Romance on the High Seas

Maida Vale Singers
John Wilson Orchestra
John Wilson *conductor*

There will be one interval

Ten years since their first Proms appearance together, John Wilson and the John Wilson Orchestra present an evening of sumptuous technicoloured scores from the Golden Age of Hollywood cinema. *See 'Music for the Dream Factory', pages 70–73.*

Broadcast tonight on BBC Four
Broadcast live on BBC Radio 3 and recorded for future broadcast on BBC Radio 2 (Prom 30)

PROMS PLUS TALK
5.45pm–6.25pm • Imperial College Union Matthew Sweet is joined by critic and broadcaster David Benedict and film critic Pamela Hutchinson to introduce tonight's Prom.
Edited version broadcast on BBC Radio 3 during tonight's interval

Saturday 10 August

PROM 31
7.30pm–c9.45pm • Royal Albert Hall

PRICE BAND B
WEEKEND PROMMING PASS *see bbc.co.uk/proms*

LISE DAVIDSEN

Brahms Variations on the St Anthony Chorale *18'*

R. Strauss Four Songs, Op. 27 *13'*

INTERVAL

Bruckner Symphony No. 4 in E flat major, 'Romantic' (1878–80 version, ed. Nowak) *68'*

Lise Davidsen *soprano*

Philharmonia Orchestra
Esa-Pekka Salonen *conductor*

Following their performance of Wagner, Mahler and Webern at last year's Proms, the Philharmonia Orchestra and Principal Conductor Esa-Pekka Salonen return with another programme of Austro-German classics. Subtitled the 'Romantic', Bruckner's Symphony No. 4 is as vividly colourful as the composer's original scenario for the work (later withdrawn) with its knights, maidens, hunting and dancing. Brahms's variations (also known as the 'Haydn' Variations) provide a vivacious opener, and prize-winning Norwegian soprano Lise Davidsen joins the orchestra in a sequence of songs by Richard Strauss, including the ecstatic 'Morgen!'.

PROMS READING
5.45pm–6.25pm • Imperial College Union William Mival, composer and Head of Composition at the Royal College of Music, discusses Bruckner's Symphony No. 4 and the challenges of writing symphonies in the late 19th century.
Edited version broadcast on BBC Radio 3 during tonight's interval

Sunday 11 August

PROM 32
11.00am–c1.10pm • Royal Albert Hall

PRICE BAND B
WEEKEND PROMMING PASS *see bbc.co.uk/proms*

JOYCE DiDONATO

Benjamin Beckman new work *5'*
UK premiere

Berlioz Les nuits d'été *30'*

INTERVAL

Strauss An Alpine Symphony *50'*

Joyce DiDonato *mezzo-soprano*

Brass of the National Youth Orchestra of Great Britain
National Youth Orchestra of the USA
Sir Antonio Pappano *conductor*

Celebrated American mezzo-soprano Joyce DiDonato is reunited with regular collaborator Sir Antonio Pappano to mark the 150th anniversary of Berlioz's death with a performance of the composer's sumptuous orchestral song-cycle *Les nuits d'été* – a musical journey from springtime love to cruellest loss. The National Youth Orchestra of the USA undertakes a journey of quite a different kind in Strauss's monumental *An Alpine Symphony*, whose vast orchestral forces and massive soundscapes conjure up the craggy drama of the Bavarian Alps. The concert opens with a new work, by Benjamin Beckman, one of the NYO-USA's two Apprentice Composers. *See 'A Life with Berlioz', pages 36–41.*

Broadcast on BBC Four on Friday 16 August

Sunday 11 August

PROM 33
8.00pm–c10.05pm • Royal Albert Hall

PRICE BAND A
WEEKEND PROMMING PASS *see bbc.co.uk/proms*

CHRISTINA GANSCH

Detlev Glanert Weites Land ('Musik mit Brahms' for orchestra) *12'*
UK premiere

Schubert, orch. D. Glanert Einsamkeit for soprano and orchestra *21'*

INTERVAL

Mahler Symphony No. 4 in G major *55'*
Henry Wood Novelties: UK premiere, 1905

Christina Gansch *soprano*

BBC Symphony Orchestra
Semyon Bychkov *conductor*

Semyon Bychkov traces the evolution and genealogy of Austro-German music in a fascinating Prom featuring three works from three different centuries. Schubert's influence on Mahler is clear from the weary loveliness and fretful anxiety of *Einsamkeit* ('Loneliness'), heard here in an elegant orchestration by contemporary composer Detlev Glanert. Mahler's Fourth Symphony, bright with sleigh bells and innocent wonder, glances back to classical models from the vantage point of *fin-de-siècle* Vienna, while Glanert takes Brahms's Fourth Symphony into the 21st century in his lyrical *Weites Land* ('Open Land'). *See 'Beyond the Bust', pages 8–13; 'New Directions', pages 42–47.*

PROMS PLUS TALK
6.15pm–6.55pm • Imperial College Union Author Patrice Lawrence and BBC Radio 3 New Generation Thinker Emma Butcher discuss children's concepts of innocence and experience.
Edited version broadcast on BBC Radio 3 during tonight's interval

Monday 12 August

PROMS AT … CADOGAN HALL 4
1.00pm–c2.00pm • Cadogan Hall

For ticket prices, see page 165

ARIS QUARTET

Schubert String Quartet No. 1 *17'*

Sirmen String Quartet No. 5 in F minor *11'*

Haydn String Quartet in B flat major, 'Sunrise' *23'*

Aris Quartet

There will be no interval

Praised for their suppleness of sound, BBC Radio 3 New Generation Artists the Aris Quartet make their Proms debut with Haydn's ebullient 'Sunrise' Quartet – nicknamed for the beautiful climbing phrase with which it opens. This late, great work is paired with two youthful pieces: Schubert's quietly innovative String Quartet No. 1, and the String Quartet No. 5 by Maddalena Laura Sirmen (born Lombardini) – the 18th-century violin virtuoso and pupil of Tartini, whose career was a defiant exception in a male-dominated profession. *See 'A History of Classical Music', pages 78–83.*

Every Prom broadcast live on BBC Radio 3

Monday 12 August

PROM 34
7.30pm–c9.30pm • Royal Albert Hall

PRICE BAND D

MARTHA ARGERICH

Schubert Symphony No. 8 in B minor, 'Unfinished' *25'*

Tchaikovsky Piano Concerto No. 1 in B flat minor *35'*

INTERVAL

Lutosławski Concerto for Orchestra *30'*

Martha Argerich *piano*

West–Eastern Divan Orchestra
Daniel Barenboim *conductor*

Daniel Barenboim and his West–Eastern Divan Orchestra return to the Proms with a programme of emotion and sensation. Legendary Argentine pianist Martha Argerich is the soloist in Tchaikovsky's Piano Concerto No. 1 – an outpouring of Romantic intensity sustained from the arresting opening chords right through to the thrilling finale. Polish folk dances pulse through Lutosławski's vibrant *Concerto for Orchestra*, with its echoes of Stravinsky and Bartók. Its bracing rhythmic energy and reticent beauty offer the perfect foil to the melodic richness of Tchaikovsky's concerto.

PROMS PLUS TALK
5.45pm–6.25pm • Imperial College Union Ahead of tonight's Prom, musicologist Adrian Thomas introduces Lutosławski's *Concerto for Orchestra*.
Edited version broadcast on BBC Radio 3 during tonight's interval

Spotlight on … BBC Conductors

13 | 14 AUG

Bramwell Tovey • Prom 56

BBC Concert Orchestra

'It's a funny feeling – I've conducted all over the world, but never at the BBC Proms.' London-born conductor Bramwell Tovey has spent the past three decades in the USA and Canada – he's currently Music Director Emeritus of the Vancouver Symphony Orchestra – and is excited to be making his Proms debut at last: 'It feels like coming home after a long time.'

Tovey will be on the podium in front of the BBC Concert Orchestra, as its Principal Conductor. 'It's such a versatile, virtuoso group,' he explains, referring to the orchestra's exceptionally broad repertoire, from established classics to contemporary music, musicals, film music and more. 'I really enjoy that – it feels like a natural fit with my own musical tastes.'

Tovey's concert celebrates the legacy of Proms founder-conductor Henry Wood, the driving force behind the very first Proms, and features music, now well established, that Wood first unveiled to British listeners, including by Debussy and Ravel. There's also a brand-new piece by Dobrinka Tabakova, the BBC Concert Orchestra's Composer-in-Residence: 'I think Sir Henry wouldhave been delighted that a concert celebrating him would feature a new work, particularly by a composer so closely aligned with the Orchestra.'

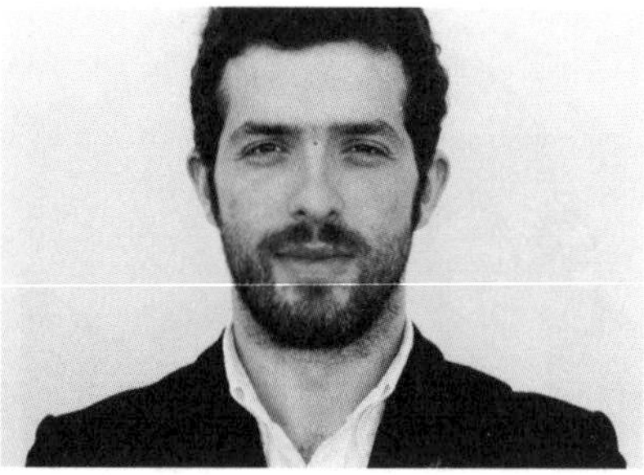

Omer Meir Wellber Proms 7 & 14

BBC Philharmonic

'Since I'm doing two Proms before I officially start, I feel it's important I should really put my stamp on the programmes.' Israeli-born conductor Omer Meir Wellber becomes the BBC Philharmonic's Chief Conductor in September, and his Proms on 23 and 29 July offer a foretaste of his far-reaching plans.

For the first, he contrasts two kinds of music-making – 'from a minority and a majority, or from an immigrant and a local'. He explains: 'Alongside Mozart and Schumann, we have the famous immigrant Schoenberg – more than half his music was written outside his home country. There's also Paul Ben-Haim, who emigrated from Germany to what became Israel and put the German school in the Mediterranean. His First Symphony is like Mahler, but with Middle Eastern melodies. These issues of accepting cultural mixtures and collaborations are serious, given everything that's going on in Europe and America at the moment.'

His second concert, featuring Haydn's oratorio *The Creation*, is inspired by his passion for the composer. 'I've become a huge admirer. Apart from period ensembles, hardly anyone plays much Haydn these days, and bigger orchestras need to be able to play his music. I'm going to be conducting a lot of Haydn with the BBC Philharmonic.'

Tuesday 13 August

PROM 35

7.00pm–c9.10pm • Royal Albert Hall

PRICE BAND A

Various Pictured Within: Birthday Variations for M. C. B. *c30'*

New 'Enigma' variations by Kalevi Aho, Sally Beamish, Sir Harrison Birtwistle, Richard Blackford, Gavin Bryars, Brett Dean, Dai Fujikura, Wim Henderickx, Colin Matthews, Anthony Payne, John Pickard, David Sawer, Iris ter Schiphorst and Judith Weir

BBC commission: world premiere

Vaughan Williams Serenade to Music *13'*

Henry Wood Novelties: world premiere, 1938

INTERVAL

Brahms Song of Destiny *18'*

Elgar 'Enigma' Variations *29'*

Nadine Benjamin *soprano*
Idunnu Münch *mezzo-soprano*
William Morgan *tenor*
David Ireland *bass-baritone*

ENO Chorus
BBC Singers
BBC Scottish Symphony Orchestra
Martyn Brabbins *conductor*

Elgar's 'Enigma' Variations is the inspiration for a new work commissioned from 14 living composers as a special birthday tribute to conductor Martyn Brabbins, who turns 60 today. Elgar's original set also features, as do Vaughan Williams's exquisite *Serenade to Music* and Brahms's 'Little Requiem', the *Song of Destiny*. See *'Beyond the Bust', pages 8–13; 'A Birthday "Enigma"', pages 24 –27; 'New Directions', pages 42–47.*

Broadcast on BBC Four on Sunday 8 September

INSPIRE CONCERT

5.00pm–6.00pm • BBC Maida Vale Studios The Aurora Orchestra performs the winning pieces of the 2019 BBC Proms Inspire Competition *(see 'Music, Inspiration … Education', pages 20–23). Tickets available from BBC Studio Audiences: bbc.co.uk/showsandtours/shows*

PROMS PLUS TALK

5.15pm–5.55pm • Imperial College Union Pianist and broadcaster David Owen Norris explores tonight's programme. *Edited version broadcast on BBC Radio 3 during tonight's interval*

Tuesday 13 August

PROM 36 • LATE NIGHT

10.15pm–c11.30pm • Royal Albert Hall

PRICE BAND E

Late-Night Mixtape

Tenebrae
12 ensemble

There willl be no interval

In the spirit of Radio 3's popular *In Tune Mixtape* – joining together an eclectic range of classical and contemporary sounds – we present a live, late-night wind-down, exploring the fringes of Minimalism and meditative listening. With radiant choral sounds and heavenly strings plus guest soloists, the Royal Albert Hall transforms into a vast ambient resonator. Pieces by the godfathers of 'holy' Minimalism, Arvo Pärt and Pēteris Vasks, emerge out of the sublime classicism of J. S. Bach and Schubert, in a Prom to calm the mind and nourish the soul.

Every Prom broadcast live on BBC Radio 3

Wednesday 14 August

PROM 37

7.00pm–c9.10pm • Royal Albert Hall

PRICE BAND B

DAME SARAH CONNOLLY

Berlioz The Childhood of Christ *95'*

Dame Sarah Connolly *mezzo-soprano*
Allan Clayton *tenor*
Roderick Williams *baritone*
Neal Davies *bass*

Britten Sinfonia Voices
Genesis Sixteen
Hallé
Sir Mark Elder *conductor*

There will be one interval

Sir Mark Elder and the Hallé continue our series marking 150 years since the death of Hector Berlioz with the composer's vividly dramatic oratorio *The Childhood of Christ*. Simple and often disarmingly direct, with emotions that unfold in some of the composer's most beautiful melodies (including the much-loved 'Shepherds' Farewell'), the oratorio follows the Holy Family as they flee from Bethlehem into Egypt, where they find safety and welcome. A superb line-up of soloists is led by Dame Sarah Connolly. *See 'A Life with Berlioz', pages 36–41; Spotlight on Roderick Williams, page 153.*

PROMS READING

5.15pm–5.55pm • Imperial College Union Berlioz originally presented an early version of *The Childhood of Christ* as the work of 'Ducré', a composer he had created as a hoax. Inspired by tonight's Prom, we explore the tradition of hoaxing in literature with discussion and readings.
Edited version broadcast on BBC Radio 3 during tonight's interval

Wednesday 14 August

PROM 38 • LATE NIGHT

10.15pm–c11.30pm • Royal Albert Hall

PRICE BAND E

SOLOMON'S KNOT

J. S. Bach

Cantata No. 130 'Herr Gott, dich loben alle wir', BWV 130 *16'*

Cantata No. 19 'Es erhub sich ein Streit', BWV 19 *21'*

Cantata No. 149 'Man singet mit Freuden vom Sieg', BWV 149 *19'*

Cantata No. 50 'Nun ist das Heil und die Kraft', BWV 50 *4'*

Solomon's Knot

There will be no interval

Singing with small forces and without a conductor, British musical collective Solomon's Knot brings a contemporary clarity and freshness to all its performances. The singers make their Proms debut with an all-Bach Late Night Prom of cantatas composed for the Feast of St Michael – the saint who, appropriately, protects against the evils of darkness and night. The programme includes the richly scored cantatas *Herr Gott, dich loben alle wir* and *Es erhub sich ein Streit*, as well as the dramatic *Man singet mit Freuden vom Sieg*, with its glorious chorale finale.

Thursday 15 August

PROM 39
7.00pm–c9.00pm • Royal Albert Hall

PRICE BAND A

CATRIONA MORISON

Mendelssohn Overture 'The Hebrides' ('Fingal's Cave') *10'*

Elgar Sea Pictures *23'*

INTERVAL

Errollyn Wallen This Frame Is Part of the Painting *c10'*
BBC commission: world premiere

Mussorgsky, orch. Ravel Pictures at an Exhibition *35'*

Catriona Morison *mezzo-soprano*

BBC National Orchestra of Wales
Elim Chan *conductor*

Winner of Cardiff Singer of the World 2017, Catriona Morison makes her Proms debut in Elgar's sumptuous *Sea Pictures*, a vivid musical portrait of the sea in its many moods. Also hanging in this musical gallery are Mussorgsky's colourful *Pictures at an Exhibition*, Mendelssohn's much-loved overture *The Hebrides* and the world premiere of Errollyn Wallen's homage to artist Howard Hodgkin, *This Frame Is Part of the Painting*. *See 'New Directions', pages 42–47; Spotlights on Catriona Morison, page 127, and Elim Chan, page 155.*

PROMS PLUS TALK
5.15pm–5.55pm • Imperial College Union (Concert Hall)
Composer Errollyn Wallen introduces her new work ahead of its world premiere, and talks about her inspiration and ideas. *Edited version broadcast on BBC Radio 3 during tonight's interval*

PROMS FAMILY WORKSHOP
5.15pm–6.00pm • Imperial College Union (Dining Hall)
Join professional musicians for a family-friendly introduction to tonight's Prom. Bring an instrument or just sit back and take it all in! *Suitable for ages 7-plus. See page 23 for details.*

Friday 16 August

PROM 40
7.30pm–c9.45pm • Royal Albert Hall

PRICE BAND C
WEEKEND PROMMING PASS *see bbc.co.uk/proms*

STEPHEN HOUGH

Sullivan Victoria and Merrie England – suite *15'*

Mendelssohn Piano Concerto No. 1 in G minor *21'*

INTERVAL

Prince Albert of Saxe-Coburg and Gotha Songs *12'*

Mendelssohn Symphony No. 3 in A minor, 'Scottish' *40'*

Alessandro Fisher *tenor*
Stephen Hough *piano*

Orchestra of the Age of Enlightenment
Adám Fischer *conductor*

The Proms celebrates the 200th anniversary of Queen Victoria's birth with a glimpse into the monarch's musical life. The programme features music by her favourite composer, Mendelssohn, including his lively 'Scottish' Symphony and First Piano Concerto, which will be performed by Stephen Hough on Victoria's own piano, loaned by HM The Queen from the Royal Collection. The concert also includes a suite from Arthur Sullivan's ballet *Victoria and Merrie England*, composed to celebrate the Queen's Diamond Jubilee, as well as songs by Prince Albert. *See 'In Parlour and Palace', pages 74–77.*

Broadcast on BBC Four on Sunday 18 August

PROMS PLUS TALK
5.45pm–6.25pm • Imperial College Union What Victorians Did for Fun – historians Kathryn Hughes and Lee Jackson discuss 19th-century entertainment.
Edited version broadcast on BBC Radio 3 during tonight's interval

Saturday 17 August

PROMS AT … HOLY SEPULCHRE LONDON
3.00pm–c4.30pm

For ticket prices, see bbc.co.uk/proms

SOFI JEANNIN

Walton Where does the uttered music go? *6'*

Britten Sacred and Profane *16'*

Ireland The Holy Boy *3'*

Thea Musgrave Rorate coeli *11'*

Maconchy Three Donne Songs – No. 1: A Hymn to God the Father *4'*

Vaughan Williams Valiant-for-truth *6'*

Judith Weir Missa del Cid *20'*

Joanna Lee At this man's hand *c3'*
BBC commission: world premiere

BBC Singers
Sofi Jeannin *conductor*

There will be no interval

The BBC Singers and Chief Conductor Sofi Jeannin take the Proms to the 'Musicians' Church', Holy Sepulchre London (aka St Sepulchure-without-Newgate), where Proms founder-conductor Henry Wood first learnt the organ and was later laid to rest. This varied conspectus of 20th-century English choral music opens with the setting of lines by the then Poet Laureate, John Masefield, that Walton composed for the unveiling of the church's Henry Wood memorial window in 1946, and is brought up to date with a new commission by Joanna Lee, *At this man's hand*, setting the verse by Masefield that is inscribed on the window itself. *See 'Beyond the Bust', pages 8–13; 'New Directions', pages 42–47.*

Saturday 17 August

PROM 41
7.30pm–c10.00pm • Royal Albert Hall

PRICE BAND (B)
WEEKEND PROMMING PASS *see bbc.co.uk/proms*

VLADIMIR JUROWSKI

Rimsky-Korsakov Mlada – suite *18'*
Henry Wood Novelties: world premiere, 1898

Rachmaninov Piano Concerto No. 1 in F sharp minor (original version, 1891) *29'*
Henry Wood Novelties: world premiere, 1900

INTERVAL

Lyadov
Baba-Yaga *4'*
Kikimora *9'*
From the Apocalypse *9'*
Henry Wood Novelties: UK premieres 1906, 1917, 1914

Glazunov Symphony No. 5 in B flat major *33'*
Henry Wood Novelties: UK premiere, 1897

Alexander Ghindin *piano*

London Philharmonic Orchestra
Vladimir Jurowski *conductor*

Vladimir Jurowski conducts an all-Russian concert of works whose world or UK premieres were given by Proms founder-conductor Henry Wood. It features Rimsky-Korsakov's dance-filled suite from his opera *Mlada*, Rachmaninov's ebullient early piano concerto, a trio of colourful tone-poems by Lyadov and Glazunov's heroic Fifth Symphony. *See 'Beyond the Bust', pages 8–13; Spotlight on Alexander Ghindin, page 157.*

PROMS PLUS TALK
5.45pm–6.25pm • Imperial College Union Wish Upon a Tsar – The Power of Russian Folk Tales, with Marina Warner and Sophie Anderson.
Edited version broadcast on BBC Radio 3 during tonight's interval

Spotlight on … BBC Radio 3 New Generation Artists

Amatis Piano Trio
Proms at … Cadogan Hall 6

BBC Radio 3 New Generation Artists, 2016–18

The Amatis Piano Trio had 'humble beginnings', according to its cellist Samuel Shepherd. 'Lea Hausmann, our violinist, and I met in Amsterdam. We needed to make some money to fund our studies, so we went busking.' The pair felt their sound gelled, so they found a pianist, the Dutch/Chinese Mengjie Han, to form a trio, and immediately scooped the audience prize at a big chamber music competition. 'We did two rehearsals and that was it. We were busking opposite the Concertgebouw, and then we were playing inside in its chamber hall.'

For its Proms debut, the trio pays homage to the great 19th-century musicians Clara and Robert Schumann. 'We built a programme of their music around Clara's Piano Trio,' says Shepherd. 'It combines the speaking quality of Classical music with the lyricism of the Romantic era. She observed the idea that, even when you're playing an instrument, the melody has to have a kind of text behind it.'

Robert's legacy of musical works may be secure today but in her own time Clara – the bicentenary of whose birth falls this year – was more famous, as a leading pianist. 'Robert and Clara shared a story of love and also professional admiration. They were total equals. That's the joy we want to express in the concert.'

Mariam Batsashvili • Prom 42

BBC Radio 3 New Generation Artist, 2017–19

When a concert features a Schumann Piano Concerto in A minor, it's still most likely to be the famous 1845 piece by Robert. But at this year's Proms it's Clara Schumann who is in the spotlight and her Piano Concerto of 1836. 'The music absolutely fits the period of Romanticism right after Viennese Classicism. It has structure and yet it is heartfelt,' says Mariam Batsashvili, who makes her Proms debut with the piece. 'When I practise it, I think, "Wow, what a talent!" We need to play her music more.'

Not that it's a simple task. The three-movement piece is 'ridiculously difficult to play,' says the Georgian pianist, one of Radio 3's current New Generation Artists. 'There are lots of jumps. I had to practise it a lot to make it look effortless, but I don't think she needed to. And I'm 25. She wrote it when she was 14.'

Clara Wieck, who was born two centuries ago, in 1819, and who married Robert Schumann in 1840, was one of the greatest pianists of the 19th century. She premiered her concerto at the Leipzig Gewandhaus, with Mendelssohn conducting. 'It's almost like chamber music,' reflects Batsashvili. 'In the second movement the whole orchestra stops and it is basically a duet between me and the cello: it's the most fascinating music for me – pure and touching.'

Sunday 18 August

PROM 42
7.30pm –c9.45pm • Royal Albert Hall

PRICE BAND A
WEEKEND PROMMING PASS *see bbc.co.uk/proms*

RAFAEL PAYARE

Beethoven Symphony No. 1 in C major 26'

C. Schumann Piano Concerto 21'

INTERVAL

Sofia Gubaidulina Fairytale Poem 10'

Shostakovich Symphony No. 1 in F minor 28'

Mariam Batsashvili *piano*

Ulster Orchestra
Rafael Payare *conductor*

Belfast's Ulster Orchestra and its dynamic Music Director Rafael Payare present the Proms premiere of Clara Schumann's Piano Concerto, performed here by BBC Radio 3 New Generation Artist Mariam Batsashvili. Begun when the then Clara Wieck was just 13 years old, it's a work whose mellow mood and lyrical melodies conceal no little technical intricacy and formal innovation. Sunny good humour also runs through both Beethoven's Symphony No. 1 – famously described as a musical 'comedy of manners' – and Shostakovich's First Symphony, lively with satirical wit and mischief. *See 'Lost Legacies', pages 96–99; Spotlight on Mariam Batsashvili, page 143.*

PROMS PLUS TALK
5.45pm–6.25pm • Imperial College Union Musicologist Natasha Loges explores the life and work of Clara Schumann.
Edited version broadcast on BBC Radio 3 during tonight's interval

Monday 19 August

PROMS AT … CADOGAN HALL 5
1.00pm–c2.00pm • Cadogan Hall

For ticket prices, see page 165

LOUISE ALDER

Schubert Gretchen am Spinnrade; Nacht und Träume; Die Forelle 10'

Mendelssohn Auf Flügeln des Gesanges; Der Mond; Neue Liebe 8'

Hensel Bergeslust; Warum sind denn die Rosen so blass?; Nach Süden 6'

Liszt Freudvoll und Leidvoll; O lieb, so lang du lieben kannst; S'il est un charmant gazon; Oh, quand je dors; Comment, disaient-ils 14'

Chopin Życzenie; Śliczny chłopiec 5'

Rossini Canzonetta spagnuola 3'

Louise Alder *soprano*
Gary Matthewman *piano*

There will be no interval

As we reach the 19th century in our Monday-lunchime survey of music spanning over 800 years, soprano Louis Alder returns, with pianist Gary Matthewman, for a solo recital of songs from across Europe, including Lieder by Schubert, and by both Mendelssohn and his sister Fanny (published under her married name of Hensel), whose final song, 'Bergeslust' – completed just a day before her death at the age of only 41 – tempers joy with a poignant ending. The many facets of love are exposed in Felix Mendelssohn's 'Der Mond' and 'Neue Liebe', as well as in Chopin's 'Śliczny chłopiec' (Handsome Lad) and songs by Liszt and Rossini. *See 'In Parlour and Palace', pages 74–77; 'A History of Classical Music', pages 78–83.*

Monday 19 August

PROM 43
7.30pm–c10.05pm • Royal Albert Hall

PRICE BAND B

ANU KOMSI

Jonathan Dove new work* c10'
BBC commission: world premiere

Dieter Ammann Piano Concerto c25'
BBC co-commission with the Boston Symphony Orchestra, Konzerthaus Wien, Lucerne Festival, Münchner Philharmoniker and Taipei Symphony Orchestra, supported by Pro Helvetia, the Swiss Arts Council: world premiere

INTERVAL

Beethoven Symphony No. 9 in D minor, 'Choral' 70'

Anu Komsi *soprano*
Hilary Summers *contralto*
Michael Weinius *tenor*
Mika Kares *bass*
Andreas Haefliger *piano*

BBC Symphony Chorus
BBC Symphony Orchestra
Sakari Oramo *conductor*
***Neil Ferris** *conductor*

Sakari Oramo conducts the annual Proms performance of Beethoven's Ninth Symphony – Finnish soprano Anu Komsi leads an international cast of soloists. It is paired with two world premieres: a new choral work by Jonathan Dove and a much-anticipated Piano Concerto by Swiss composer Dieter Ammann, performed by his compatriot Andreas Haefliger. *See 'New Directions', pages 42–47; Spotlight on Andreas Haefliger, page 132.*

PROMS READING
5.45pm–6.25pm • Imperial College Union Seán Williams introduces readings from the works of Friedrich Schiller.
Edited version broadcast on BBC Radio 3 during tonight's interval

Tuesday 20 August

PROM 44
7.30pm–c9.25pm • Royal Albert Hall

PRICE BAND C

SIR SIMON RATTLE

Koechlin Les bandar-log *16'*

Varèse Amériques (original version, 1921) *25'*

INTERVAL

Walton Belshazzar's Feast *34'*

Gerald Finley *baritone*

Orfeó Català
Orfeó Català Youth Choir
London Symphony Chorus
London Symphony Orchestra
Sir Simon Rattle *conductor*

Sir Simon Rattle conducts a concert of sonic spectacle, bringing one of the great English oratorios together with an American orchestral classic. Walton's choral masterpiece *Belshazzar's Feast* gets the Proms treatment with a 300-strong choir and Canadian baritone Gerald Finley as soloist. More than 10 percussionists are needed to bring Varèse's *Amériques* – a celebration of the modern city in sound – to life, while Charles Koechlin's *Jungle Book*-inspired *Les bandar-log* transports listeners to the primeval forest, where all the noise comes from the monkeys.

Broadcast on BBC Four on Friday 23 August

PROMS PLUS TALK
5.45pm–6.25pm • Imperial College Union The jungle of Rudyard Kipling's reputation is explored by novelist Frances Hardinge and academic Sue Walsh, chaired by BBC Radio 3 New Generation Thinker Anindya Raychaudhuri.
Edited version broadcast on BBC Radio 3 during tonight's interval

Wednesday 21 August

PROM 45
7.30pm–c10.00pm • Royal Albert Hall

PRICE BAND C

NINA SIMONE

Mississippi Goddam: A Homage to Nina Simone

Ledisi

Metropole Orkest
Jules Buckley *conductor*

There will be one interval

Singer, songwriter, arranger and political activist – Nina Simone is a giant of jazz history. She's celebrated here in all her guises in a concert led by Jules Buckley and the Metropole Orkest, featuring titles including 'Feeling Good', 'My Baby Just Cares for Me' and 'I Put a Spell on You'. *See 'I Put a Spell on You', pages 100–103.*

Broadcast on BBC Four on Friday 30 August
Recorded for future broadcast on BBC Radio 2

PROMS PLUS TALK
5.45pm–6.25pm • Imperial College Union The life, work and legacy of great African-American singer-songwriter Nina Simone, discussed by poet Zena Edwards and singer Ayanna Witter-Johnson.
Edited version broadcast on BBC Radio 3 during tonight's interval

Thursday 22 August

PROM 46
7.30pm–c9.40pm • Royal Albert Hall

PRICE BAND A

SHEKU KANNEH-MASON

Howell Lamia *12'*
Henry Wood Novelties: world premiere, 1919

Elgar Cello Concerto in E minor *31'*

INTERVAL

Knussen The Way to Castle Yonder *8'*

Weinberg Symphony No. 3 in B minor *32'*
London premiere

Sheku Kanneh-Mason *cello*

City of Birmingham Symphony Orchestra
Mirga Gražinytė-Tyla *conductor*

The CBSO and Music Director Mirga Gražinytė-Tyla celebrate the centenary of Mieczysław Weinberg – the man Shostakovich hailed as 'one of the most outstanding composers' of his day – with a rare performance of his Symphony No. 3, a work that combines folk melodies and dances with confessional urgency. That intensity is shared by Elgar's passionate Cello Concerto, performed here by 2016 BBC Young Musician winner Sheku Kanneh-Mason. The concert opens with Dorothy Howell's radiant tone-poem *Lamia* (first performed, like Elgar's concerto, 100 years ago) and also includes *The Way to Castle Yonder*, a suite from the much-missed Oliver Knussen's opera *Higglety Pigglety Pop!*. *See 'Beyond the Bust', pages 8–13.*

Broadcast on BBC Four on Sunday 25 August

PROMS PLUS TALK
5.45pm–6.25pm • Imperial College Union An exploration of the life and work of Mieczysław Weinberg with musicologist and broadcaster Erik Levi.
Edited version broadcast on BBC Radio 3 during tonight's interval

Spotlight on … Premiere Soloists

Nora Fischer • Prom 67

Louis Andriessen: The Only One

Nora Fischer caught the attention of composer Louis Andriessen in an unexpected way at the first rehearsal of his opera *Theatre of the World*. 'In the score was a very high note marked "screaming", so I thought I would really scream it out,' recalls the singer. 'Everyone was shocked. This was Dutch National Opera – and you don't do these things! But Andriessen was impressed, especially that it was in tune.'

The Dutch composer was so taken with her voice that he has penned her a song cycle, *The Only One*, which she performs on 8 September. He aimed, says Fischer, for it to be a showcase of everything she does as a performer. 'Vocally, it goes in all directions. There's lyrical stuff, screaming, lows, highs, ugliness, beauty, jazz and classical,' she explains. 'It's not entirely clear what the poems, by the Flemish poet Delphine Lecompte, are about. You get a glimpse into someone's confused mind – they are dynamic, abstract, colourful, an inner world of association.'

Finished last summer, the piece has in rehearsal become a 'playground' for Fischer, who loves to challenge audiences and fuse musical genres. 'I sing it at home and mess around with it. It's going to be one of those pieces that sound different every time. It thrives on a sense of spontaneity.'

Paul Lewis • Prom 52

Ryan Wigglesworth: Piano Concerto

'It's going to be a very Mozart-focused concert, that's for sure!' British pianist Paul Lewis is talking about the theme behind his BBC Proms performance in Prom 52, which features music by the great Austrian composer alongside tributes from more recent figures. 'Mozart is constantly challenging,' Lewis continues, 'but in the best possible way. As a pianist you always have to emulate the vocal quality in his music. The piano can certainly sing, but it doesn't sing by itself – you have to achieve that somehow.'

Ryan Wigglesworth joins Lewis not only as conductor, but also as composer and co-soloist. 'We've worked together several times before and we've always felt we've seen eye to eye,' Lewis explains. He's the soloist in Wigglesworth's own tribute to Mozart, giving the British composer's Piano Concerto its very first performance. And, the two men team up as joint soloists in Mozart's own Concerto for two pianos, which Lewis considers more exacting than you perhaps might expect. 'It's always a challenge for two pianists to play together,' says Lewis. 'If it doesn't work, I actually think the sound of two pianos together isn't great. You have to integrate your sound with that of the other pianist. But, when it works, you feel something of the sheer delight of playing the piano, which I hugely enjoy.'

Friday 23 August

PROM 47

7.30pm–c9.55pm • Royal Albert Hall

PRICE BAND C

WEEKEND PROMMING PASS *see bbc.co.uk/proms*

ANDRIS NELSONS

J. S. Bach

Fantasia in G minor, BWV 542 *4'*

Cantata No. 147 'Herz und Mund und Tat und Leben', BWV 147 – Chorale 'Jesus bleibet meine Freude' (transcr. Schmidt-Mannheim) *3'*

Prelude in E flat major, BWV 552 *7'*

Chorale Prelude 'Wachet auf, ruft uns die Stimme', BWV 645 *3'*

Fugue in E flat major, BWV 552 *7'*

INTERVAL

Bruckner Symphony No. 8 in C minor (1890 version, ed. Haas) *80'*

Michael Schönheit *organ*

Gewandhausorchester Leipzig
Andris Nelsons *conductor*

The Leipzig Gewandhaus Orchestra returns to the Proms for the first time under new Music Director Andris Nelsons. At the heart of their programme is Bruckner's Symphony No. 8 – a work as vast in scope as size, a mighty orchestral monologue whose monumental finale the composer considered 'the most significant movement of my life'. Before the broad unfolding of Bruckner, Michael Schönheit presents the meticulous detail of Bach in a series of solo organ works including the lovely chorale 'Wachet auf'.

PROMS PLUS TALK

5.45pm–6.25pm • Imperial College Union A discussion about the relationship between music and architecture with broadcaster and writer Stephen Johnson.
Edited version broadcast on BBC Radio 3 during tonight's interval

Saturday 24 August

PROM 48
7.30pm–c9.55pm • Royal Albert Hall

PRICE BAND B
WEEKEND PROMMING PASS *see bbc.co.uk/proms*

SEONG-JIN CHO

Silvestri Three Pieces for strings *11'*

Prokofiev Piano Concerto No. 2 in G minor *32'*

INTERVAL

Rachmaninov Symphony No. 2 in E minor *56'*

Seong-Jin Cho *piano*

BBC Symphony Orchestra
Cristian Măcelaru *conductor*

Rachmaninov's mighty Symphony No. 2 sits at the centre of this concert given by Cristian Măcelaru and the BBC Symphony Orchestra. From a brooding opening it moves through a lovely slow movement to an ecstatic close – one of the most triumphant in the repertoire. There's more drama and still greater virtuosity in Prokofiev's demanding Piano Concerto No. 2, performed here by 2015 Chopin International Piano Competition winner Seong-Jin Cho. The concert opens with the folk-inspired Three Pieces for strings by the Romanian composer-conductor Constantin Silvestri, who defected to the West in 1956 and died in London 50 years ago. *See Spotlight on Cristian Măcelaru, page 158.*

PROMS PLUS TALK
5.45pm–6.25pm • Imperial College Union An exploration of the Russian symphonic tradition, with musicologist Geoffrey Norris.
Edited version broadcast on BBC Radio 3 during tonight's interval

Sunday 25 August

PROM 49
5.30pm–c7.30pm • Royal Albert Hall

PRICE BAND H

THE LOST WORDS

The Lost Words

A programme based on the book by Robert Macfarlane and Jackie Morris, including works by John Luther Adams, Kerry Andrew, James Burton, Beethoven, Rautavaara, Vaughan Williams and Vivaldi, plus a new commission by Alissa Firsova

Stephanie Childress *violin*
Jason Singh *beatboxer*
Angie Newman *British Sign Language Interpreter*

The Lost Words – Spell Song *folk group*
National Youth Choir of Great Britain
Southbank Sinfonia
Jessica Cottis *conductor*

There will be one interval

We celebrate the rich musical landscape of nature in a Prom inspired by the bestselling book *The Lost Words*, which revives disappearing words that describe the natural world. With a brand-new 'spell' by the book's author Robert Macfarlane, and live paintings from Jackie Morris, who created the original artwork, the programme includes the nightingale, quail and cuckoo calls from Beethoven's 'Pastoral' Symphony, the Arctic bird cries of Rautavaara's *Cantus arcticus* and the carefree flight of Vaughan Williams's *The Lark Ascending*. A unique event for all the family. *See 'New Directions', pages 42–47; 'Lost Words in the Name of the Earth', pages 48–51.*

PROMS FAMILY WORKSHOP
3.45pm–4.30pm • Imperial College Union Join Robert Macfarlane for a special family-friendly workshop taking you and your children into the world of spell-writing and *The Lost Words. Suitable for all the family (ages 7-plus). Places must be booked in advance: see page 23.*

Monday 26 August

PROMS AT … CADOGAN HALL 6
1.00pm–c2.00pm • Cadogan Hall

For ticket prices, see page 165

AMATIS PIANO TRIO

R. Schumann Adagio and Allegro, Op. 70 *9'*

C. Schumann
Three Romances, Op. 22 *9'*
Piano Trio in G minor, Op. 17 *28'*

Amatis Piano Trio

There will be no interval

The prize-winning Amatis Piano Trio, current BBC Radio 3 New Generation Artists, make their Proms debut with chamber works by husband-and-wife composers Robert and Clara Schumann. The climax is Clara Schumann's Piano Trio: one of her finest works, it combines lyrical themes with new contrapuntal invention and scope. The programme also includes Clara's Three Romances for violin and piano, composed for virtuoso Joseph Joachim, as well as Robert's attractive Adagio and Allegro for cello and piano, its wistful slow movement giving way to an energetic Allegro. *See 'A History of Classical Music', pages 78–83; 'Lost Legacies', pages 96–99; Spotlight on Amatis Piano Trio, page 143.*

PROMS FAMILY ORCHESTRA & CHORUS
10.00am–1.00pm • Royal Albert Hall Join professional musicians on the stage of the Royal Albert Hall to create an environment-themed piece inspired by author Robert Macfarlane and artist Jackie Morris's spell book *The Lost Words. Suitable for all the family (ages 7-plus). Places must be booked in advance: see page 23.*

Monday 26 August

PROM 50
7.30pm–c9.30pm • Royal Albert Hall

PRICE BAND B
WEEKEND PROMMING PASS *see bbc.co.uk/proms*

DANIEL HARDING

R. Schumann Genoveva – overture *9'*

Jörg Widmann Babylon Suite *30'*
London premiere

INTERVAL

Beethoven Symphony No. 6 in F major, 'Pastoral' *39'*

Orchestre de Paris
Daniel Harding *conductor*

Town or country? That's the choice offered here by Daniel Harding and the Orchestre de Paris. Scored for a 90-strong orchestra, Jörg Widmann's explosive *Babylon Suite* (adapted from his 2012 opera) invites listeners into the all-consuming sonic chaos of the city – a babel of sound and sensation. Beethoven's Symphony No. 6, by contrast, takes listeners through fields and past brooks in its evocative portrait of pastoral life. The concert opens with the gathering storm-clouds of the overture to Schumann's only opera, *Genoveva*. *See 'New Directions', pages 42–47.*

PROMS PLUS TALK
5.45pm–6.25pm • Imperial College Union A mind-walk around the sights and insights of British landscapes, ancient and modern, with Horatio Clare and MC/rapper Testament.
Edited version broadcast on BBC Radio 3 during tonight's interval

Tuesday 27 August

PROM 51
7.00pm–c10.15pm • Royal Albert Hall

PRICE BAND D

SOFIA FOMINA

Mozart The Magic Flute *155'*
(semi-staged; sung in German, with surtitles)

David Portillo *Tamino*
Sofia Fomina *Pamina*
Björn Bürger *Papageno*
Alison Rose *Papagena*
Brindley Sherratt *Sarastro*
Caroline Wettergreen *Queen of the Night*
Jörg Schneider *Monostatos*
Esther Dierkes *First Lady*
Marta Fontanals-Simmons *Second Lady*
Katharina Magiera *Third Lady*
Michael Kraus *Speaker*
Martin Snell *First Priest/Second Man in Armour*
Thomas Atkins *Second Priest/First Man in Armour*

Glyndebourne
Orchestra of the Age of Enlightenment
Antonello Manacorda *conductor*

There will be one interval

Glyndebourne's new production of *The Magic Flute* comes to the Proms in a special semi-staging. Mozart's final opera is a beguiling mix of enchantment and Enlightenment politics. A score overflowing with melody and invention and a fairy-tale cast of characters together create one of the composer's best-loved comedies. Antonello Manacorda conducts an exciting young cast including Sofia Fomina, Björn Bürger and David Portillo. *See Spotlight on Caroline Wettergreen, page 153.*

PROMS PLUS TALK
5.15pm–5.55pm • Imperial College Union An introduction to *The Magic Flute* with musicologist Tim Jones.
Edited version broadcast on BBC Radio 3 during tonight's interval

Wednesday 28 August

PROM 52
7.30pm–c10.05pm • Royal Albert Hall

PRICE BAND A

PAUL LEWIS

Mozart Concerto in E flat major for two pianos *26'*

Tchaikovsky Suite No. 4, 'Mozartiana' *25'*
Henry Wood Novelties: UK premiere, 1897

INTERVAL

Ryan Wigglesworth Piano Concerto *c25'*
BBC co-commission with Melbourne Symphony Orchestra: world premiere

Stravinsky Divertimento: The Fairy's Kiss *24'*

Paul Lewis *piano*

Britten Sinfonia
Ryan Wigglesworth *piano/conductor*

Arranging four pieces by Mozart in his Suite No. 4, Tchaikovsky pays homage to the composer he regarded as a 'divinity'. Tchaikovsky himself was the inspiration for Stravinsky's ballet *The Fairy's Kiss*, shot through with Tchaikovsky's melodies. Conductor Ryan Wigglesworth also features as both pianist – alongside Paul Lewis in Mozart's Concerto for two pianos – and composer, with the world premiere of his own Piano Concerto. *See 'Beyond the Bust', pages 8–13; 'New Directions', pages 42–47; Spotlight on Paul Lewis, page 146.*

PROMS PLUS TALK
5.45pm–6.25pm • Imperial College Union Ahead of tonight's Prom, musicologist Jonathan Cross introduces Stravinsky's *Divertimento: The Fairy's Kiss.*
Edited version broadcast on BBC Radio 3 during tonight's interval

Thursday 29 August

PROM 53

7.00pm–c9.00pm • Royal Albert Hall

PRICE BAND B

SIR ANDREW DAVIS

Vaughan Williams Fantasia on a Theme by Thomas Tallis *16'*

Hugh Wood Scenes from Comus *28'*

INTERVAL

Elgar The Music Makers *38'*

Stacey Tappan *soprano*
Dame Sarah Connolly *mezzo-soprano*
Anthony Gregory *tenor*

BBC Symphony Chorus
BBC Symphony Orchestra
Sir Andrew Davis *conductor*

Sir Andrew Davis conducts the BBC Symphony Orchestra and Chorus and mezzo-soprano Dame Sarah Connolly in Elgar's last great choral work. *The Music Makers* is the musical culmination of a career, drawing together quotations from many of the composer's best-loved pieces, including the 'Enigma' Variations and *Sea Pictures*, and weaving them into a musical manifesto for the power of art. The concert also includes Vaughan Williams's luminous *Fantasia on a Theme by Thomas Tallis* for double string orchestra and Hugh Wood's lyrical setting of scenes from Milton's pastoral masque *Comus*.

PROMS PLUS TALK

5.15pm–5.55pm • Imperial College Union Musicologist Kate Kennedy introduces Elgar's *The Music Makers*.
Edited version broadcast on BBC Radio 3 during tonight's interval

Thursday 29 August

PROM 54 • LATE NIGHT

10.15pm–c11.40pm • Royal Albert Hall

PRICE BAND F

DUKE ELLINGTON

Duke Ellington's Sacred Music

Monty Alexander *piano*
Annette Walker *tap dancer*

BBC Singers
Carleen Anderson and the UK Vocal Assembly
Nu Civilisation Orchestra
Peter Edwards *conductor*

There will be no interval

Jazz, showbiz swagger and spirituality come together as never before in Duke Ellington's spectacular Sacred Concerts. Described by Ellington himself as 'the most important thing I have ever done', these sacred revues, blending big-band jazz, gospel and Broadway-style melodies, bring all the legendary musician's originality and energy to Christian subjects, and generated three critically acclaimed, boundary-crossing albums. Drawing on these, the Proms premieres a brand-new Sacred Concert – an exhilarating evening of dance, song and spectacle.

Broadcast on BBC Four on Friday 6 September

Every Prom broadcast live on BBC Radio 3

Friday 30 August

PROM 55

7.00pm–c10.00pm • Royal Albert Hall

PRICE BAND B
WEEKEND PROMMING PASS *see bbc.co.uk/proms*

ALLAN CLAYTON

Handel Jephtha *138'*

Allan Clayton *Jephtha*
Jeanine De Bique *Iphis*
Hilary Summers *Storgè*
Tim Mead *Hamor*
Cody Quattlebaum *Zebul*
Rowan Pierce *Angel*

SCO Chorus
Scottish Chamber Orchestra
Richard Egarr *harpsichord/conductor*

There will be one interval

Following on from the success of last year's *Theodora*, the multi-year Proms Handel cycle continues with the composer's last, and perhaps greatest, oratorio – *Jephtha*. Period-performance specialist Richard Egarr conducts the Scottish Chamber Orchestra and Chorus in the devastating story of the warrior Jephtha commanded by God to sacrifice his daughter Iphis. Tenor Allan Clayton is the conflicted Jephtha, with Trinidadian soprano Jeanine De Bique as Iphis.
See Spotlight on Jeanine De Bique, page 150.

PROMS PLUS TALK

5.15pm–5.55pm • Imperial College Union The concept of sacrifice in the Old Testament is discussed by Revd Richard Coles and Deborah Rooke.
Edited version broadcast on BBC Radio 3 during tonight's interval

Spotlight on ... Opera/Oratorio Soloists

Jeanine De Bique • Prom 55

Iphis, *Jephtha*

It was a case of the virtual becoming reality when Jeanine De Bique took the stage with Chineke! at the Proms in 2017. 'Chi-chi Nwanoku [founder of Chineke!] contacted me on social media,' says De Bique. 'Some colleagues had passed her a video of mine, and she really wanted me to sing. She had faith in me.'

The Trinidadian soprano, a former member of the Vienna State Opera who has performed around the world, sang music by Joseph Bologne, Chevalier de Saint-Georges, and Handel – and the Prom was a hit. 'It was an extraordinary experience to work with that orchestra,' she reflects. 'They created such magic on stage.' This year, De Bique returns to sing Iphis in Handel's *Jephtha* with the Scottish Chamber Orchestra. 'Handel and Mozart sit really well with my voice. I love Handel as there's always the possibility to create new things in the music,' she says. 'In his time, the artists would have been so proficient with the style that they were composing on the spot. It's almost like jazz.'

Preparation, though, is the key to successful spontaneity. 'It's like running a race. There's only one time to run that 100 metres,' she says. 'An athlete imagines it from the moment they walk on to the track and, for me, singing an aria is like that – imagining how I get from the start to the finish.'

Benjamin Hulett • Prom 14

Uriel, *The Creation*

Benjamin Hulett's Proms performance on 29 July will be far from the first time that the young British tenor has performed as soloist in Haydn's great oratorio *The Creation*. 'I've sung it with choral societies and symphony orchestras, in opera houses and churches – even in the Haydnsaal at Esterházy Castle, where Haydn himself worked.' What keeps bringing him back to the work? 'Its joy, its beauty and its humour – the work really endears itself to audiences and performers through those aspects.'

Is *The Creation* in any sense operatic, or does it at least draw on his opera training? 'Although we as soloists are given the names of angels, we actually function more as commentators or narrators on the Creation process. The characterisation of my role, the angel Uriel, comes from the interplay between voice and orchestra – sometimes I'm responding to a new musical depiction in the ensemble, and sometimes I'm singing text to which the orchestra responds.' How does he compare his experiences in the opera house with those on concert stages? 'There are so many differences! In concert, we're able to present our own personalities, or what we want the audience to see, and to enjoy engaging directly with an audience – in this case, to allow the Prommers to share a smile with us, and feel the electricity of the Royal Albert Hall.'

Saturday 31 August

PROM 56

7.30pm–*c*9.50pm • Royal Albert Hall

PRICE BAND A

WEEKEND PROMMING PASS *see bbc.co.uk/proms*

Ravel Rapsodie espagnole *16'*

Henry Wood Novelties: UK premiere, 1909

Ireland Piano Concerto *24'*

Henry Wood Novelties: world premiere, 1930

INTERVAL

Dobrinka Tabakova new work *c10'*

BBC commission: world premiere

Debussy, orch. Wood Préludes, Book 1 – La cathédrale engloutie *6'*

Granados, orch. Wood Danzas españolas – Andaluza *5'*

Wagner, arr. Wood Wesendonck Lieder – Träume *5'*

Grainger, arr. Wood Handel in the Strand *4'*

Ravel La valse *12'*

Henry Wood Novelties: UK premiere, 1921

Nathaniel Anderson-Frank *violin*
Leon McCawley *piano*

BBC Concert Orchestra
Bramwell Tovey *conductor*

A 150th-anniversary tribute to Henry Wood, founder-conductor of the Proms, featuring works he premiered and arranged, and reflecting his wide musical tastes, from Wagner to John Ireland, Ravel to Percy Grainger. *See 'Beyond the Bust', pages 8–13; 'New Directions', pages 42–47; Spotlight on Bramwell Tovey, page 140.*

Broadcast on BBC Four on Sunday 1 September

PROMS FAMILY WORKSHOP

5.45pm–6.30pm • Imperial College Union Join professional musicians for a family-friendly introduction to tonight's Prom. Bring an instrument or just sit back and take it all in! *Suitable for ages 7-plus.* *See page 23 for details.*

Sunday 1 September

PROM 57
11.00am–c1.00pm • Royal Albert Hall

PRICE BAND B
WEEKEND PROMMING PASS *see bbc.co.uk/proms*

ERIC LU

Qigang Chen Wu Xing (The Five Elements) *11'*

Mozart Piano Concerto No. 23 in A major *28'*

INTERVAL

Rachmaninov Symphonic Dances *36'*

Eric Lu *piano*

Shanghai Symphony Orchestra
Long Yu *conductor*

The Shanghai Symphony Orchestra and Music Director Long Yu make their first appearance at the Proms. They are joined by Eric Lu, winner of the 2018 Leeds International Piano Competition, for Mozart's Piano Concerto No. 23 with its quasi-operatic humour and wistful slow movement. The programme also includes Chinese composer Qigang Chen's evocative tone-poem *The Five Elements* and Rachmaninov's triptych of *Symphonic Dances*: a passionate Allegro, an uneasy waltz and, finally, a ferocious dance of death. *See 'Chinese Revolutions', pages 92–95; Spotlight on Eric Lu, page 134.*

Broadcast on BBC Four on Friday 6 September

Sunday 1 September

PROM 58
7.30pm–c9.30pm • Royal Albert Hall

PRICE BAND A
WEEKEND PROMMING PASS *see bbc.co.uk/proms*

GEORGIA JARMAN

Linda Catlin Smith new work *c15'*
BBC commission: world premiere

Janáček The Fiddler's Child *12'*
Henry Wood Novelties: UK premiere, 1924

Szymanowski Love Songs of Hafiz, Op. 26 *22'*

INTERVAL

Tchaikovsky Symphony No. 2 in C minor, 'Little Russian' *32'*

Georgia Jarman *soprano*

BBC Scottish Symphony Orchestra
Ilan Volkov *conductor*

Folk songs and folk tales run through this programme from the BBC SSO and Principal Guest Conductor Ilan Volkov. A runaway success at its premiere, Tchaikovsky's Symphony No. 2 takes a different Ukrainian folk melody as the theme for each of its four movements, including the dizzyingly inventive finale, while a gruesome Czech legend provides the starting point for Janáček's atmospheric orchestral ballad *The Fiddler's Child*. Szymanowski's exotic songs based on texts by the 14th-century Persian mystic poet Hafiz and a world premiere by American composer Linda Catlin Smith complete the concert. *See 'Beyond the Bust', pages 8–13; 'New Directions', pages 42–47.*

PROMS PLUS TALK
5.45pm–6.25pm • Imperial College Union Ahead of tonight's Prom, cultural historian Rosamund Bartlett discusses Tchaikovsky and the Russian folk tradition.
Edited version broadcast on BBC Radio 3 during tonight's interval

Monday 2 September

PROMS AT … CADOGAN HALL 7
1.00pm–c2.00pm • Cadogan Hall

For ticket prices, see 165

SILESIAN STRING QUARTET

Weinberg String Quartet No. 7 in C major *25'*

Bacewicz Piano Quintet No. 1 *24'*

Wojciech Świtała *piano*
Silesian String Quartet

There will be no interval

Celebrations of the 100th anniversary of Mieczysław Weinberg – the composer Shostakovich famously hailed as his musical successor – continue with an all-Polish programme from the first half of the 20th century that sets Weinberg's own music alongside that of his great contemporary Grażyna Bacewicz. Folk themes take on a new sophistication, cleverly manipulated and moulded in Bacewicz's mature masterpiece the Piano Quintet No. 1. Poland's award-winning Silesian String Quartet are joined here by pianist Wojciech Świtała. *See 'A History of Classical Music', pages 78–83.*

Every Prom broadcast live on BBC Radio 3

Monday 2 September

PROM 59
7.00pm–c10.15pm • Royal Albert Hall

PRICE BAND C

SIR JOHN ELIOT GARDINER

Berlioz Benvenuto Cellini *154'*
(concert performance; sung in French, with surtitles)

Cast to include:

Michael Spyres *Benvenuto Cellini*
Sophia Burgos *Teresa*
Matthew Rose *Balducci*
Tareq Nazmi *Pope Clement VII*
Krystian Adam *Francesco*
Ashley Riches *Bernardino*

Monteverdi Choir
Orchestre Révolutionnaire et Romantique
Sir John Eliot Gardiner *conductor*

There will be one interval

Sir John Eliot Gardiner brings his five-year series of Berlioz performances to a triumphant close, and this summer's 150th-anniversary celebrations to a spectacular climax, with the composer's rarely performed opera *Benvenuto Cellini*, based on the life and loves of the Renaissance sculptor – culminating in the forging of a vast masterwork. With its sprawling storytelling and vastly demanding score, this is a piece built for the scope of the Royal Albert Hall. American tenor Michael Spyres sings the title-role. *See 'A Life with Berlioz', pages 36–41.*

PROMS PLUS TALK
5.15pm–5.55pm • Imperial College Union Historian and broadcaster Sarah Lenton introduces Berlioz's *Benvenuto Cellini.*
Edited version broadcast on BBC Radio 3 during tonight's interval

Tuesday 3 September

PROM 60
7.30pm–c9.55pm • Royal Albert Hall

PRICE BAND D

BERNARD HAITINK

Beethoven Piano Concerto No. 4 in G major *34'*

INTERVAL

Bruckner Symphony No. 7 in E major (ed. Nowak) *65'*

Murray Perahia *piano*

Vienna Philharmonic
Bernard Haitink *conductor*

In a year that marks both his 90th birthday and the 65th anniversary of his conducting debut, Bernard Haitink conducts the first of the Vienna Philharmonic's two concerts this season. Making his first Proms appearance since 2012, legendary American pianist Murray Perahia is the soloist in Beethoven's revolutionary Piano Concerto No. 4 – written by the composer as his own farewell to the performing stage. A farewell of a different kind runs through Bruckner's Symphony No. 7. Completed shortly after Wagner's death, the work's heartfelt slow movement, with its poignant closing elegy, pays homage to the man and mentor Bruckner described as his 'dearly beloved Master'.

BBC MUSIC INTRODUCING SHOWCASE
5.45pm–6.25pm • Imperial College Union BBC Music Introducing presents a special showcase of live music from rising young artists.
Recorded for future broadcast in Radio 3's 'In Tune'

Wednesday 4 September

PROM 61
7.00pm–c9.10pm • Royal Albert Hall

PRICE BAND D

LEONIDAS KAVAKOS

Dvořák The Noonday Witch *14'*
Henry Wood Novelties: UK premiere, 1896

Korngold Violin Concerto *26'*

INTERVAL

Dvořák Symphony No. 9 in E minor, 'From the New World' *43'*

Leonidas Kavakos *violin*

Vienna Philharmonic
Andrés Orozco-Estrada *conductor*

Dvořák's 'New World' Symphony, with its wistful slow movement, is the centrepiece of the second concert from the Vienna Philharmonic – a programme of Central European works that showcases the orchestra's distinctively rich sound. Andrés Orozco-Estrada pairs it with the composer's colourful, folk-infused tone-poem *The Noonday Witch*, in which a mother's threats inadvertently summon a witch into her home. Cinematic drama is also a hallmark of Korngold's richly orchestrated and unashamedly romantic Violin Concerto, performed here by soloist Leonidas Kavakos. *See 'Beyond the Bust', pages 8–13; 'A Vehicle for Virtuosity?', pages 64–69.*

PROMS PLUS TALK
5.15pm–5.55pm • Imperial College Union Musicologist Ben Winters discusses Korngold and America.
Edited version broadcast on BBC Radio 3 during tonight's interval

Wednesday 4 September

PROM 62 • LATE NIGHT

10.15pm–c11.30pm • Royal Albert Hall

PRICE BAND E

CANZONIERE GRECANICO SALENTINO

Canzoniere Grecanico Salentino
with
Justin Adams *guitar*
Ballaké Sissoko *kora*

There will be no interval

Inspired by the ancient ritual of *pizzica tarantata*, the frenzied trance-like dance said to purge the bite of the tarantula spider, Canzoniere Grecanico Salentino's shows are an explosion of life that summons up the wildness behind the classical tarantella. The Italian band creates a spectacle full of dance, passion, rhythm and mystery – as they say, 'We still have our own demons to exorcise today'. They renew their traditions by inviting musicians to join them at their home in Southern Italy, and two of those guests join them onstage – Robert Plant's guitarist Justin Adams and legendary kora player Ballaké Sissoko.

Every Prom broadcast live on BBC Radio 3

Spotlight on … Opera/Oratorio Soloists

Caroline Wettergreen Prom 51

Queen of the Night, *The Magic Flute*

'I call it the forcefield!' That's how Caroline Wettergreen feels when she's singing the Queen of the Night, one of Mozart's most extreme and testing roles. 'There's a power to it that's hard to explain. It feels like you're Superwoman. On a good day, it's as if you're standing in the middle of the eye of a tornado.'

The Norwegian soprano is part of the *Magic Flute* cast, decamping from Glyndebourne for the company's annual trip to the Royal Albert Hall, following her 2018 appearance in Massenet's *Cendrillon* for the Glyndebourne Tour. Being present in the moment and preparing well are crucial for hitting the stratospheric notes in the aria 'Der Hölle Rache', says Wettergreen. 'I try to pair roles in that top range – you have to stay up there to feel fresh. Before Glyndebourne I'm singing the Queen in Oslo, as well as Blonde in *The Abduction from the Seraglio*, which is similar.'

Once Wettergreen realised she could reach those top Fs, singing the Queen of the Night was a 'dream' for her. 'Every singer has a love–hate relationship with Mozart. His music is so ridiculously see-through,' she says. 'When you master it, it's like being in love. But I think he made his music extra hard just for the fun of it. He was a little devil!'

Roderick Williams • Prom 37

Joseph, *The Childhood of Christ*

Roderick Williams is fascinated by Berlioz, who is, he says, 'a complete one-off'. 'His flights of fancy are extraordinary and there doesn't seem to be a logic to his music in the way that a lot of composers adhere to,' says the British baritone, who first came across Berlioz's music as a cellist at school. 'As a part-time composer myself, I sit in the foothills, look up and think, "How did you do that? And why!"'

Williams feels wrong-footed when he sings Berlioz too. 'His melodies always go in a different direction to where you think. The rest of the Western world seems to think in groups of two, four and eight bars. Berlioz composed them to be whatever length he wished.' Yet it's this ability to take an unexpected path that makes the 19th-century French composer's music so appealing. Take *The Childhood of Christ*, in which Williams sings the role of Joseph this summer. 'At Christmas time we all revel in stories of the Nativity, but what about just afterwards, when the angels and kings have packed up and the stars' light has faded?' asks Williams. 'It took Berlioz to think of that.' The 1854 oratorio also contains 'one of the most extraordinarily beautiful arias' Williams knows. 'Berlioz takes Herod the child-slayer and makes him almost human. He gets inside the mind of a despotic tyrant. It's a moment of pathos.'

Thursday 5 September

PROM 63
7.30pm–c9.40pm • Royal Albert Hall

PRICE BAND D

YUJA WANG

Rachmaninov Piano Concerto No. 3 in D minor *41'*

INTERVAL

Brahms Symphony No. 2 in D major *43'*

Yuja Wang *piano*

Staatskapelle Dresden
Myung-Whun Chung *conductor*

Explosively virtuosic and a thrilling live performer, Yuja Wang is the soloist in Rachmaninov's emotionally expansive and technically demanding Third Piano Concerto – one of the most challenging in the repertoire. She joins conductor Myung-Whun Chung and the Staatskapelle Dresden – the second of this week's visiting European orchestras – for a concert that also includes Brahms's genial Symphony No. 2, whose freshness and spontaneity have drawn comparisons with Beethoven's 'Pastoral' Symphony.

PROMS PLUS TALK
5.45pm–6.25pm • Imperial College Union Novelist Mark Haddon on updating the legend of Pericles, popularised by Shakespeare, from the sea-faring to the aviation age.
Edited version broadcast on BBC Radio 3 during tonight's interval

Friday 6 September

PROM 64
8.00pm–c9.45pm • Royal Albert Hall

PRICE BAND C
WEEKEND PROMMING PASS *see bbc.co.uk/proms*

GRAFFITI ART

The Breaks

Soul Mavericks, featuring Terra & Eddie, Sunni and Lagaet
Mr Switch
Alice Russell *vocals*
Vula Malinga *vocals*
Brendan Reilly *vocals*

Heritage Orchestra
Jules Buckley *conductor*

There will be no interval

A non-stop exploration into 'the breaks' – the beat-driven music that has influenced the world of scratch DJs and b-boying/b-girling (*ie* breakdancing) since the 1970s. One of the four pillars of hip-hop culture – along with MC-ing, DJ-ing and graffiti art – breaking has developed from its original roots tobecome a global phenomenon with a virtuosity all of its own. *See 'These Are the Breaks', pages 52–55.*

THE VERB
5.40pm–6.55pm • Imperial College Union Poet and broadcaster Ian McMillan hosts a special edition of BBC Radio 3's *The Verb*, his showcase of poetry and the spoken word, with guest writers and performers.
Edited version broadcast later on BBC Radio 3

Saturday 7 September

PROM 65
7.30pm–c10.05pm • Royal Albert Hall

PRICE BAND B
WEEKEND PROMMING PASS *see bbc.co.uk/proms*

DANAE KONTORA

Mozart
The Abduction from the Seraglio – overture *5'*
Aria: 'Popoli di Tessaglia! – Io non chiedo, eterni dei' *11'*
Cassation No. 1 in G major – Andante *3'*
Aria: 'No, no, che non sei capace' *4'*
Symphony No. 35 in D major, 'Haffner' *21'*

INTERVAL

R. Strauss
Capriccio – sextet *7'*
Ariadne auf Naxos – 'Grossmächtige Prinzessin!' *11'*

Beethoven Symphony No. 7 in A major *39'*

Danae Kontora *soprano*

Deutsche Kammerphilharmonie Bremen
Constantinos Carydis *conductor*

Greek coloratura soprano Danae Kontora makes her Proms debut with a sequence of Mozart and Strauss arias, while Mozart's 'Haffner' Symphony is filled with operatic ornamentation and dramatic effects. The vitality of Beethoven's Symphony No. 7 led to its being famously described by Wagner as 'the apotheosis of the dance'. *See Spotlight on Danae Kontora, page 158.*

PROMS PLUS TALK
5.45pm–6.25pm • Imperial College Union Musicologist Barbara Eichner explores the connections between the music of Mozart and Strauss.
Edited version broadcast on BBC Radio 3 during tonight's interval

Sunday 8 September

PROM 66

11.00am–c11.55am • Royal Albert Hall

PRICE BAND E

WEEKEND PROMMING PASS *see bbc.co.uk/proms*

JOHN LUTHER ADAMS

John Luther Adams In the Name of the Earth *50'*

European premiere

Choirs to include:

BBC Symphony Chorus
Crouch End Festival Chorus
London International Gospel Choir
London Philharmonic Choir
London Symphony Chorus
LSO Community Choir

There will be no interval

Pulitzer Prize-winning American composer John Luther Adams is a master of large-scale musical spectacles – sonic installations that take the natural world not just as their inspiration but also as a stage. *In the Name of the Earth* celebrates the elements in a musical meditation on rivers, lakes, mountains and deserts. The Proms audience immersed in the sound of eight choirs – totalling more than 600 singers – placed around the auditorium. Marshalling these huge vocal forces are conductors Neville Creed, Neil Ferris, Simon Halsey and David Temple. *See 'New Directions', pages 42–47; 'Lost Words in the Name of the Earth', pages 48–51.*

10.40am: Audience members who would like to participate in this morning's performance are invited to a preparatory sing-through of the final theme of 'In the Name of the Earth'.

Every Prom broadcast live on BBC Radio 3

Spotlight on … Proms Debut Artists

Leonardo García Alarcón
Proms at … Cadogan Hall 2

harpsichord/organ/director

When Argentine-born conductor Leonardo García Alarcón first arrived in Europe at the age of 20, he headed straight for the Continent's biggest, most historic libraries – including the Vatican, Lisbon, Paris and Vienna. 'The forgotten music I found was enough to serve several generations!' He founded his period-instrument ensemble Cappella Mediterranea specifically to rediscover these rarely heard works – though they have expanded their repertoire in the 14 years since then, performing Bach, Handel, Monteverdi and others alongside lesser-known composers.

For his BBC Proms debut, though, Alarcón offers a dialogue between two leading students of Francesco Cavalli: Barbara Strozzi and Antonia Bembo, two women composers who were famous in their time and benefited from the relative compositional freedom that was permitted in Venice.

'Strozzi composed music of sensual emotion,' says Alarcón, 'and Bembo's music has a dramatic sensitivity deriving from a mixture of her French and Italian music inspirations.' Alarcón's Proms programme features excerpts from Bembo's opera *Ercole amante* ('Hercules in Love'), as well as an excerpt from Cavalli's opera on the same subject.

Elim Chan • Prom 39

conductor

'Colourful!' That's the word Elim Chan chooses to sum up the programme she's conducting for her Proms debut. 'It explores the deeper, darker colours that speak to you in an inner, emotional way – which I love. The sheer power of the orchestra speaks in this programme, but there's this subtlety to it too.'

The salty tang of the ocean unites Mendelssohn's overture *The Hebrides* and Elgar's *Sea Pictures* in the first half, while Errollyn Wallen's *This Frame Is Part of the Painting* and Mussorgsky's *Pictures at an Exhibition* both offer musical reflections on visual art. 'A highlight will be conducting mezzo-soprano Catriona Morison in the Elgar and Wallen,' says the Hong Kong-born conductor. 'She's an artist I have really been wanting to work with.'

In 2014 Chan became the first female winner of the Donatella Flick Conducting Competition. Just five years on, after a stint with the LSO, she is Principal Guest Conductor of the Royal Scottish National Orchestra and about to become Chief Conductor of the Antwerp Symphony Orchestra. Two conductors in particular have inspired her journey: 'Carlos Kleiber embodies joy, his spirit energises me,' she says. 'And one of my mentors is Sir Antonio Pappano. He's such a good role model: for every opera and concert he gives his all.'

8 | 10 SEPT

Sunday 8 September

PROM 67

7.30pm–*c*9.30pm • Royal Albert Hall

PRICE BAND A

WEEKEND PROMMING PASS *see bbc.co.uk/proms*

NORA FISCHER

Mussorgsky, orch. Rimsky-Korsakov A Night on the Bare Mountain *11'*

Henry Wood Novelties: UK premiere, 1898

Louis Andriessen The Only One *25'*

BBC co-commission with the Los Angeles Philharmonic and NTR ZaterdagMatinee: UK premiere

INTERVAL

Judith Weir Forest *13'*

Sibelius Symphony No. 5 in E flat major (final version, 1919) *32'*

Nora Fischer *singer*

BBC Symphony Orchestra
Sakari Oramo *conductor*

A Prom celebrating Nature in all her moods. A flight of 16 swans was the catalyst for Sibelius's stirring Fifth Symphony, with its ambiguous, mysterious ending, while for Judith Weir it was nature's process – forests sprouting outwards from a single seed, endlessly growing and multiplying – that offered inspiration. Nature turns menacing in Mussorgsky's vivid tone-poem *A Night on the Bare Mountain*. Boundary-breaking singer Nora Fischer is the soloist in the UK premiere of *The Only One* by Dutch composer Louis Andriessen, who turned 80 this year. *See 'Beyond the Bust', pages 8–13; 'New Directions', pages 42–47; Spotlight on Nora Fischer, page 146.*

PROMS PLUS TALK

5.45pm–6.25pm • Imperial College Union Historian Suzannah Lipscomb and activist Laura Bates discuss witchcraft, witch trials and the image of the witch.

Edited version broadcast on BBC Radio 3 during tonight's interval

Monday 9 September

PROMS AT … CADOGAN HALL 8

1.00pm–*c*2.00pm • Cadogan Hall

For ticket prices, see page 165

RYAN WIGGLESWORTH

Knussen … upon one note – Fantasia after Purcell *3'*

Sir Harrison Birtwistle Fantasia upon all the notes *9'*

Freya Waley-Cohen new work *5'*

BBC commission: world premiere

Knussen Study for 'Metamorphosis' *5'*

Hans Abrahamsen Herbstlied *6'*

Alastair Putt Halazuni *8'*

Knussen Songs without Voices *8'*

Knussen Chamber Orchestra
Ryan Wigglesworth *piano/conductor*

There will be no interval

The final concert in this year's Proms at … Cadogan Hall series, tracing over 800 years of music history, brings us from the late 20th century right up to the present day. A giant of British contemporary music, composer Oliver Knussen is celebrated a year on from his death in a special performance by the newly formed Knussen Chamber Orchestra. Made up of orchestral principals and rising young musicians from across the UK, the ensemble is conducted by Knussen's protégé Ryan Wigglesworth. Knussen's own Purcell-inspired *… upon one note*, lyrical *Songs without Voices* and *Study for 'Metamorphosis'* for solo bassoon are framed by works from Sir Harrison Birtwistle, Alastair Putt and a newly commissioned work by Freya Waley-Cohen. *See 'New Directions', pages 42–47; 'A History of Classical Music', pages 78–83.*

Monday 9 September

PROM 68

7.30pm–*c*9.45pm • Royal Albert Hall

PRICE BAND C

CHRISTINE GOERKE

Wagner Night

Weber Der Freischütz – overture *10'*

Wagner Siegfried – Forest Murmurs *9'*

Franck Le chasseur maudit *14'*

INTERVAL

Wagner
Götterdämmerung – Dawn; Duet 'Zu neuen Taten, teurer Helde'; Siegfried's Rhine Journey; Siegfried's Death and Funeral March; Brünnhilde's Immolation Scene *55'*

Christine Goerke *soprano*
Stephen Gould *tenor*

Royal Philharmonic Orchestra
Marc Albrecht *conductor*

Composer-themed evenings were a distinctive and popular feature of Henry Wood's early Proms seasons: if it was Monday, it was Wagner Night. We revive this tradition with a concert whose first half explores the enchanted forest (both beguiling and darkly supernatural) – a key symbol of the German Romantic movement. The second half presents pivotal scenes from *Götterdämmerung*, the climax of Wagner's four-opera magnum opus *The Ring of the Nibelung* – including Siegfried's Death and Funeral Music and the vocal tour de force of Brünnhilde's Immolation Scene. *See 'Beyond the Bust', pages 8–13.*

PROMS PLUS TALK

5.45pm–6.25pm • Imperial College Union In the third of our series on Henry Wood, Hannah French considers the Proms founder-conductor's relationship with Wagner's music.

Edited version broadcast on BBC Radio 3 during tonight's interval

Tuesday 10 September

PROM 69
7.00pm–c9.10pm • Royal Albert Hall

PRICE BAND C

ELENA STIKHINA

Smetana The Bartered Bride – overture and Three Dances *19'*

Tchaikovsky Eugene Onegin – Letter Scene *12'*
Henry Wood Novelties: UK premiere, 1892

INTERVAL

Shostakovich Symphony No. 8 in C minor *65'*
Henry Wood Novelties: UK premiere, 1944

Elena Stikhina *soprano*

Czech Philharmonic
Semyon Bychkov *conductor*

The dancing rhythms and swirling colours of Smetana's opera *The Bartered Bride* launch a concert of big musical gestures and even bigger emotions. First love blazes hot in the Letter Scene from Tchaikovsky's opera *Eugene Onegin*, as Tatyana (sung here by soprano Elena Stikhina) pours out her heart in music as romantic as anything the composer ever wrote. War, not love, drives the pulsing heartbeat of Shostakovich's Eighth Symphony – the most personal and direct of the composer's many attempts 'to express the terrible tragedy of war'. *See 'Beyond the Bust', pages 8–13.*

PROMS PLUS TALK
5.15pm–5.55pm • Imperial College Union Bestselling crime novelist Ruth Ware and epistolary historian Shaun Usher discuss the function of letters in literature and life.
Edited version broadcast on BBC Radio 3 during tonight's interval

Spotlight on ... Pianists

Leif Ove Andsnes • Prom 18

When Leif Ove Andsnes gave his very first performance at the BBC Proms, he chose to play Britten's Piano Concerto. That was back in 1992, when the Norwegian pianist was 22. Now he's bringing the piece back to the Royal Albert Hall and it will, he says, 'be wonderful to return!' Particularly, he adds, as he'll be working with Edward Gardner, currently Chief Conductor of the Bergen Philharmonic, the orchestra in Andsnes's home town.

Andsnes first got to know Britten's Piano Concerto through the recording the composer himself conducted, with Sviatoslav Richter at the keyboard. 'I started loving and playing the concerto when I was 21, 22 – before I learnt the Beethoven concertos. I wanted to champion not so well-known pieces.' Written when Britten was 24 as a showcase for his own piano playing, the concerto is 'full of young man's ambition and virtuosic display'. Andsnes greatly admires the British composer's playing, captured in his mature recordings of songs and chamber music: 'He was so sensitive, full of colour and characterisation. It would be so interesting to have recordings of his playing when he was young.' The spirit of his playing is, however, encapsulated in the concerto. 'It always pleases audiences,' says Andsnes. 'It's an exuberant, sunny piece. Although there are shadows and loneliness, it's lively and optimistic.'

Alexander Ghindin • Prom 41

'It's a concerto composed by a young, really talented person, who is not beaten by life. It's by the guy who feels everything is ahead,' says Alexander Ghindin of Rachmaninov's First Piano Concerto. Completed in 1891, the piece was given its world premiere at the Proms in 1900, under the baton of Henry Wood. Rachmaninov later revised it, but Ghindin will be playing his preferred first version this summer.

'It's full of influences from Tchaikovsky, Grieg, Chopin – all the composers he played while he was studying,' says Ghindin. 'He wrote melody for melody's sake. In this concerto the melodies are so pure and full of energy.' By the time of the 1917 revision, Rachmaninov had become, in Stravinsky's words, the six-foot scowl. 'The language is very chromatically complicated and pessimistic,' notes Ghindin of the later version. 'In his youth, melody was like a song.' Why then has the First Concerto been so ignored? 'Compare it to the Second Concerto, which is more mature, more "perfect",' says Ghindin, who has given live concert cycles of all four Rachmaninov concertos and has recorded the original First. 'In the First Concerto, there's better and worse. The Second is composed by God working through a person, the First is composed just by a person. But because of that it's very interesting, very personal.'

Spotlight on … Proms Debut Artists

Danae Kontora • Prom 65

soprano

'Should I be nervous?' laughs soprano Danae Kontora, looking ahead to her BBC Proms debut. 'It's a big deal, I know. I always wondered: would I sing there one day? What would it be like?' The Greek-born singer is a fast-rising star on both concert and opera stages, but her programme – virtuosic coloratura arias by Mozart and Richard Strauss – understandably induced some apprehension. 'I was amazingly excited and terrified at the same time. In one way, it's cut out for me, but these pieces are so technical and so emotional, and I'll need huge stamina.'

Her two Mozart insertion arias bring to her mind the volatile music of *The Magic Flute*'s Queen of the Night, a role she's sung several times. 'You can never overestimate that part, but, because I've done it so much, it doesn't feel like a threat. These arias are like huge versions of what the Queen sings.' She is also singing Zerbinetta's aria from Strauss's *Ariadne auf Naxos*. 'Strauss is one of my favourite composers, so it kind of comes naturally: my voice knows how to work on it.'

What's the difference between performing in an opera house and in concert? 'In the opera house you create the character with your acting, gestures, movement and voice. In a concert you need to pour all of that into your voice. It's tricky, but very interesting. Plus in a concert you get to choose your own dress!'

Cristian Măcelaru • Prom 48

conductor

When Romanian conductor Cristian Măcelaru makes his debut at the Proms, he'll be bringing a piece from his home country. 'The Three Pieces for strings by Constantin Silvestri is a wonderful, charming work,' he says. 'It's based on Romanian folk music and it lies somewhere between Bartók and Ligeti. Silvestri is best known in the UK for conducting the Bournemouth Symphony Orchestra, but he was a fabulous composer too.'

There's also a personal connection to Rachmaninov's Symphony No. 2, as Măcelaru has worked extensively with the Philadelphia Orchestra, with whom the composer was closely associated. 'I had the opportunity to look in the library at Rachmaninov's own scores,' he explains. 'I have never seen such perfect calligraphy, penmanship and handwriting. It was flawless. It made me look at the music differently.' Măcelaru now values the music's nobility: 'It has this royal quality. It's full of passion, but it's implied rather than overtly exposed.' He also feels Rachmaninov's music needs the flexibility at which the BBC SO excels. 'It's the kind of piece where one needs to respond to the feeling on stage,' he says. And there's another reason he's looking forward to working again with these musicians: 'I enjoy the occasional tongue-in-cheek joke and I love the dry humour of the British ensembles!'

Tuesday 10 September

PROM 70 • LATE NIGHT

10.15pm–c11.30pm • Royal Albert Hall

PRICE BAND F

DANIEL PIORO

Biber Mystery (Rosary) Sonatas No. 16 – Passacaglia in G minor *6'*

Krzysztof Penderecki Sinfonietta for strings – Vivace *5'*

Jonny Greenwood
Three Miniatures from Water – No. 3 *5'*
88 (No. 1) *7'*

Steve Reich Pulse *15'*

Jonny Greenwood Horror vacui – for solo violin and 68 strings *c22'*
BBC commission: world premiere

Daniel Pioro *violin*
Katherine Tinker *piano*
Jonny Greenwood *bass guitar/tanpura*

BBC Proms Youth Ensemble
BBC National Orchestra of Wales
Hugh Brunt *conductor*

There will be no interval

Jonny Greenwood's talents range from being lead guitarist of Radiohead to writing award-winning film scores. Here he curates a Late Night Prom culminating in the world premiere of his *Horror vacui*, which explores characteristics of electronically created music and transfers them into the acoustic arena. The programme includes Biber's almost Bachian Passacaglia for solo violin and Minimalist master Steve Reich's radiantly throbbing *Pulse*. *See 'New Directions', pages 42–47; 'A Vehicle for Virtuosity?', pages 64–69.*

Broadcast on BBC Four on Friday 13 September

Wednesday 11 September

PROM 71
7.30pm–c9.45pm • Royal Albert Hall

PRICE BAND A

JOHN BUTT

Bach Night

J. S. Bach
Orchestral Suite No. 4 in D major, BWV 1069 *19'*
Orchestral Suite No. 1 in C major, BWV 1066 *21'*

INTERVAL

J. S. Bach
Orchestral Suite No. 2 in B minor, BWV 1067 *20'*
Orchestral Suite No. 3 in D major, BWV 1068 *20'*

interspersed with four new works inspired by dance movements from the suites, from Stuart MacRae, Nico Muhly, Ailie Robertson and Stevie Wishart (BBC co-commissions with the Dunedin Consort: world premieres)

Dunedin Consort
John Butt *conductor*

Bach specialist John Butt and his period-instrument Dunedin Consort continue our series of composer-themed nights as a tribute to Proms founder-conductor Henry Wood. They pair Bach's four Orchestral Suites with four newly commissioned works taking inspiration from the suites' dance movements – providing both companions and contrasts. *See 'Beyond the Bust', pages 8–13.*

FRONT ROW
5.15pm–5.45pm • Imperial College Union Join the audience for a special edition of *Front Row*, BBC Radio 4's arts programme, with news from the worlds of art, literature, film and music.
Recorded by BBC Radio 4 for broadcast this evening at 7.15pm

Thursday 12 September

PROMS 72 & 73
7.00pm–c8.30pm & 10.15pm–c11.45pm
Royal Albert Hall

PRICE BAND B

NICHOLAS COLLON

Berlioz Symphonie fantastique (orchestral theatre staging) *80'*

Mathew Baynton *actor*
Blind Summit Theatre

Aurora Orchestra
Nicholas Collon *conductor*

There will be no interval

A diabolical witches' sabbath, a riotous ball, a march to the gallows and an unrequited passion make up the hallucinatory narrative of Berlioz's *Symphonie fantastique*. Inspired by the composer's own romantic infatuation with a young actress, the score is a cinematic fantasy full of tragedy and passion, a work teeming with orchestral drama – by turns gorgeous and grotesque. Nicholas Collon and the Aurora Orchestra perform this grandiose work from memory, in a specially devised production incorporating elements of design, lighting and choreography, as well as Berlioz's own words about his music. *See 'A Life with Berlioz', pages 36–41.*

Broadcast on BBC Four on Friday 13 September (Prom 73)
Broadcast live on BBC Radio 3 (Prom 72)

PROMS POETRY COMPETITION
4.55pm–5.55pm • Imperial College Union Poet Malika Booker joins host Ian McMillan, presenter of The Verb, and Judith Palmer, director of the Poetry Society, to judge this year's BBC Proms Poetry competition and hear the winning entries.
For further information, visit www.bbc.co.uk/proms.
Edited version broadcast later tonight on BBC Radio 3

Friday 13 September

PROM 74
7.30pm–c9.50pm • Royal Albert Hall

PRICE BAND C

ELIZABETH WATTS

Beethoven Night

Handel, arr. Manze Music for the Royal Fireworks *15'*

Beethoven Concert aria 'Ah! perfido' *13'*

J. S. Bach, arr. Elgar Fantasia and Fugue in C minor, BWV 537 *9'*

INTERVAL

Beethoven
Fidelio – overture *7'*
Fidelio – 'Abscheulicher! … Komm, Hoffnung, lass den letzten Stern' *8'*
Symphony No. 5 in C minor *35'*

Elizabeth Watts *soprano*

NDR Radiophilharmonie Hannover
Andrew Manze *conductor*

Proms founder-conductor Henry Wood's tradition of composer-themed nights continues here with Beethoven. The composer's revolutionary Fifth Symphony provides the climax of a programme that also includes music from his dramatic 'rescue' opera *Fidelio*. Bach's music was a passion shared by Beethoven and Wood, and is represented here by Elgar's orchestration of the Fantasia and Fugue in C minor for organ. *See 'Beyond the Bust', pages 8–13.*

PROMS PLUS TALK
5.45pm–6.25pm • Imperial College Union Beethoven's only opera, *Fidelio*, and his Fifth Symphony are two of his most iconic works. Benjamin Walton examines Beethoven's social standing in the early years of the 19th century.
Edited version broadcast on BBC Radio 3 during tonight's interval

Saturday 14 September

PROM 75
7.15pm–c10.30pm • Royal Albert Hall

PRICE BAND G

JAMIE BARTON

Last Night of the Proms 2019

Programme to include:

Daniel Kidane Woke c9'
BBC commission: world premiere

Falla The Three-Cornered Hat – Suite No. 2 13'

Elgar Sospiri 5'
Henry Wood Novelties: world premiere, 1914

Laura Mvula Sing to the Moon 4'

Bizet Carmen – 'L'amour est un oiseau rebelle' (Habanera) 2'

Saint-Saëns Samson and Delilah – 'Mon coeur s'ouvre à ta voix' 7'

Verdi
Don Carlos – 'O don fatale' 5'
Aida – Triumphal March 5'

Offenbach Orpheus in the Underworld – overture 9'

Grainger Marching Song of Democracy 7'

Maconchy Proud Thames 6'

Arlen The Wizard of Oz – 'Over the Rainbow' 5'

arr. Wood Fantasia on British Sea-Songs 17'

Arne, arr. Sargeant Rule, Britannia! 4'

Elgar Pomp and Circumstance March No. 1 in D major ('Land of Hope and Glory') 8'

Parry, orch. Elgar Jerusalem 2'

arr. Britten The National Anthem 3'

Trad., arr. Paul Campbell
Auld Lang Syne 2'

Jamie Barton *mezzo-soprano*

BBC Singers
BBC Symphony Chorus
BBC Symphony Orchestra
Sakari Oramo *conductor*

There will be one interval

From orchestral dances and marches to songs and arias, Offenbach's light-footed musical comedy to Verdi's operatic tragedies, world premieres to traditional favourites, this year's Last Night of the Proms is a spectacular climax to the world's largest classical music festival. Charismatic American mezzo-soprano Jamie Barton, whose lustrous voice has established her as one of the most exciting performers of her generation, joins Sakari Oramo and the BBC Symphony Orchestra and Chorus to lead the musical celebrations. *See 'Beyond the Bust', pages 8–13; 'New Directions', pages 42–47.*

First half live on BBC Two, second half live on BBC One

PROMS PLUS EVENT
5.00pm–5.45pm • Imperial College Union (Metric Bar) Join us for an informal look back at the 2019 BBC Proms season.

Saturday 14 September

PROMS IN THE PARK

Gates open 3.00pm • Entertainment from 5.00pm • Hyde Park, London

MICHAEL BALL

Michael Ball *presenter*

BBC Concert Orchestra
Richard Balcombe *conductor*

Join in the Last Night of the Proms celebrations in Hyde Park, hosted by Michael Ball. The open-air concert celebrates the night with a host of stars from the worlds of classical music, rock and pop, choirs and musical theatre – nearly 150 performers in all! Proms in the Park favourites, the 60-piece BBC Concert Orchestra, conducted by Richard Balcombe, will again perform all the traditional Last Night anthems live on the Hyde Park stage. Forty thousand voices will join them for the mass singalong as the evening brings to a close two months of music-making with a spectacular fireworks display.

Listen to BBC Radio 2 from Tuesday 23 April for announcements of headline artists and special guests.

Broadcast live on BBC Radio 2

Booking tickets

Tickets (£46.00 plus booking fee) available from 11.00am on Friday 26 April from the Royal Albert Hall. Ticket requests may also be included in the Proms Planner and submitted online from 9.00am on Saturday 11 May *(see page 163 for booking timetable).*

Online bbc.co.uk/promsinthepark

By phone from the Royal Albert Hall on 020 7070 4441 (a booking fee of 2% of the total value – plus £2.00 per ticket up to a maximum of £25.00 – applies for telephone bookings).

In person at the Royal Albert Hall Box Office (no fees apply to tickets bought in person).

By post see bbc.co.uk/proms.

For details of how to order a picnic hamper for collection on the day, or to find out about VIP packages and corporate hospitality, visit bbc.co.uk/promsinthepark.

Experience the Last Night magic around the UK!

Northern Ireland
Scotland
Wales

The BBC Proms in the Park events offer live concerts featuring high-profile artists, well-loved presenters and BBC Big Screen link-ups to the Royal Albert Hall, when you can join with audiences across the nations. So gather your friends and your Last Night spirit for an unforgettable evening.

Keep checking bbc.co.uk/promsinthepark for announcements of artists, venues and booking information.

Highlights of the Last Night celebrations around the UK will feature as part of the live television coverage of the Last Night on BBC One and BBC Two and you can watch more at bbc.co.uk/proms.

Booking

17 April

Create your Proms Plan online

On Wednesday 17 April, go to bbc.co.uk/proms and fill in your Proms Planner (which must be completed by 11.59pm on Friday 10 May)

9 May

Book your passes

From 9.00am on Thursday 9 May, book your Season and Weekend Promming Passes for the Royal Albert Hall or Proms at … Cadogan Hall Series Passes. (These are not included in the Proms Planner)

10 May

CBeebies and Relaxed Proms

From 9.00am on Friday 10 May, book your tickets for the CBeebies Proms (Proms 3 & 5), the Relaxed Prom (Prom 24) and The Lost Words (Prom 49), including a limited number of Promming tickets

11 May

General booking opens

From 9.00am on Saturday 11 May, submit your Proms Planner or book online via bbc.co.uk/proms, in person or by phone. See bbc.co.uk/proms for details of how to book

14 June

Book your Proms at … tickets and Proms Learning events

From 9.00am on Friday 14 June, book your tickets for Proms at … Battersea Arts Centre and Proms at … Holy Sepulchre London. Booking for the Proms Inspire Day (13 August), Proms Family Workshop (25 August) and Proms Family Orchestra & Chorus (26 August) opens at 10.00am

Online
bbc.co.uk/proms or royalalberthall.com

By phone
on 020 7070 4441 †

In person
at the Royal Albert Hall Box Office (no booking fee)

By post
BBC Proms, Box Office, Royal Albert Hall, London SW7 2AP ‡

BOOKING FEES
A booking fee of 2% of the total value – plus £2.00 per ticket (£1.00 per ticket for the Relaxed Prom) up to a maximum of £25.00 – applies to all bookings (including Season and Weekend Promming Passes), other than those made in person at the Royal Albert Hall.

† CALL COSTS
Standard geographic charges from landlines and mobiles will apply. All calls may be recorded and monitored for training and quality-control purposes.

‡ POSTAL BOOKINGS
General postal bookings will be processed from 9.00am on Saturday 11 May. Please see bbc.co.uk/proms for details required for all postal bookings.

Royal Albert Hall ticket prices

Seated tickets for all BBC Proms concerts at the Royal Albert Hall fall into one of eight price bands, indicated beside each concert listing on pages 121–160. For Promming, see page opposite.

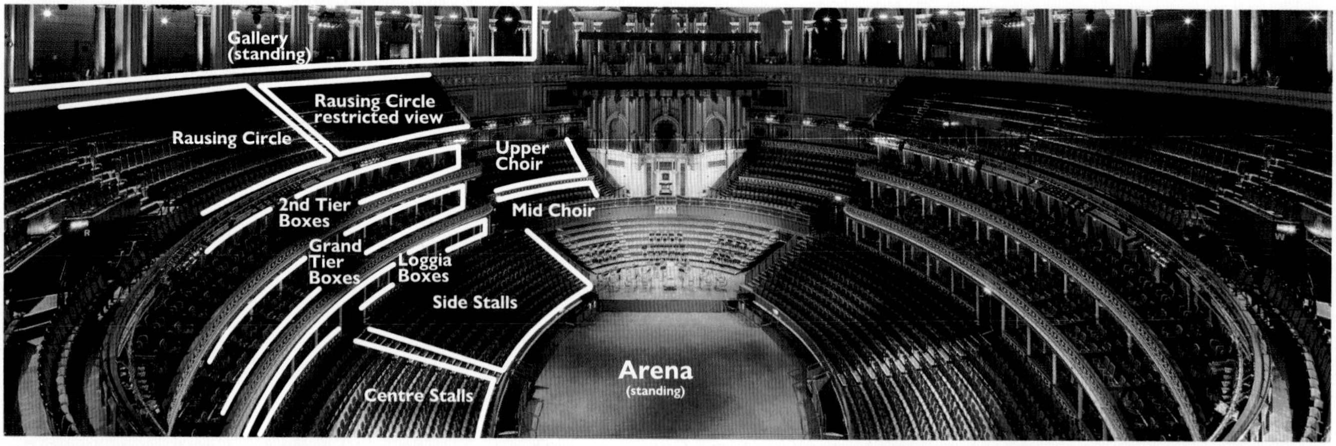

PRICE BANDS	A	B	C	D	E	F	G	H	
GRAND TIER BOXES 12 seats, price per seat*	£41.00	£52.00	£62.00	£72.00	£26.00	£35.00	£105.00	£20.00	Relaxed Prom: all tickets £12.00/ £6.00
LOGGIA AND 2ND TIER BOXES Loggia: 8 seats, price per seat 2nd Tier: 5 seats, price per seat	£36.00	£47.00	£57.00	£67.00	£26.00	£35.00	£100.00	£20.00	
CENTRE STALLS	£32.00	£42.00	£52.00	£64.00	£22.00	£30.00	£95.00	£16.00	
SIDE STALLS	£29.00	£39.00	£49.00	£59.00	£22.00	£30.00	£90.00	£16.00	
MID CHOIR	£26.00	£30.00	£34.00	£45.00	£22.00	£30.00	£65.00	£16.00	
UPPER CHOIR	£19.50	£22.00	£29.00	£38.00	£15.00	£20.00	£62.00	£12.00	
RAUSING CIRCLE FRONT	£19.50	£22.00	£29.00	£38.00	£15.00	£20.00	£62.00	£12.00	
RAUSING CIRCLE MID	£17.00	£20.00	£24.00	£30.00	£15.00	£20.00	£58.00	£12.00	
RAUSING CIRCLE REAR	£12.50	£15.50	£19.50	£25.00	£15.00	£20.00	£47.00	£12.00	
RAUSING CIRCLE RESTRICTED VIEW	£7.50	£9.50	£14.00	£18.00	£7.50	£10.00	£27.00	£7.50	

Please note: a booking fee of 2% of the total value – plus £2.00 per ticket (£1.00 per ticket for the Relaxed Prom) up to a maximum of £25.00 – applies to all bookings (including Season and Weekend Promming Passes), other than those made in person at the Royal Albert Hall. As the Royal Albert Hall approaches its 150th birthday in 2021, a multimillion-pound programme of restoration will be undertaken. In order to help fund this restoration, an optional £1.50 per ticket Restoration Levy will be added to tickets for concerts at the Royal Albert Hall only. *As most Grand Tier Boxes are privately owned, availability is limited.

Advance seats

There is a Prom for every music-lover, whether you're a first-timer or seasoned regular. To view the whole season at a glance, see our calendar on pages 122–123. Advance seats start at just £7.50 (plus booking fee).

Prom on the day for £6.00

The popular tradition of Promming (standing in the Arena or Gallery areas of the Royal Albert Hall) is central to the unique and informal atmosphere of the BBC Proms.

Up to 1,350 Promming (standing) places in the Arena and Gallery are available on the day of each concert, for just £6.00. A limited number of these tickets are released online between 9.00am and 12 noon and the rest are sold in person when the doors open.

Save by buying a Season or Weekend Promming Pass (exclusions apply).

Promming tickets for Proms at … venues are available on the day from each venue.

Online booking

The 'Select Your Own Seat' option is not available via the Proms Planner or during the first few days that Proms tickets are on sale. You will be allocated the best available places within your chosen seating area.

It is not possible to book entire boxes online. If you would like to book a complete box, call the Box Office on 020 7070 4441.

18s and under go half-price

Tickets for persons aged 18 and under can be purchased at half-price in any seating area for all Proms except the Last Night and in any price band (except for £6.00 tickets) at any venue.

Great savings for groups

Groups of 10 or more attending concerts at the Royal Albert Hall can claim a 5% discount on the price of selected tickets (not including the Last Night). Call the Group Booking Information line on 020 7070 4408 for details.

Proms at … Cadogan Hall

Stalls: £16.00, Centre Gallery: £13.00 (booking fees apply). Promming tickets are available on the day from Cadogan Hall, or purchase a Proms at … Cadogan Hall Series Pass.

Other 'Proms at …' concerts

Advance tickets can be bought from the Royal Albert Hall Box Office from Friday 14 June. See bbc.co.uk/proms for details of prices and how to buy Promming tickets on the day.

Last Night of the Proms

Owing to high demand, the majority of tickets for the Last Night of the Proms are allocated by ballot.

The Five-Concert Ballot

Customers who purchase tickets for at least five other concerts at the Royal Albert Hall are eligible to enter the Five-Concert Ballot. For details on how to enter, see bbc.co.uk/proms. The Five-Concert Ballot closes on **Thursday 6 June**.

If you require a wheelchair space for the Last Night of the Proms, you will still need to book for five other concerts, but you must phone the Access Information Line (020 7070 4410) by **Thursday 6 June** and ask to be entered into the separate ballot for wheelchair spaces.

The Open Ballot

One hundred Centre Stalls seats (priced £95.00 each, plus booking fee) and 100 Front Circle seats (priced £62.00 each, plus booking fee) for the Last Night of the Proms at the Royal Albert Hall will be allocated by Open Ballot, which closes on **Thursday 4 July**.

Please complete the official Open Ballot Form for 2019, which is available to download from bbc.co.uk/promstickets.

General availability for the Last Night

Any remaining tickets for the Last Night will go on sale at 9.00am on **Friday 12 July** by phone or online only. Only one application (for a maximum of two tickets) can be made per household. There is exceptionally high demand for Last Night tickets, but returns occasionally become available.

Promming at the Last Night

Whole Season Promming Passes include admission to the Last Night.

A limited allocation of Last Night tickets (priced £6.00) is also reserved for Prommers who have attended five or more concerts (in either the Arena or the Gallery). They are eligible to purchase one ticket each for the Last Night on presentation of their used tickets (which will be retained) at the Box Office. For details, see bbc.co.uk/proms.

On the night

A limited number of Promming tickets will be available on the Last Night itself (priced £6.00, one per person). No previous ticket purchases are necessary.

Proms in the Park

BBC Proms in the Park, Hyde Park, London, Saturday 14 September. Tickets (standard admission): £46.00 (booking fees apply). See bbc.co.uk/promsinthepark for details.

Visit bbc.co.uk/proms for full details of how to book, booking fees and terms and conditions

Tickets not available for your favourite Prom? Don't give up! Prom on the day for £6.00

At just £6.00, Promming tickets are available on the day and can be purchased in person by cash or contactless payment.

Buy Promming tickets online

A limited number of Promming tickets are released online between 9.00am and 12.00pm on the day of each concert.

All Promming tickets purchased online are subject to a booking fee of 2% of the total value plus £1.00 per ticket.

How to Prom

Visit bbc.co.uk/proms for our guide to Promming, including limited Promming places for wheelchair-users and ambulant disabled concert-goers.

Promming is easy!

Just turn up, queue, take your place in the magnificent Royal Albert Hall and enjoy world-class performances from just a few feet away (subject to availability).

Booking

Access at the Proms

ACCESS INFORMATION LINE
020 7070 4410 (9.00am–9.00pm daily).

Full information on the facilities offered to disabled concert-goers at the Royal Albert Hall is available online at royalalberthall.com or by calling the Access Information Line. The Royal Albert Hall has a Silver award from the Attitude is Everything Charter of Best Practice.

All disabled concert-goers (and one companion) receive a 50% discount on all ticket prices (except Arena and Gallery areas) for concerts at the Royal Albert Hall and Cadogan Hall. To book, call the Access Information Line on 020 7070 4410 or purchase in person at the Royal Albert Hall.

Twenty spaces are bookable for wheelchair-users with adjacent companion seats for the majority of concerts. To book, please call the Access Information Line or visit the Royal Albert Hall Box Office in person.

Six additional Side Stalls wheelchair spaces are available for Proms 56–75 from Saturday 31 August.

For information on wheelchair spaces available for the Last Night of the Proms via the Five-Concert Ballot, see page 165.

The Gallery can accommodate up to four wheelchair-users.

A limited number of seats are available in the Arena and Gallery for reservation each day by ambulant disabled Prommers: see bbc.co.uk/proms for details.

A limited number of car parking spaces for disabled concert-goers can be reserved close to the Hall; please contact the Access Information Line to book.

Ramped venue access is available at Doors 1, 3, 8, 9 and 12. The most convenient set-down points for vehicle arrival are near Doors 3 and 9.

Public lifts are located at Doors 1 and 8.

All bars and restaurants are wheelchair-accessible.

Other services available on request:
The Royal Albert Hall auditorium has an infra-red system with a number of personal headsets for use with or without hearing aids. Headsets can be collected on arrival from the Information Desk on the Ground Floor at Door 6.

Assistance dogs are very welcome and can be easily accommodated in the boxes. If you prefer to sit elsewhere, please call the Access Information Line for advice. The Royal Albert Hall stewards will be happy to look after your dog while you enjoy the concert.

Transfer wheelchairs are available for customer use. The Royal Albert Hall has busy corridors and therefore visitors using mobility scooters are asked to enter via Door 3 or Door 8 and will be offered a transfer wheelchair on arrival. Scooters can be stored in designated places. We are unable to offer charging facilities for scooters.

To request any of the above services, please call the Access Information Line or complete an accessibility request form online at royalalberthall.com 48 hours before you attend. Alternatively you can make a request upon arrival at the Information Desk at Door 6, subject to availability.

Assisted Proms
The CBeebies Proms (Proms 3 and 5) and the Relaxed Prom (Prom 24) will be British Sign Language-interpreted. Please book your tickets online in the usual way. If you require good visibility of the signer, please choose the Stalls Signer Area online when selecting your tickets, or call the Access Information Line and request this area.

For information about the Relaxed Prom, including Audio Description services, visit bbc.co.uk/proms.

BBC Proms Festival Guide – audio, Braille and large-print formats

Audio CD (read by BBC Radio presenters and authors) and Braille versions of this Festival Guide are available in two parts, 'Articles' and 'Concert Listings/Booking Information', priced £3.50 each. For more information and to order, call the RNIB Helpline on 0303 123 9999.

A text-only large-print version of this Festival Guide is available, priced £7.00.

To order, please call Deborah Fether on 07716 225658, or email PromsPublications@bbc.co.uk. (Allow 10 working days for delivery.)

BBC Proms concert programmes in large print

Large-print concert programmes can be purchased on the night (at the same price as the standard programme), if ordered at least five working days in advance.

Large-print sung texts and opera librettos (where applicable) are available with the purchase of a standard programme, if ordered at least five working days in advance. To order, please call Deborah Fether on 07716 225658, or email PromsPublications@bbc.co.uk.

The programmes and texts will be left for collection at the Door 6 Merchandise Desk one hour before the start of the concert.

A Royal Albert Hall steward will be happy to read excerpts of the concert programme to visually impaired visitors. Please call the Access Information Line or complete an accessibility request form online at royalalberthall.com 48 hours before you attend.

Royal Albert Hall

Kensington Gore, London SW7 2AP
www.royalalberthall.com • 020 7070 4441

The Royal Albert Hall of Arts and Sciences was officially opened by Queen Victoria on 29 March 1871. When, in 1867, Victoria laid the foundation stone for the building (which today can be found underneath K stalls, row 11, seat 87 in the main auditorium), she announced that it was to be named after her husband Prince Albert, who had died six years previously.

The Grade I listed building is encircled by an 800-foot mosaic frieze that depicts the advancement of the Arts and Sciences of all nations and topped by a glazed-iron roof that measures 20,000 square feet.

The world's leading figures in music, dance, sport and politics have appeared on stage at the Royal Albert Hall since it opened, including members of the Women's Social and Political Union (the suffragettes), Albert Einstein, Muhammad Ali and Winston Churchill. The BBC Proms moved to the Royal Albert Hall in 1941, after the Queen's Hall was gutted by fire in an air raid. The Hall has since hosted over 4,500 Proms concerts.

Eleven Royal Albert Hall Stars – stones engraved with the names of prominent characters and events from the Hall's history – were launched last year. This walk of fame under the canopy of the building includes Adele, Shirley Bassey, Eric Clapton and, of course, the BBC Proms.

Latecomers
Latecomers will only be admitted if and when there is a suitable break in the performance.

Security
Please do not bring large bags to the Royal Albert Hall. All bags and visitors may be subject to security checks as a condition of entry.

Children under 5
Children under 5 are welcome at the CBeebies Proms (Proms 3 and 5) and the Relaxed Prom (Prom 24). Out of consideration for audience and artists, we recommend that children attending other Proms are aged 5 and over.

Dress code
Come as you are: there is no dress code at the Proms.

Proms merchandise and programmes
Merchandise is available at Doors 6 and 12 and on the Rausing Circle level at Doors 4 and 8. Programmes are on sale throughout the building. Merchandise and programmes are also available online at shop.royalalberthall.com.

South Kensington (Piccadilly, Circle & District Lines – please note there are planned works at this station so check before you travel); Gloucester Road (Piccadilly, Circle & District Lines); High Street Kensington (Circle & District Lines)

Enjoy a wide range of food and drink from two and a half hours before each concert – see royalalberthall.com

Cloakroom available. A charge of £1.00 per item applies. Cloakroom season tickets, priced £20.40, are also available *(conditions apply – see royalalberthall.com)*

Wheelchair-accessible *(see page 166 for details)*

Beit Venues, Imperial College Union

Prince Consort Road, London SW7 2BB
www.beitvenues.org

Free pre-Prom events
Pre-concert events are held in the Concert Hall at Beit Venues, Imperial College Union. Family Workshops are held in the Dining Hall. Entry for all events is through Beit Quad, Prince Consort Road.

Pre-concert events are free of charge and unticketed (seating is unreserved), with the exception of selected recordings of radio programmes as detailed in the concert listings, for which free tickets will be available from BBC Studio Audiences (bbc.co.uk/showsandtours/shows).

Places must be reserved in advance for the Proms Family Workshop on Sunday 25 August . Visit bbc.co.uk/proms or call 020 7765 0557.

Please note: prommers who have joined the Royal Albert Hall queue and wish to attend a pre-Prom event should make sure they take a numbered slip from one of the Royal Albert Hall stewards to secure their place back in the queue in time for doors opening. Event times vary, so please check concert listings before you attend.

Seating at Beit Venues, Imperial College Union, is limited and all pre-Prom events are subject to capacity. We advise arriving early for the more popular events. Latecomers will be admitted where possible but, as many of these events are recorded for broadcast, you may have to wait until a suitable break. The event stewards will guide you.

- See Royal Albert Hall *(opposite)*
- Bar on site
- Cloakroom available
- Wheelchair-accessible

Cadogan Hall

5 Sloane Terrace, London SW1X 9DQ
www.cadoganhall.com • 020 7730 4500

The Cadogan Hall concert hall opened in June 2004, taking over the building in Sloane Square that housed the congregation of the New Christian Science Church from 1907 until 1996.

Although an organ installed in 1911 was dismantled and transferred to another church in the Midlands, its casing was put in store, along with timber panelling and balustrading, during the building's conversion to a performance space. Once restored, the organ screen was discovered to have unique column capitals and carvings around the arching balustrade, adding to the building's rich character.

The stained-glass windows at Cadogan Hall were designed by the Danish nobleman Baron Arild Rosenkrantz, who learnt his craft while working at Tiffany in New York. There are no allegorical images in the windows, featuring instead simple Celtic knot motifs.

The Royal Philharmonic Orchestra is resident at Cadogan Hall and the venue has hosted the BBC Proms Monday-lunchtime chamber music series every year since 2005.

- Sloane Square (Circle & District Lines)
- Bar on site
- Cloakroom available
- Wheelchair-accessible

Booking

Battersea Arts Centre

Lavender Hill, London SW11 5TN
www.bac.org.uk • 020 7223 2223

Battersea Arts Centre is the guardian of the former Battersea Town Hall, built in 1893 by Edward Mountford. The building was a focal point in the early days of the Trade Union movement, Independent Labour Party and the campaign for women's suffrage. It has hosted influential activists and artists from Emmeline Pankhurst to The Jam, Paul Robeson to Grayson Perry and Stewart Lee to Stormzy.

A local campaign to save the building from demolition in 1965 resulted in its Grade II* listing in 1970. It has been an arts centre since 1974 and an independent arts theatre since 1981, welcoming over 160,000 people a year to its performances, projects, workshops and events.

Battersea Arts Centre's Grand Hall was severely damaged in a major fire in 2015, although its large Hope-Jones pipe organ was off-site for cleaning and has since been restored. The Grand Hall repoened in September last year after an extensive refurbishment led by architects Haworth Tompkins.

- Clapham Junction (Overground); Clapham Common (Northern Line); Stockwell (Victoria Line)
- Bar on site
- Cloakroom available
- Wheelchair-accessible

Holy Sepulchre London

Holborn Viaduct, London EC1A 2DQ
www.hsl.church • 020 7236 1145

There has been a worshipping community at Holy Sepulchre since 1137 and its ministers have included the 16th-century Bible-translator John Rogers.

The current building dates from *c*1450 but the interior was completely rebuilt after it was gutted in the Great Fire of London in 1666.

There are two significant chapels in the church, The Royal Fusiliers Chapel (dedicated in 1950) in the south-east of the church and The Musicians' Chapel (dedicated in 1955) on the north side of the Nave.

Henry Wood, founder-conductor of the Proms, learnt the organ at the church as a teenager and his ashes were interred there in 1955. He is depicted in a stained-glass memorial window above his grave.

- City Thameslink; St Paul's (Central Line); Blackfriars (District & Circle Lines)
- Wheelchair-accessible

FOR TICKET PRICES, SEE PAGE 164

BBC Proms
BBC Proms

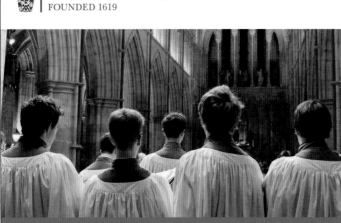

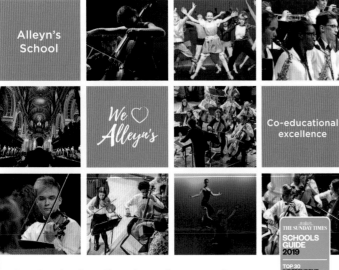

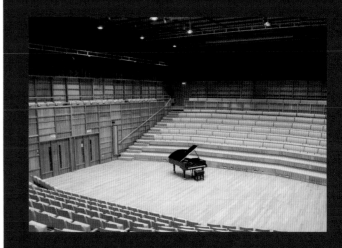

Music Scholarships available
• World class facilities
• Outstanding opportunities
• Bespoke music pathways
• Specialist provision
• Ensemble excellence
• Thriving concert programme
For more information please call Admissions on 01458 444296 or email admissions@millfieldschool.com
millfieldmusic.com
MILLFIELD

ST GEORGE'S SCHOOL WINDSOR CASTLE
Day and boarding school for girls and boys aged 3-13 and home to the Choristers of St George's Chapel
Love Learning
Music Scholarships are offered from Year 5
Join us at one of our Open Mornings or contact registrar@stgwindsor.org to arrange an individual tour
www.stgwindsor.org/admissions | 01753 865553

Imagine
@Music_WHS
Music Scholarships at 11+ and 16+
WIMBLEDON HIGH SCHOOL
EX HUMILIBUS EXCELSA
GDST
Registered charity no. 306983

Oakham
SCHOOL
"A clear-eyed, energetic, forward-thinking school" - The Good Schools Guide
Music scholarships offered at 11+ 13+ and 16+
Looking for a top music school?
We are a fully co-educational boarding and day school for 10-18 year olds, offering the IB Diploma and A-Levels, located in the heart of rural England.
Come and see us:
admissions@oakham.sch.uk
01572 758758
oakham.rutland.sch.uk/Arrange-A-Visit

MERCHANT TAYLORS'
School
Music Scholarships for instrumentalists and singers at 11+ 13+ 16+
www.mtsn.org.uk
Coaches: Hampstead, Highgate, Ealing & St John's Wood
Moor Park (Baker Street 35 minutes)
Merchant Taylors' School, Sandy Lodge, Northwood, Middlesex HA6 2HT
Tel. +44 (0)1923 845514
Email. admissions@mtsn.org.uk
Excellence, integrity and distinction since 1561
For boys 3 - 18

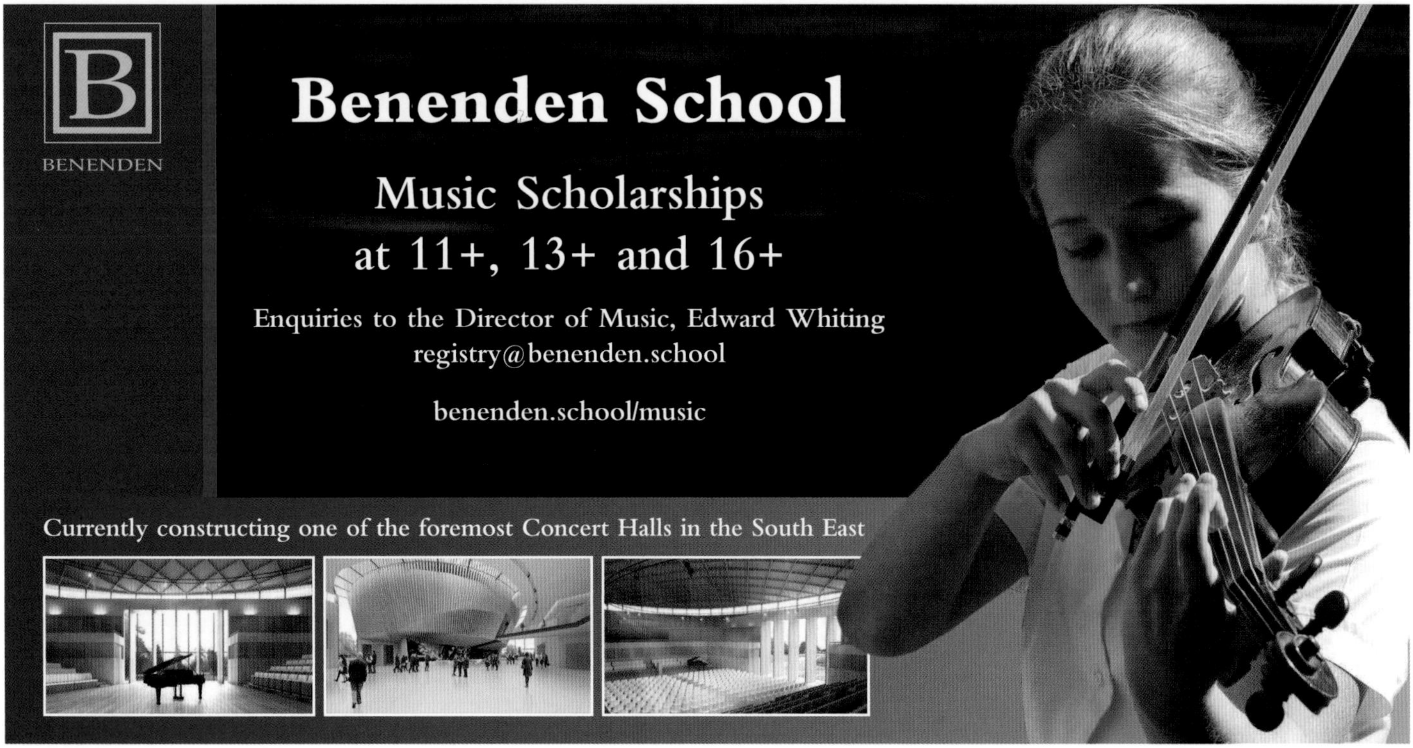

B
BENENDEN
Benenden School
Music Scholarships at 11+, 13+ and 16+
Enquiries to the Director of Music, Edward Whiting
registry@benenden.school
benenden.school/music
Currently constructing one of the foremost Concert Halls in the South East

Index of Artists

Bold italic *figures refer to Prom numbers*

P@CH *'Proms at … Cadogan Hall' chamber music concerts, 1.00pm Mondays*
P@BAC *'Proms at … Battersea Arts Centre', Saturday 27 July*
P@HSL *'Proms at … Holy Sepulchre London', Saturday 17 August*

**first appearance at a BBC Henry Wood Promenade Concert*
†current / ‡former member of BBC Radio 3's New Generation Artists scheme

A —

Krystian Adam *tenor* ***59***
Justin Adams* *guitar* ***62***
Timo Alakotila* *harmonium* ***20***
Leonardo García Alarcón* *harpsichord/organ/director* ***P@CH 2***
Marc Albrecht *conductor* ***68***
Louise Alder *soprano* ***P@CH 5***
Monty Alexander* *piano* ***54***
Robert Ames *conductor* ***27***
Nathaniel Anderson-Frank* *violin* ***56***
Leif Ove Andsnes *piano* ***18***
Martha Argerich *piano* ***34***
Thomas Atkins* *tenor* ***51***

B —

Daniel Barenboim *conductor* ***34***
Jamie Barton *mezzo-soprano* ***75***
Lisa Batiashvili‡ *violin* ***17***
Mariam Batsashvili*† *piano* ***42***
Mathew Baynton* *actor* ***72, 73***
Joshua Bell *violin* ***2***
Stephen Bell *conductor* ***11***
Nicola Benedetti *violin* ***12***
Nadine Benjamin* *soprano* ***35***
Jeroen Berwaerts* *trumpet* ***9***
Kristian Bezuidenhout *harpsichord* ***P@CH 3***
Jeanine De Bique *soprano* ***55***
Martyn Brabbins *conductor* ***35***
Sarah-Jane Brandon* *soprano* ***14***
YolanDa Brown *presenter* ***3, 5***
Hugh Brunt *conductor* ***70***
Jules Buckley *conductor* ***45, 64***
Björn Burger *baritone* ***51***
Sophia Burgos* *soprano* ***59***
John Butt *conductor* ***71***
Semyon Bychkov *conductor* ***33, 69***

C —

Karina Canellakis *conductor* ***1***
Constantinos Carydis* *conductor* ***65***
Elim Chan* *conductor* ***39***
Stephanie Childress* *violin* ***49***
Seong-Jin Cho* *piano* ***48***
Myung-Whun Chung *conductor* ***63***
Allan Clayton‡ *tenor* ***37, 55***
Oliver Coates* ***P@BAC***
Nicholas Collon *conductor* ***72, 73***
Dame Sarah Connolly *mezzo-soprano* ***37, 53***
Jessica Cottis *conductor* ***49***
Neville Creed* *conductor* ***66***

D —

Thomas Dausgaard *conductor* ***19, 20***
Lise Davidsen *soprano* ***31***
Neal Davies *bass* ***37***
Sir Andrew Davis *conductor* ***53***
Joyce DiDonato *mezzo-soprano* ***32***
Esther Dierkes* *soprano* ***51***
Sunnyboy Dladla *tenor* ***26***
Oleg Dolgov* *tenor* ***28***

E —

Peter Edwards* *conductor* ***54***
Richard Egarr *harpsichord/conductor* ***55***
James Ehnes *violin* ***6***
Sir Mark Elder *conductor* ***37***
Ladislav Elgr* *tenor* ***1***
Peter Eötvös *conductor* ***8***

F —

Isabelle Faust *violin* ***8***
Neil Ferris* *conductor* ***43, 66***
Gerald Finley *baritone* ***44***
Adám Fischer *conductor* ***40***
Nora Fischer* *singer* ***67***
Alessandro Fisher*† *tenor* ***40***
Justin Fletcher *presenter* ***3, 5***
Mariana Flores *soprano* ***P@CH 2***
Sofia Fomina* *soprano* ***51***
Marta Fontanals-Simmons *mezzo-soprano* ***51***

G —

Sol Gabetta *cello* ***25***
Christina Gansch *soprano* ***33***
Sir John Eliot Gardiner *conductor* ***59***
Edward Gardner *conductor* ***6, 18***
Alexander Gavrylyuk *piano* ***23, 24***
Ben Gernon *conductor* ***23, 24***
Alexander Ghindin* *piano* ***41***
Christine Goerke *soprano* ***68***
Stephen Gould* *tenor* ***68***
Mirga Gražinytė-Tyla *conductor* ***46***
Jonny Greenwood* *bass guitar/tanpura* ***70***
Anthony Gregory* *tenor* ***53***
Asmik Grigorian* *soprano* ***1***

H —

Andreas Haefliger *piano* ***43***
Bernard Haitink *conductor* ***60***
Simon Halsey *conductor* ***66***
Håkan Hardenberger *trumpet* ***9***
Daniel Harding *conductor* ***50***
David Hockings* *percussion* ***13***
Nicolas Hodges *piano* ***13***
Taito Hoffrén* *singer* ***20***
Peter Holder* *organ* ***1***
Stephen Hough *piano* ***40***
Jakub Hrůša *conductor* ***2***
Benjamin Hulett *tenor* ***14***

I —

David Ireland* *bass-baritone* ***35***

J —

Mariss Jansons *conductor* ***15, 17***
Georgia Jarman* *soprano* ***58***
Chris Jarvis *presenter* ***3, 5***
Sofi Jeannin *conductor* ***P@HSL***
Jennifer Johnston‡ *mezzo-soprano* ***1***
Vladimir Jurowski *conductor* ***41***

K —

Sheku Kanneh-Mason *cello* ***46***
Kirill Karabits *conductor* ***4***
Mika Kares* *bass* ***43***
Leonidas Kavakos *violin* ***61***
Angélique Kidjo* *singer* ***16***
Anu Komsi *soprano* ***43***
Danae Kontora* *soprano* ***65***
Ilona Korhonen* *singer* ***20***
Michael Kraus *baritone* ***51***
Pekka Kuusisto *violin* ***20***

L —

Olivier Latry *organ* ***21***
Ledisi* ***45***
Paul Lewis *piano* ***52***
Eric Lu* *piano* ***57***

M —

Cristian Măcelaru* *conductor* ***48***
Katharina Magiera* *contralto* ***51***
Claudia Mahnke* *mezzo-soprano* ***18***
Vula Malinga* *vocals* ***64***
Antonello Manacorda* *conductor* ***51***
Andrew Manze *conductor* ***74***
Gary Matthewman* *piano* ***P@CH 5***
Leon McCawley *piano* ***56***
Tim Mead *counter-tenor* ***55***
Alexander Melnikov *piano* ***19***
Maddie Moate* *presenter* ***3, 5***
William Morgan* *tenor* ***35***
Catriona Morison*† *mezzo-soprano* ***39***
Idunnu Münch* *mezzo-soprano* ***35***

N —

Tareq Nazmi *bass* ***59***
Alex Neal* *percussion* ***13***
Andris Nelsons *conductor* ***47***
Angie Newman *British Sign Language Interpreter* ***3, 5, 49***

O —

Sakari Oramo *conductor* ***13, 43, 67, 75***
Andrés Orozco-Estrada *conductor* ***61***
Tadaaki Otaka *conductor* ***28***
Martin Owen *horn* ***13***
Eric Owens *bass-baritone* ***1***

P —

Sir Antonio Pappano *conductor* ***32***
Rafael Payare *conductor* ***42***
Murray Perahia *piano* ***60***
Rowan Pierce *soprano* ***55***
Daniel Pioro* *violin* ***70***
Christoph Pohl *baritone* ***14***
David Portillo* *tenor* ***51***

Q —

Cody Quattlebaum* *bass-baritone* ***55***

R —

Nemanja Radulović* *violin* ***4***
Sir Simon Rattle *conductor* ***44***
Brendan Reilly* *vocals* ***64***
Ashley Riches *bass-baritone* ***59***
Natalya Romaniw* *soprano* ***28***
Alison Rose *soprano* ***51***
Matthew Rose *bass* ***59***
Kathryn Rudge‡ *mezzo-soprano* ***26***
Alice Russell* *vocals* ***64***
Kwamé Ryan* *conductor* ***3, 5***

S —

Fatma Said* ‡ *soprano* ***26***
Esa-Pekka Salonen *conductor* ***31***
Cat Sandion* *presenter* ***3, 5***
Jörg Schneider *tenor* ***51***
Michael Schönheit* *organ* ***47***
Brindley Sherratt *bass* ***51***
David Shipley *bass* ***26***
Jason Singh *beatboxer* ***49***
Ballaké Sissoko* *kora* ***62***
Stuart Skelton *tenor* ***18***
Martin Snell* *baritone* ***51***
Yeol Eum Son* *piano* ***7***
Michael Spyres *tenor* ***59***
Christopher Stark *conductor* ***10***
Dalia Stasevska* *conductor* ***25***
Markus Stenz *conductor* ***9***
Elena Stikhina* *soprano* ***69***
John Storgårds *conductor* ***22***
Nathalie Stutzmann *conductor* ***26***
Hilary Summers *contralto* ***43, 55***
Wojciech Świtała* *piano* ***P@CH 7***
Mr Switch ***64***

T —

Minna-Liisa Tammela* *singer* ***20***
Stacey Tappan* *soprano* ***53***
David Temple *conductor* ***66***
Vilma Timonen* *kantele* ***20***
Katherine Tinker* *piano* ***70***
Bramwell Tovey *conductor* ***56***

V —

Ilan Volkov *conductor* ***58***

W —

Annette Walker* *tap dancer* ***54***
Jennifer Walshe* ***P@BAC***
Yuja Wang *piano* ***63***
Elizabeth Watts *soprano* ***74***
Michael Weinius *tenor* ***43***
Omer Meir Wellber* *conductor* ***7, 14***
Caroline Wettergreen* *soprano* ***51***
Mark Wigglesworth *conductor* ***12***
Ryan Wigglesworth *piano/ conductor* ***52, P@CH 8***
Roderick Williams *baritone* ***37***
John Wilson *conductor* ***29, 30***

Y —

Long Yu *conductor* ***57***

GROUPS

12 ensemble* ***36***
Amatis Piano Trio* † ***P@CH 6***
Aris Quartet* † ***P@CH 4***
Aurora Orchestra ***72, 73***
Bamberg Symphony Orchestra ***2***
Bavarian Radio Symphony Orchestra ***15, 17***
BBC Concert Orchestra ***11, 56***
BBC National Chorus of Wales ***26, 28***
BBC National Orchestra of Wales ***9, 26, 28, 39, 70***
BBC Philharmonic ***7, 14, 22, 23, 24***
BBC Proms Youth Choir ***14***
BBC Proms Youth Ensemble ***70***
BBC Scottish Symphony Orchestra ***19, 20, 35, 58***
BBC Singers ***1, 35, 54, 75, P@HSL***
BBC Symphony Chorus ***1, 43, 53, 66, 75***
BBC Symphony Orchestra ***1, 8, 13, 18, 25, 33, 43, 48, 53, 67, 75***
Blind Summit Theatre* ***72, 73***
Bournemouth Symphony Orchestra ***4***
Brass of the National Youth Orchestra of Great Britain ***32***
Britten Sinfonia ***52***
Britten Sinfonia Voices* ***37***
Canzoniere Grecanico Salentino* ***62***
Cappella Mediterranea* ***P@CH 2***
Carleen Anderson and the UK Vocal Assembly* ***54***
CBeebies Prom Choir* ***3, 5***
Chineke! ***3, 5***
City of Birmingham Symphony Orchestra ***46***
Crewdson & Cevanne* ***P@BAC***
Crouch End Festival Chorus ***66***
Czech Philharmonic ***69***
Deutsche Kammerphilharmonie Bremen ***65***
Dunedin Consort ***71***
The English Concert ***P@CH 3***
ENO Chorus ***35***
Genesis Sixteen* ***37***
Gewandhausorchester Leipzig ***47***
Glyndebourne ***51***
Hallé ***37***
Heritage Orchestra ***64***
John Wilson Orchestra ***29, 30***
Knussen Chamber Orchestra* ***P@CH 8***
London Contemporary Orchestra ***27***
London International Gospel Choir* ***66***
London Philharmonic Choir ***66***
London Philharmonic Orchestra ***41***
London Symphony Chorus ***44, 66***
London Symphony Orchestra ***44***
The Lost Words – Spell Song* ***49***
LSO Community Choir* ***66***
Maida Vale Singers ***29, 30***
Metropole Orkest ***45***
Monteverdi Choir ***59***
The Multi-Story Orchestra ***10***
National Youth Choir of Great Britain ***49***
National Youth Orchestra of Great Britain ***12***
National Youth Orchestra of the USA ***32***
NDR Radiophilharmonie Hannover ***74***
Nu Civilisation Orchestra* ***54***
Orchestre de Paris ***50***
Orchestra of the Age of Enlightenment ***40, 51***
Orchestra of the Royal Academy of Music and The Juilliard School ***6***
Orchestre Révolutionnaire et Romantique ***59***
Orfeó Català ***44***
Orfeó Català Youth Choir* ***44***
Philharmonia Chorus ***28***
Philharmonia Orchestra ***31***
Public Service Broadcasting* ***10***
Royal Philharmonic Orchestra ***68***
SCO Chorus* ***55***
Scottish Chamber Orchestra ***55***
Shanghai Symphony Orchestra* ***57***
Silesian String Quartet* ***P@CH 7***
Singapore Symphony Orchestra* ***57***
Solomon's Knot* ***38***
Soul Mavericks* ***64***
Southbank Sinfonia* ***49***
Staatskapelle Dresden ***63***
Tenebrae ***36***
Trinity Boys Choir ***4***
Ulster Orchestra ***42***
Vienna Philharmonic ***60, 61***
VOCES8* ***P@CH 1***
West–Eastern Divan Orchestra ***34***
Will Gregory Moog Ensemble* ***11***

'The Henry Wood Effect' image credits *(see inside front cover)*
Bridgeman Images (young Henry Wood); Chris Christodoulou/BBC (Proms Youth Ensemble, Prom 44, 2017; BBC Radio 3's Petroc Trelawny); Mirrorpix/Bridgeman Images (Henry Wood conducting); Julie Howden (Catriona Morison); Dorling Kindersley/UIG/ Bridgeman Images (Holy Sepulchre London); Saara Salmi (Outi Tarkiainen); BBC (Henry Wood); Kirsten McTernan/BBC (Donna Williams, Prom 59, 2018); Roberto Herrett/Alamy (Queen's Hall plaque); Chris Christodoulou/Bridgeman Images (Henry Wood bust)

Index of Works

A —

Hans Abrahamsen *(born 1952)*
Herbstlied* ***P@CH 8***
John Adams *(born 1947)*
Short Ride in a Fast Machine ***3, 4, 5***
John Luther Adams *(born 1953)*
In the Name of the Earth*[4] ***66***
Kalevi Aho *(born 1949)*
Pictured Within: Birthday Variations for M. C. B. – Variation 12*[1] ***35***
Prince Albert of Saxe-Coburg and Gotha *(1819–61)*
Songs* ***40***
Dieter Ammann *(born 1962)*
Piano Concerto*[2] ***43***
Louis Andriessen *(born 1939)*
The Only One*[3] ***67***
Harold Arlen *(1905–86)*
Blues in the Night – excerpt* ***29, 30***
The Wizard of Oz – 'Over the Rainbow' ***75***
Thomas Arne *(1710–78)*
Rule, Britannia! (arr. Sargent) ***75***
Malcolm Arnold *(1921–2006)*
Peterloo Overture ***23***
Lera Auerbach *(born 1973)*
Icarus*[6] ***12***

B —

Grażyna Bacewicz *(1909–69)*
Piano Quintet No. 1* ***P@CH 7***
Johann Sebastian Bach *(1685–1750)*
Cantata No. 19 'Es erhub sich ein Streit', BWV 19* ***38***
Cantata No. 50 'Nun ist das Heil und die Kraft', BWV 50 ***38***
Cantata No. 130 'Herr Gott, dich loben alle wir', BWV 130* ***38***
Cantata No. 147 'Herz und Mund und Tat und Leben', BWV 147 – Chorale 'Jesus bleibet meine Freude' (transcr. Schmidt-Mannheim)* ***47***
Cantata No. 149 'Man singet mit Freuden vom Sieg', BWV 149 ***38***
Chorale Prelude 'Wachet auf, ruft uns die Stimme', BWV 645 ***47***
Fantasia and Fugue in C minor, BWV 537 (arr. Elgar) ***74***
Fantasia in G minor, BWV 542 ***47***
Orchestral Suites Nos. 1–4, BWV 1066–9 ***71***
Prelude and Fugue in E flat major, BWV 552 ***47***
Toccata and Fugue in D minor, BWV 565 ***21***
Samuel Barber *(1910–81)*
Violin Concerto ***4***
Béla Bartók *(1881–1945)*
Dance Suite † ***8***
Sally Beamish *(born 1956)*
Pictured Within: Birthday Variations for M. C. B. – Variation 3*[1] ***35***
Benjamin Beckman *(born 2000)*
new work*[5] ***32***
Ludwig van Beethoven *(1770–1827)*
Adagio in F major (for mechanical clock)* ***21***
Concert aria 'Ah! perfido' ***74***
Fidelio – 'Abscheulicher! … Komm Hoffnung, lass den letzten Stern'; overture ***74***
Piano Concerto No. 4 in G major ***60***
Symphony No. 1 in C major ***42***
Symphony No. 2 in D major ***15***
Symphony No. 5 in C minor ***74***
Symphony No. 6 in F major, 'Pastoral' ***50***
Symphony No. 7 in A major ***65***
Symphony No. 9 in D minor, 'Choral' ***43***
Antonia Bembo *(c1640–c1720)*
Ercole amante – 'Mingannasti in verità'; 'Volgete altrove il guardo'* ***P@CH 2***
Paul Ben-Haim *(1897–1984)*
Symphony No. 1* ***7***
Hector Berlioz *(1803–69)*
Benvenuto Cellini ***59***
The Childhood of Christ ***37***
Les nuits d'été ***32***
Symphonie fantastique (orchestral theatre staging) ***72, 73***
Heinrich Ignaz Franz von Biber *(1644–1704)*
Mystery (Rosary) Sonatas No. 16 – Passacaglia in G minor* ***70***
Sir Harrison Birtwistle *(born 1934)*
Fantasia upon all the notes* ***P@CH 8***
Pictured Within: Birthday Variations for M. C. B. – Variation 9*[1] ***35***
Georges Bizet *(1838–75)*
Carmen – 'L'amour est un oiseau rebelle' (Habanera) ***75***
Richard Blackford *(born 1954)*
Pictured Within: Birthday Variations for M. C. B. – Variation 8*[1] ***35***
Alexander Borodin *(1833–87)*
Prince Igor – Polovtsian Dances † ***28***
Johannes Brahms *(1833–97)*
Song of Destiny ***35***
Symphony No. 1 in C minor ***9***
Symphony No. 2 in D major ***63***
Tragic Overture ***26***
Variations on the St Anthony Chorale ***31***
Benjamin Britten *(1913–76)*
Piano Concerto (revised version, 1945) † ***18***
Sacred and Profane ***P@HSL***
Violin Concerto ***6***
The Young Person's Guide to the Orchestra – Fugue (finale) ***3, 5***
arr. Britten
The National Anthem ***75***
Tobias Broström *(born 1978)*
Nigredo – Dark Night of the Soul*[3] ***9***
Anton Bruckner *(1824–96)*
Symphony No. 4 in E flat major, 'Romantic' (1878–80 version, ed. Nowak) ***31***
Symphony No. 7 in E major (ed. Nowak) ***60***
Symphony No. 8 in C minor (1890 version, ed. Haas) ***47***
Gavin Bryars *(born 1943)*
Pictured Within: Birthday Variations for M. C. B. – Variation 11*[1] ***35***
William Byrd *(c1540–1623)*
Sing joyfully* ***P@CH 1***

C —

Francesco Cavalli *(1602–76)*
Ercole amante – 'E vuol dunque Ciprigna'* ***P@CH 2***
Qigang Chen *(born 1951)*
Wu Xing (The Five Elements)* ***57***
Frédéric Chopin *(1810–49)*
Śliczny chłopiec* ***P@CH 5***
Życzenie* ***P@CH 5***
Aaron Copland *(1900–90)*
Fanfare for the Common Man ***3, 5***

D —

Brett Dean *(born 1961)*
Pictured Within: Birthday Variations for M. C. B. – Variation 6*[1] ***35***
Claude Debussy *(1862–1918)*
Prélude à l'après-midi d'un faune † ***8***
Préludes, Book 1 – La cathédrale engloutie (orch. Wood) ***56***
Zosha Di Castri *(born 1985)*
Long Is the Journey – Short Is the Memory*[1] ***1***
Jonathan Dove *(born 1959)*
new work*[1] ***43***
Vadam et circuibo civitatem* ***P@CH 1***
Antonín Dvořák *(1841–1904)*
The Golden Spinning Wheel ***1***
The Noonday Witch † ***61***
Symphony No. 9 in E minor, 'From the New World' ***61***
Violin Concerto in A minor ***2***

E —

Edward Elgar *(1857–1934)*
Cello Concerto in E minor ***46***
'Enigma' Variations ***35***
The Music Makers ***53***
Pomp and Circumstance March No. 1 in D major ('Land of Hope and Glory') ***75***
Sea Pictures ***39***
Sospiri † ***75***
Peter Eötvös *(born 1944)*
Alhambra (violin concerto)*[3] ***8***

F —

Manuel de Falla *(1876–1946)*
El amor brujo – Ritual Fire Dance (transcr. Latry) ***21***
The Three Cornered Hat – Suite No. 2 ***75***
César Franck *(1822–90)*
Le chasseur maudit ***68***
Dai Fujikura *(born 1977)*
Pictured Within: Birthday Variations for M. C. B. – Variation 1*[1] ***35***

G —

Orlando Gibbons *(1583–1625)*
O clap your hands ***P@CH1***
Eugène Gigout *(1844–1925)*
Air célèbre de la Pentecôte* ***21***
Detlev Glanert *(born 1960)*
Weites Land ('Musik mit Brahms' for orchestra)*[5] ***33***
Alexander Glazunov *(1865–1936)*
Symphony No. 5 in B flat major † ***41***
Percy Grainger *(1882–1961)*
Handel in the Strand (arr. Wood) ***56***
Marching Song of Democracy ***75***
Enrique Granados *(1867–1916)*
Danzas españolas – Andaluza (orch. Wood) ***56***
Jonny Greenwood *(born 1971)*
88 (No. 1)* ***70***
Horror vacui – for solo violin and 68 strings*[1] ***70***
Three Miniatures from Water – No. 3* ***70***
Sofia Gubaidulina *(born 1931)*
Fairytale Poem* ***42***

H —

George Frideric Handel *(1685–1759)*
Jephtha ***55***
Music for the Royal Fireworks (arr. Manze) ***74***
Trio Sonata in G major* ***P@CH 3***
Joseph Haydn *(1732–1809)*
The Creation ***14***
String Quartet in B flat major, 'Sunrise'* ***P@CH 4***
Wim Henderickx *(born 1962)*
Pictured Within: Birthday Variations for M. C. B. – Variation 7*[1] ***35***
Fanny Hensel *(1805–47)*
Bergeslust* ***P@CH 5***
Nach Süden* ***P@CH 5***
Warum sind denn die Rosen so blass?* ***P@CH 5***
Hildegard of Bingen *(1098–1179)*
Spiritus sanctus vivificans* ***P@CH 1***
Gustav Holst *(1874–1934)*
The Planets ***4***
Dorothy Howell *(1898–1982)*
Lamia † ***46***

I —

John Ireland *(1879–1962)*
The Holy Boy* ***P@HSL***
Piano Concerto † ***56***

J —

Élisabeth Jacquet de la Guerre *(1665–1729)*
Violin Sonata in D minor* **P@CH 3**
Leoš Janáček *(1854–1928)*
The Fiddler's Child † **58**
Glagolitic Mass (final version, 1928) † **1**
Josquin des Prez *(c1450/55–1521)*
Ave Maria … Virgo serena* **P@CH 1**

K —

Aram Khachaturian *(1903–78)*
Gayane – Sabre Dance (transcr.Kiviniemi) **21**
Daniel Kidane *(born 1986)*
Woke*[1] **75**
Oliver Knussen *(1952–2018)*
Songs without Voices* **P@CH 8**
Study for 'Metamorphosis'* **P@CH 8**
… upon one note – Fantasia after Purcell* **P@CH 8**
The Way to Castle Yonder* **46**
Charles Koechlin *(1867–1950)*
Les bandar-log **44**
Erich Wolfgang Korngold *(1897–1957)*
The Constant Nymph – excerpt* **29, 30**
The Sea Hawk – excerpt **29, 30**
Violin Concerto **61**
Jed Kurzel *(born 1976)*
Alien: Covenant – excerpt* **27**

L —

Orlande de Lassus *(1530/32–1594)*
Missa 'Bell'Amfitrit'altera' – Gloria* **P@CH 1**
Joanna Lee *(born 1982)*
At this man's hand*[1] **P@HSL**
Mica Levi *(born 1987)*
Under the Skin – excerpt* **27**
Franz Liszt *(1811–86)*
Comment, disaient-ils* **P@CH 5**
Freudvoll und Leidvoll **P@CH 5**
O lieb, so lang du lieben kannst **P@CH 5**
Oh, quand je dors **P@CH 5**
Prelude and Fugue on BACH (arr. Guillou) **21**
S'il est un charmant gazon* **P@CH 5**
Frederick Loewe *(1901–88)*
Camelot – excerpt **29, 30**
My Fair Lady – excerpt **29, 30**
Witold Lutosławski *(1913–94)*
Concerto for Orchestra **34**
Anatoly Lyadov *(1855–1914)*
Baba-Yaga † **41**
From the Apocalypse † **41**
Kikimora † **41**

M —

Sir James MacMillan *(born 1959)*
The Confession of Isobel Gowdie **19**
Elizabeth Maconchy *(1907–94)*
Proud Thames **75**
Three Donne Songs – No. 1: A Hymn to God the Father* **P@HSL**
Stuart MacRae *(born 1976)*
new work*[2] **71**
Gustav Mahler *(1860–1911)*
Das Lied von der Erde † **18**
Symphony No. 4 in G major † **33**
Clint Mansell *(born 1963)*
Moon – excerpt* **27**
Louis Marchand *(1669–1732)*
Pièces de Clavecin, Book 1 – Allemande* **P@CH 3**
Colin Matthews *(born 1946)*
Pictured Within: Birthday Variations for M. C. B. – Variation 4*[1] **35**
Felix Mendelssohn *(1809–47)*
Auf Flügeln des Gesanges **P@CH 5**
Der Mond* **P@CH 5**
Neue Liebe **P@CH 5**
Overture 'The Hebrides' ('Fingal's Cave') **39**
Piano Concerto No. 1 in G minor **40**
Symphony No. 3 in A minor, 'Scottish' **40**
Olivier Messiaen *(1908–92)*
Des canyons aux étoiles … **13**
Jean Mouton *(before 1459–1522)*
Nesciens mater virgo virum **P@CH 1**
Wolfgang Amadeus Mozart *(1756–91)*
The Abduction from the Seraglio – overture **65**
Cassation No. 1 in G major – Andante **65**
Concerto in E flat major for two pianos **52**
The Magic Flute **51**
Aria: 'No, no, che non sei capace' **65**
Piano Concerto No. 15 in B flat major **7**
Piano Concerto No. 23 in A major **57**
Aria: 'Popoli di Tessaglia! – Io non chiedo, eterni Dei' **65**
Requiem in D minor (compl. Süssmayr) **26**
Symphony No. 35 in D major, 'Haffner' **65**
Symphony No. 40 in G minor – finale (4th mvt) **3, 5**
Nico Muhly *(born 1981)*
new work*[2] **71**
John Murphy *(born 1965)*
Sunshine – excerpt* **27**
Thea Musgrave *(born 1928)*
Rorate coeli **P@HSL**
Modest Mussorgsky *(1839–81)*
A Night on the Bare Mountain (orch. Rimsky-Korsakov) † **67**
Pictures at an Exhibition (orch. Ravel) **39**
Laura Mvula *(born 1986)*
Sing to the Moon **75**

N —

Alex North *(1910–91)*
A Streetcar Named Desire – excerpt* **29, 30**

O —

Jacques Offenbach *(1819–80)*
Orpheus in the Underworld – overture **75**

P —

Giovanni Pierluigi da Palestrina *(c1525–1594)*
Magnificat primi toni* **P@CH 1**
Carly Paradis *(born 1980)*
The Innocents – excerpt* **27**
Hubert Parry *(1848–1918)*
Jerusalem (orch. Elgar) **75**
Anthony Payne *(born 1936)*
Pictured Within: Birthday Variations for M. C. B. – Variation 13*[1] **35**
Krzysztof Penderecki *(born 1933)*
Sinfonietta for strings – Vivace **70**
Pérotin *(fl c1200)*
Viderunt omnes – excerpt **P@CH 1**
John Pickard *(born 1963)*
Pictured Within: Birthday Variations for M. C. B. – Variation 14*[1] **35**
Steven Price *(born 1977)*
Gravity – excerpt* **27**
Sergey Prokofiev *(1891–1953)*
Piano Concerto No. 2 in G minor **48**
Romeo and Juliet – suite **12**
Violin Concerto No. 2 in G minor † **17**
Giacomo Puccini *(1858–1924)*
Madam Butterfly – Humming Chorus **3, 5**
Henry Purcell *(1659–95)*
Chacony **P@CH 3**
The Fairy Queen – Hornpipe **P@CH 3**
The Indian Queen – Rondeau **P@CH 3**
The Virtuous Wife – First Act Tune*; overture*; Second Music* **P@CH 3**
Alastair Putt *(born 1983)*
Halazuni* **P@CH 8**

R —

Sergey Rachmaninov *(1873–1943)*
The Bells † **28**
The Isle of the Dead † **22**
Piano Concerto No. 1 in F sharp minor (original version, 1891) † **41**
Piano Concerto No. 3 in D minor **63**
Rhapsody on a Theme of Paganini **23, 24**
Symphonic Dances **57**
Symphony No. 2 in E minor **48**
Maurice Ravel *(1875–1937)*
Rapsodie espagnole † **56**
La valse † **56**
Steve Reich *(born 1936)*
Pulse* **70**
Nikolay Rimsky-Korsakov *(1844–1908)*
Mlada – suite † **41**
Ailie Robertson *(born 1983)*
new work*[2] **71**
Gioachino Rossini *(1792–1868)*
Canzonetta spagnuola* **P@CH 5**

S —

Camille Saint-Saëns *(1835–1921)*
Danse macabre (arr. Lemare) **21**
Samson and Delilah – 'Mon coeur s'ouvre à ta voix' **75**
David Sawer *(born 1961)*
Pictured Within: Birthday Variations for M. C. B. – Variation 2*[1] **35**
Iris ter Schiphorst *(born 1956)*
Pictured Within: Birthday Variations for M. C. B. – Variation 5*[1] **35**
Arnold Schoenberg *(1874–1951)*
Five Orchestral Pieces † **7**
Franz Schubert *(1797–1828)*
Einsamkeit for soprano and orchestra (orch. D. Glanert)* **33**
Die Forelle **P@CH 5**
Gretchen am Spinnrade **P@CH 5**
Nacht und Träume **P@CH 5**
String Quartet No. 1* **P@CH 4**
Symphony No. 8 in B minor, 'Unfinished' **34**
Clara Schumann *(1819–96)*
Piano Concerto* **42**
Piano Trio in G minor, Op. 17 **P@CH 6**
Three Romances, Op. 22* **P@CH 6**
Robert Schumann *(1810–56)*
Adagio and Allegro, Op. 70 **P@CH 6**
Genoveva – overture **50**
Piano Concerto in A minor **19**
Symphony No. 4 in D minor (revised version, 1851) **7**
Dmitry Shostakovich *(1906–75)*
Symphony No. 1 in F minor **42**
Symphony No. 8 in C minor † **69**
Symphony No. 10 in E minor **15**
Symphony No. 11 in G minor, 'The Year 1905' **22**
Jean Sibelius *(1865–1957)*
Karelia – suite † **25**
Symphony No. 1 in E minor † **17**
Symphony No. 5 in E flat major (original version, 1915) **20**
Symphony No. 5 in E flat major (final version, 1919) **67**
Violin Concerto in D minor † **20**
Constantin Silvestri *(1913–69)*
Three Pieces for strings* **48**
Maddalena Laura Sirmen *(1745–1818)*
String Quartet No. 5 in F minor* **P@CH 4**
Alexia Sloane *(born 2000)*
Earthward*[1] **P@CH 1**
Bedřich Smetana *(1824–84)*
The Bartered Bride – overture and Three Dances **69**
Má vlast **2**
Linda Catlin Smith *(born 1957)*
new work*[1] **58**
Max Steiner *(1888–1971)*
Now, Voyager – excerpt* **29, 30**
The Treasure of the Sierra Madre – excerpt* **29, 30**
Richard Strauss *(1864–1949)*
An Alpine Symphony **32**
Also sprach Zarathustra **19**
Ariadne auf Naxos – 'Grossmächtige Prinzessin!' **65**

Capriccio – sextet **65**
Four Songs, Op. 27 **31**
Der Rosenkavalier – suite **17**
Till Eulenspiegels lustige Streiche **9**
Igor Stravinsky *(1882–1971)*
Divertimento: The Fairy's Kiss **52**
The Firebird – suite (1919) † **8**
The Rite of Spring **6**
Barbara Strozzi *(1619–77)*
L'amante segreto* **P@CH 2**
Che si può fare* **P@CH 2**
Lagrime mie* **P@CH 2**
Sino alla morte* **P@CH 2**
Jule Styne *(1905–94)*
Romance on the High Seas – excerpt* **29, 30**
Arthur Sullivan *(1842–1900)*
Victoria and Merrie England – suite **40**
Karol Szymanowski *(1882–1937)*
Love Songs of Hafiz, Op. 26* **58**

T —

Dobrinka Tabakova *(born 1980)*
new work*[1] **56**
Tōru Takemitsu *(1930–96)*
Twill by Twilight **28**
Outi Tarkiainen *(born 1985)*
Midnight Sun Variations*[1] **22**
Pyotr Ilyich Tchaikovsky *(1840–93)*
Eugene Onegin – Letter Scene † **69**
Piano Concerto No. 1 in B flat minor **34**
Swan Lake – excerpts **23, 24**
Suite No. 4, 'Mozartiana' † **52**
Symphony No. 2 in C minor, 'Little Russian' **58**
Symphony No. 6 in B minor, 'Pathétique' **25**
Violin Concerto in D major **12**
Georg Philipp Telemann *(1681–1767)*
Sonata in A minor, TWV 43:a 5* **P@CH 3**
Anna Thorvaldsdottir *(born 1977)*
Metacosmos*[5] **6**
Traditional
Auld Lang Syne (arr. Paul Campbell) **75**

V —

Edgard Varèse *(1883–1965)*
Amériques (original version, 1921) **44**
Ralph Vaughan Williams *(1872–1958)*
Fantasia on a Theme by Thomas Tallis **53**
Serenade to Music † **35**
Valiant-for-truth **P@HSL**
Giuseppe Verdi *(1813–1901)*
Aida – Triumphal March **75**
Don Carlos – 'O don fatale' **75**
Tomás Luis de Victoria *(1548–1611)*
Regina coeli a 8* **P@CH 1**

W —

Richard Wagner *(1813–83)*
Dawn; Duet 'Zu neuen Taten, teurer Helde'; Siegfried's Rhine Journey; Siegfried'sDeath and Funeral March; Brünnhilde's Immolation Scene **68**
Siegfried – Forest Murmurs **68**
Tristan and Isolde – Prelude and Liebestod (orchestral version) **26**
Wesendonck Lieder – Träume (arr. Wood) **56**
Freya Waley-Cohen *(born 1989)*
new work*[1] **P@CH 8**
Errollyn Wallen *(born 1958)*
This Frame Is Part of the Painting*[1] **39**
William Walton *(1902–83)*
Belshazzar's Feast **44**
Where does the uttered music go? **P@HSL**
Huw Watkins *(born 1976)*
The Moon*[1] **28**
Carl Maria von Weber *(1786–1826)*
Der Freischütz – overture **68**
Mieczysław Weinberg *(1919–96)*
Cello Concerto*[6] **25**
String Quartet No. 7 in C major* **P@CH 7**
Symphony No. 3 in B minor*[6] **46**
Judith Weir *(born 1954)*
Forest* **67**
Missa del Cid **P@HSL**
Pictured Within: Birthday Variations for M. C. B. – Variation 10*[1] **35**
Jörg Widmann *(born 1973)*
Babylon Suite*[6] **50**
Charles-Marie Widor *(1844–1937)*
Bach's Memento – No. 4: Marche du veilleur de nuit* **21**
Ryan Wigglesworth *(born 1979)*
Piano Concerto*[1] **52**
Stevie Wishart *(born 1959)*
new work*[2] **71**
arr. Henry Wood *(1869–1944)*
Fantasia on British Sea-Songs **75**
Hugh Wood *(born 1932)*
Scenes from Comus **53**

Z —

Hans Zimmer *(born 1957)*
Earth*[1] **3, 5**
Interstellar – excerpt* **27**

MISCELLANEOUS

1969: The Sound of a Summer **11**
Bach Night **71**
Beethoven Night **74**
CBeebies Prom: A Musical Trip to the Moon **3, 5**
Duke Ellington's Sacred Music **54**
The Breaks **64**
Late-Night Mixtape **36**
The Lost Words **49**
Mississippi Goddam: A Homage to Nina Simone **45**
The Race for Space **10**
Relaxed Prom **24**
The Sound of Space: Sci-Fi Film Music **27**
Wagner Night **68**
The Warner Brothers Story **29, 30**

BBC Proms 2019

Director, BBC Proms David Pickard
Controller, BBC Radio 3 Alan Davey
Personal Assistant Yvette Pusey

Editor, BBC Radio 3 Emma Bloxham

Head of Marketing, Publications and Learning Kate Finch

Business Co-ordinator Tricia Twigg

Concerts and Planning Helen Heslop (Manager), Hannah Donat (Artistic Producer), Alys Jones, Holly Cumming-Wesley (Event Producers), Alison Dancer, Victoria Gunn, Marianne Tweedie (Event Co-ordinators)

Learning Helen White (Senior Learning Manager), Lauren Creed, Beatrice Carey, Melanie Fryer (Managers), Siân Bateman, Rebecca Burns, Catherine Humphrey, Naomi Selwyn (Co-ordinators), Abigail Willer (Administrator)

Marketing Emily Caket (Manager), Sanjeet Riat (Co-ordinator)

Press and Communications Camilla Dervan (Communications Manager), Anna Hughes (Publicist), Joe Horsman (Assistant Publicist)

Music Television Jan Younghusband (Head of Commissioning, BBC Music TV), Livewire Pictures Ltd (Production)

Digital Rory Connolly (Editor, BBC Music), David Prudames (Assistant Commissioner, BBC Music Digital), Andrew Downs (Lead Producer, BBC Proms Digital), Rhian Roberts (Digital Editor, BBC Radio 3)

BBC Music Library Natalie Dewar (Archive Collections Manager), Joseph Schultz (Proms Co-ordinator), Michael Jones (Hire Co-ordinator), Tim Auvache, Anne Butcher, Raymond Howden, Richard Malton, Steven Nunes, David Vivian Russell, Chris Williams (Music Librarians), Alison John, Claire Martin (Archive Assistants)

Commercial Rights and Business Affairs Emily Bevington, Simon Brown, Sue Dickson, Hilary Dodds, Maddie Hennessy, Emma MacDonald, Emma Trevelyan, Pamela Wise

---

Publications Editor Petra Abbam
Editorial Manager Edward Bhesania
Sub-Editor Úna-Frances Clarke
Publications Designer Reenie Basova
Junior Publications Designer Lydia Ricketts
Publications Co-ordinator Deborah Fether

Advertising John Good Ltd
Cover illustration BBC Creative/BBC
Published by BBC Proms Publications, Room 3015, Broadcasting House, London W1A 1AA
Distributed by Bloomsbury Publishing, 50 Bedford Square, London WC1B 3DP

Printed by APS Group

APS Group holds ISO 14001 environmental management, FSC® and PEFCTM certifications. Printed using vegetable-based inks on FSC-certified paper. Formed in 1993 as a response to concerns over global deforestation, FSC (Forest Stewardship Council®) is an independent, non-governmental, not-for-profit organisation established to promote the responsible management of the world's forests. For more information, please visit www.fsc-uk.org.

FSC www.fsc.org MIX Paper from responsible sources FSC® C003270

ISBN 978-1-912114-03-0

1 *BBC commission: world premiere*
2 *BBC co-commission: world premiere*
3 *BBC co-commission: UK premiere*
4 *European premiere*
5 *UK premiere*
6 *London premiere*

** first appearance at a BBC Henry Wood Promenade Concert* † *Henry Wood Novelties: works given their world, UK or local premieres by Henry Wood, whether at the Proms or elsewhere*